About *The Way Into...*

The Way Into... is a major series that provides an accessible and highly usable "guided tour" of the Jewish faith and people, its history and beliefs—in total, a basic introduction to Judaism for adults that will enable them to understand and interact with sacred texts.

The Authors

Each book in the series is written by a leading contemporary teacher and thinker. While each of the authors brings his or her own individual style of teaching to the series, every volume's approach is the same: to help you to learn, in a life-affecting way, about important concepts in Judaism.

The Concepts

Each volume in *The Way Into...* series explores one important concept in Judaism, including its history, its basic vocabulary, and what it means to Judaism and to us. In the Jewish tradition of study, the reader is helped to interact directly with sacred texts.

The topics to be covered in *The Way Into...* series:

Torah
Jewish Prayer
Encountering God in Judaism
Jewish Mystical Tradition
Tikkun Olam (Repairing the World)
Judaism and the Environment
The Varieties of Jewishness
Covenant and Commandment
Holiness and Chosenness (*Kedushah*)
Time
Zion
Money and Ownership
Women and Men
The Relationship between Jews and Non-Jews

The Way Into

Judaism and the Environment

Jeremy Benstein, PhD

דרך למוד דרך למוד דרך למוד
דרך למוד

JEWISH LIGHTS Publishing

Woodstock, Vermont

The Way Into Judaism and the Environment

2006 First Printing
© 2006 by Jeremy Benstein

Library of Congress Cataloging-in-Publication Data
Benstein, Jeremy, 1961–
The way into Judaism and the environment / Jeremy Benstein.
    p. cm. — (The way into—)
Includes bibliographical references and index.
ISBN-13: 978-1-58023-268-5 (hardcover)
ISBN-10: 1-58023-268-X (hardcover)
1. Human ecology—Religious aspects—Judaism. 2. Nature—Religious aspects—Judaism. 3. Environmental law (Jewish law) I. Title.
BM538.H85B46 2006
296.3'8—dc22

                                                          2006023902

The publisher gratefully acknowledges the contribution of Rabbi Sheldon Zimmerman to the creation of this series. In his lifelong work of bringing a greater appreciation of Judaism to all people, he saw the need for *The Way Into...* and inspired us to act on it.

10   9   8   7   6   5   4   3   2   1

Manufactured in the United States of America
Jacket Design: Glenn Suokko and Jenny Buono
Text Design: Glenn Suokko
♻ Printed on recycled paper

Published by Jewish Lights Publishing
A Division of LongHill Partners, Inc.
Sunset Farm Offices, Route 4, P.O. Box 237
Woodstock, VT 05091
Tel: (802) 457-4000   Fax: (802) 457-4004
www.jewishlights.com

For Noam and Yonah,
and the *alma de'atei,* the world-that-is-coming,
their world.

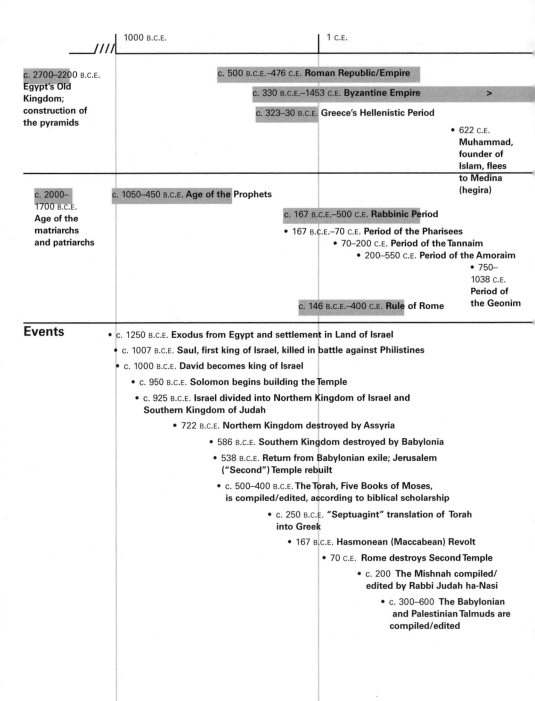

1000 B.C.E.   1 C.E.

c. 2700–2200 B.C.E.
Egypt's Old
Kingdom;
construction of
the pyramids

c. 500 B.C.E.–476 C.E. **Roman Republic/Empire**

c. 330 B.C.E.–1453 C.E. **Byzantine Empire** >

c. 323–30 B.C.E. **Greece's Hellenistic Period**

• 622 C.E.
**Muhammad,
founder of
Islam, flees
to Medina
(hegira)**

c. 2000–
1700 B.C.E.
Age of the
matriarchs
and patriarchs

c. 1050–450 B.C.E. **Age of the** Prophets

c. 167 B.C.E.–500 C.E. **Rabbinic Period**

• 167 B.C.E.–70 C.E. **Period of the Pharisees**
  • 70–200 C.E. **Period of the Tannaim**
    • 200–550 C.E. **Period of the Amoraim**
      • 750–
      1038 C.E.
      **Period of
      the Geonim**

c. 146 B.C.E.–400 C.E. **Rule** of Rome

Events

• c. 1250 B.C.E. **Exodus from Egypt and settlement in Land of Israel**

• c. 1007 B.C.E. **Saul, first king of Israel, killed in battle against Philistines**

• c. 1000 B.C.E. **David becomes king of Israel**

• c. 950 B.C.E. **Solomon begins building the Temple**

• c. 925 B.C.E. **Israel divided into Northern Kingdom of Israel and
  Southern Kingdom of Judah**

• 722 B.C.E. **Northern Kingdom destroyed by Assyria**

• 586 B.C.E. **Southern Kingdom destroyed by Babylonia**

• 538 B.C.E. **Return from Babylonian exile; Jerusalem
  ("Second") Temple rebuilt**

• c. 500–400 B.C.E. **The Torah, Five Books of Moses,
  is compiled/edited, according to biblical scholarship**

• c. 250 B.C.E. **"Septuagint" translation of Torah
  into Greek**

• 167 B.C.E. **Hasmonean (Maccabean) Revolt**

• 70 C.E. **Rome destroys Second Temple**

• c. 200 **The Mishnah compiled/
  edited by Rabbi Judah ha-Nasi**

• c. 300–600 **The Babylonian
  and Palestinian Talmuds are
  compiled/edited**

1000 C.E.   2000 C.E.

- c. 1040–1105 **Rashi, French Bible and Talmud scholar and creator of line-by-line commentary on the Torah**
  - 1178 **Maimonides (1135–1204) completes his code of Jewish law, the *Mishneh Torah***
    - c. 1295 ***The Zohar*, Kabbalistic work of mystical teaching, composed**
      - 1492 **Jews expelled from Spain**
        - 1565 **Joseph Caro publishes *Shulchan Arukh*, the standard code of Jewish law and practice**
          - 1654 **First Jewish settlement in North America at New Amsterdam**
            - 1700–1760 **Israel Baal Shem Tov, founder of Hasidism**
              - 1729–1786 **Moses Mendelssohn, "Father of the Jewish Enlightenment"**
                - 1801–1888 **Samson Raphael Hirsch, founder of "modern Orthodoxy"**
                  - 1836 **Yeshiva University founded**
                  - 1873; 1875 **Reform Judaism in U.S. establishes Union of American Hebrew Congregations and Hebrew Union College**
                    - 1887 **Conservative Judaism's Jewish Theological Seminary founded**
                    - 1897 **Theodor Herzl convenes first Zionist Congress**
                      - 1933–1945 **The Holocaust (Shoah)**
                      - 1935 **Mordecai Kaplan establishes the Jewish Reconstructionist Foundation**
                      - 1948 **Birth of the State of Israel**

Contents

About *The Way Into ...*   **i**

Timeline   **vi**

Acknowledgments   **xiii**

***Torat Chayim:* Books and Our Lives**   **1**

    A Bridge in Two Directions   1

    On Relevance and Authenticity   4

    Midrash and Halacha, Sources as Resources   5

    Reading This Book   7

    Concluding Reflection   8

    A Note on the Translation   9

1. *Emet Ve'emunot:* Environmentalism, Religion, and the Environmental Crisis in Context   **11**

    Nature, the Environment, and Sustainability   11

    Crises and Opportunities, Nightmares and Dreams   13

    Religion as Problem: Lynn White Throws Down the Gauntlet   14

    Re-evaluating Religion in Light of Environmental Concerns   17

    The Humble Ruler and the Stuff of Nature   20

    Religion and Environmentalism: Common Ground and Unique Messages   23

    Unnatural Judaism: From Alienation to Reconnection   25

2. *Bereishit Bara':* Creator, Creating, Creation, Creatures, and Us   **33**

    Biblical Beginnings: Readers, Reading, Readings, How to Read—and Us   33

    Stories of Creations: Biblical Cubism   35

Genesis 1 and 2: Comparative Readings 36

Genesis 1: Master and Rule—The Demands
of Dominion 42

Genesis 2: Serve and Preserve—The Stipulations
of Stewardship 47

Between Apes and Angels: On Being a Part of,
and Apart From 53

The Rest of the Story: Where Does Creation
Stop and History Begin ... 58

Concluding Thoughts: On Goodness, Settlement,
and Chaos 66

3. *Lishmor La'asot U'lekayem:* Traditional Sources and Resources 71

Nature: Is It and Does It Matter (I)—Heaven v. Earth 72

Nature: Is It and Does It Matter (II)—Torah v. *Teva*
(Nature) 74

More on the Nature of Nature 79

Wind, Rain, Mountains, and Fields 84

Bein Adam Le'olam? Jewish Legal and Moral
Categories Regarding Nature 88

Bal Tashchit I: From Battlefield Forestry to
Environmental Values 93

Bal Taschchit II: Negotiating Needs and Wants 98

Empathy and Ethics: The Pain of Living Things 101

Tikkun and Partnership, Flax and Foreskins 107

4. *Olam Umelo'o:* Contemporary Topics and Issues 113

Multiply and Fill Up the Earth: Are We There Yet? 114

Eat and Be Satisfied: How Much Is Enough? 118

Of Pits and Piety, or Torah and Toxics 127

Tzedek and the City: Justice, Land Use, and Urban Life 131

Wilderness and Worship 139

Melo' Kol Ha'aretz Kevodo—The Fullness of the
Earth Is God's Glory 143

Mazon Ve'chazon—Food and Vision, or the Duties
of the Diet 149

Sustainability and Sustenance: How to Keep on
Keepin' On 159

5. *Chagim Uzmanim:* Cycles in Time, Sacraments in Life 165

Lu'ach ve'Ru'ach—Of Calendars and Culture,
Nature and History 166

Yamim Tovim—Good Days: The High
Holidays and Pilgrimage Festivals 170

The Nature of Hanukkah 176

The Four Faces of Tu B'Shvat—A New Year
of the Trees 179

Shabbat—A Day of Worldly Rest 182

Shmitah—The Radical Social-Environmental Vision
of a Yearlong Sabbath 188

Blessings and Worship: From Appraising to Praising 192

6. *Ha'am Ve'Ha'aretz:* The Land of Israel and a Jewish Sense of Place 201

Bein Adam "LaMakom"—On the Importance of Place 204

On Wandering and Return: The Jew as Native 207

The Cultural Contradictions of Israeli
Environmentalism 215

Back to Bridge-Building: The Environment as Deep
Common Concern 225

Talmud VeMa'aseh: Where to Go from Here—
   Suggestions for Further Study   231
Notes   235
Glossary   247
Index   254

Acknowledgments

Although written over the course of a year, this book is the product of more than two decades of study, teaching, reflection, and activism, and a life that goes back much further. The memory and writings of my grandfather, Rabbi Morris Adler, *zatzal,* who was tragically killed when I was a boy, and my grandmother Goldie have always inspired me to be who I am and do what I do. Their daughter, Shulamith, my late mother, and my father Eli, and now my stepmother Fagie have been and continue to be sources of love and support that have known no bounds. Siblings Judy, Joel, and Miriam have contributed in their own ways more than they know.

After parents and home, the formative experiences in my life occurred in Gar'in Pardes, the group with whom I made *aliyah* to Israel, and at Kibbutz Ketura, the place where I have spent more of my life than any other. It was there in the desert of the Southern Arava and in the educational work of Keren Kolot that I first began to think seriously about Judaism and the natural world. Part of me will remain there forever.

The inspiring and indefatigable Alon Tal, along with the good people at Ketura, later founded the Arava Institute, where many of the ideas for this book were tried out on unsuspecting students, and of which I continue to be a proud affiliate.

My college roommate, (now Rabbi) Brad Artson, has been a soul mate and, despite the geographical distance, has intellectually inspired and spiritually nourished me and my work over the years.

Likewise, I express gratitude to the wonderful Jewish community of the Tivon Havura, and in particular Zev and Edna Gorny-Labinger, each with their own perfect synthesis of art and environment, nature and culture.

Other people whom I have learned with and from, in friendship and in myriad important ways, include: Gil Troy, Noah Efron, Noam Zion, Alon Tal, Nigel Savage, Dan and Kay Ehrenkrantz, Ayalon Edelstein, Orit and Yehonadav Perlman, Miriam Sivan, Matthew Sigman, Melila Helner-Eshed, David Seidenberg, Joshua Yarden, Golan Ben Horin, Samuel Chain, and Avner de Shalit.

My first forays into writing on these topics were enabled and encouraged by Gershom Gorenberg, and they were improved by his editorial talents at the *Jerusalem Report*. I am grateful as well to the good people at Jewish Lights—publisher Stuart M. Matlins, editorial vice president Emily Wichland, and my always gracious editor, Alys Yablon Wylen—for inviting me to attempt this work and for their patience in my bringing it to completion.

When all is said and done, my professional, intellectual, spiritual, and personal sides meet at one place: the Heschel Center for Environmental Learning and Leadership in Tel Aviv. I am proud to have been there since its inception, and to be part of the Israeli environmental movement, working for a just and sustainable Israel. Special thanks to the members of that movement, especially the growing family of staff and the environmental fellows at the Center, and in particular Lia Ettinger, my awe-inspiring professional partner for the better part of a decade.

None of this would have occurred at all were it not for Eilon Schwartz. From the *gar'in,* through the kibbutz, and now at the Heschel Center: for the past twenty-five years ours has been a shared adventure. Eilon is a personal example, an intellectual powerhouse, a moral role model, and a fellow traveler. His thoughts and our relationship are present on every page of this book, not just the ones where I've actually taken the trouble to quote him.

Acharona chaviva, my bride and life partner, Elisheva: for your love and patience, and for the values that we share. And for the fruit of our love, Noam Shlomi and Yonah Mishael, to whom this book is dedicated.

Jeremy Benstein
Kiryat Tivon, Israel

תורת חיים
Torat Chayim

Books and Our Lives

A Bridge in Two Directions

The engagement of Judaism—Jewish texts, values, traditions—with environmental issues is not simple or straightforward. Although the challenges and opportunities raised are compelling both for Jewish life and for environmental thought, there are several possible ways to understand the application of biblical, Talmudic, or medieval categories and values to our contemporary problems.

One approach maintains that "there is nothing new under the sun" (Eccles. 1:4–11), and therefore *chazal*, the early rabbinic sages, knew all that is necessary to deal successfully with global warming and other modern threats. According to this view, all the questions and answers have been revealed, and the process of applying ancient texts to modern problems is relatively uncomplicated, done by authorities trained primarily in those texts.

The contrasting approach understands the challenges we face to be largely unprecedented, with no simple or automatic answers to be found in premodern sources. The uniquely modern nature of the problems makes classical texts irrelevant. Moreover, the decidedly religious character of those texts makes them doubly archaic and arcane in relation to our technological lives, with their singular opportunities and threats. These challenges will be met then, according to this view, not by religious authorities trained in

1

ancient wisdom, but by scientists and technocrats familiar with the latest innovations and their applications.

The doubts of the skeptic are understandable: Aren't the lives of primitive, small-scale farmers and modern urbanites fundamentally incommensurable? Are we trying to reproduce those antique life forms? Is there only one type of sustainability? That is, does the equilibrium they found in their world determine the limits of ours? Can we actually learn from ancient agrarian tales relevant lessons for our modern technological lives?

My answers to these questions are: no, no, no, no—and yes. I would argue that there are certain eternal unchanging truths about the human condition and nature–human relations that a patina of modern technological sophistication doesn't fundamentally alter. That is, one can accept the essential newness of many of the issues we face in the twenty-first century and still embrace the need for guiding values and insight from timeless sources. Although some of the problems of our own day, such as soil erosion and health-impairing pollution, were known in the ancient world, the phenomena that make up the issues of today's environmental movement are relatively without historic parallel. It is the underlying questions, however, that have remained unchanged over millennia of human culture and religious thought: what is the appropriate relationship between humanity and the rest of creation, between the material and the spiritual in our lives? What are our responsibilities to future generations regarding the world we shall bequeath them?

This is a third approach in understanding Judaism's relation to the environment, and it is the working assumption of this book. Torah and traditional sources are crucially relevant, yet their meaningful application to our lives is far from automatic and therefore requires creative interpretation on our part. We become an integral and active part of the process of creating the complex interface between word and world.

An important implication of this understanding is that the skills and knowledge necessary for the successful undertaking of this task are not on one side or the other of the textual/technological divide; they must span that chasm. It's not enough to be extensively trained in the intricacies of Talmudic thought without a thorough grounding in the details and data of contemporary environmental discourse. And mere technical knowledge, as wide-ranging as it may be, can never by itself address the real underlying questions, which are issues of values, beliefs, and worldviews, requiring wisdom, not (just) data.

This book attempts both to present and to deepen a dialogue that has begun over the past decade, which recognizes the importance of the bridge between the two sides, and no less crucial, the fact that it is a bridge in two directions. One direction is from the "bulkhead" of the tradition ("the book"), to current reality ("life"), applying classical categories to contemporary issues; the other direction is from life, from today's problems and challenges, back to the sources, looking for precedents and relevant traditional language in which to frame our debate.

The affirmation of both of these poles and the need for ongoing communication between them is in itself something of an innovation, because unfortunately it has been all too common for writers and activists with proficiency in one or the other of these specializations to end up with superficial claims that don't do justice to the depth and complexity of the other side. Thus, there are works that address current challenges and threats intelligently, but try to "Judaize" the discussion with a few "green" verses mined judiciously from some anthology. Likewise, there exist learned disquisitions on Jewish environmental values, which display a knowledge of what's going on in the world that stops at the *boursakai*, the tanner of Talmudic times whose business gave off noxious fumes. The only real dialogue that can occur is one that flows from deep familiarity and commitment both to the book and to life, and to their creative interaction.

On Relevance and Authenticity

Through my work, which has combined environmental thought, activism, and Jewish education, I have come across a wide range of Jews to whom this sort of imaginative, informed dialogue appeals. At one end of the spectrum are the "woodsy and unchurched"— environmentally inclined, but religiously untutored and uncommitted, who can be taught to express their concern for the world in relationship to Jewish values and sources. At the other end are the "*frum* and ungreen," Jewishly involved but environmentally uninitiated, who will discover that environmental concerns are not at all peripheral to their faith commitments and the demands of traditional Judaism. It is important to note that the polyphonic dialogue I am trying to establish is not only between contemporary Jews and the historic sources, but also between the different Jewish people and communities of our own day: both of the foregoing polar examples, and everyone in between.

An important challenge in this dialogue is the dilemma between relevance (the grounding in "life") and authenticity[1] (with a strong basis in "the book"). A person grounded in the need for maximal authenticity, while looking for connections to current concerns, may be suspicious of programs that seem to pander to today's agendas and fads; on the other hand, the ecological true believer, coming from the frontlines of relevancy, though searching for authentic traditional viewpoints, may have low tolerance for discussions that seem stuck in musty old dogmas and outmoded belief systems. The solution will be found in the doing, in the unfolding of the conversation.

There is a third type of potential reader—either somewhere in the middle, or off this spectrum entirely—one who is neither overly Jewishly committed or learned, nor very environmentally aware or active. This type presents a different sort of challenge. In Israel, for instance, trying to promote connections between Judaism and environmentalism among the predominantly secular majority is doubly problematic. A good deal of that population is apprehensive of Judaism and all the restrictions promulgated in its name, which seem antithetical to the demands and the pleasures of modern life. Environmentalism, with its own list of virtues and vices, is suspect on exactly the same grounds. Similarly, in the American context, it might not be hugely effective to market environmentalism as consonant with a thing called Judaism, which is often no more than something distasteful remembered from Hebrew school or Sunday school.

Both environmentalism and Judaism are seen here as value systems, pluralistic within certain bounds, that propose alternatives to the media- and market-driven lifestyles so prevalent in our contemporary society. Judaism, all too often a ritualistic adornment to our spiritual complacency, can be and needs to be a faith with teeth: a striving, a confrontation, whether in the lofty call to be a "holy people" or simply to actualize prophetic visions of justice and caring. This type of Judaism has something to say about our lives and our world—and it is often a critique. And those who are searching for or have embraced some sort of critique of contemporary life will be most open to one or both of these languages of *cheshbon nefesh,* self-criticism, literally "soul accounting."

Midrash and Halacha, Sources as Resources

Formulating a critique of one's own lifestyle and civilization is far from easy. We are so embedded in our society that it's hard to transcend its worldview, in which we have so much invested, and look at it from without. Judaism, as an age-old tradition, can help us do that, and so this book connects Jewish sources and values to a critique of contemporary society, in the context of issues that are the focus of environmentalism, such as consumerism and the challenges of material abundance, the notion of human progress through technological innovation (involving the intensifying manipulation of nature), and the culture of individualism (often at the expense of communal well-being). My goal, then, is to develop a language in which to formulate ideas and challenge preconceptions, not lay down any particular law on any given issue.

I often begin lectures by disabusing audiences of the belief that what we're going to talk about is "what Judaism says about" for two reasons. First, quite simply, there is no such thing as "Judaism," some reified entity that speaks in its own name. Moreover, even given some overarching conception ("Judaism" or "Jewish tradition") that refers to the plethora of books, people, schools of thought, historical periods, and ideological orientations, there are very few issues about which one thing is said. Judaism is thus not a set of rigid answers to fixed questions, but an ongoing dialogue in which the questions arise, along with various answers from different times and places, and even more generally, a language in which to engage in the dialogue and formulate the questions in the first place. Clearly, there are also more authoritarian approaches in our history, but without going into these weighty denominational questions, we can find *asmachta,* support for this interpretive or dialogic approach, in the basic structural expressions of Jewish learning.

One of those modes of learning is midrash, the ongoing creative and pluralistic interpretation and application of traditional texts in light of changing contemporary insight and needs. But lest this creativity and plurality degenerate into a free-for-all, let us recognize that in our approach of *lidrosh et haketuvim* (lit. "demanding from," or interpreting the texts), that is, doing *midrash*, not only are we making demands, making claims on the text in our creative interpretation, but the texts are also *making claims on us;* thus, both the necessity to interpret and the freedom to do so are based on our commitment to the texts as having a guiding role in our lives.[2] Postmodern literary fashion notwithstanding, mere intellectual engagement is not enough; midrash can only take place in the context of a covenantal commitment to the text and its teachings.

Another great mode of Jewish learning that is relevant here is Halacha—usually translated as "Jewish law," but more literally "the path," that which is to be done (and not just spoken about). Halachic discourse, while certainly motivated by the desire for *p'sak,* the final authoritative decision, takes place in the medium of *mahloket* (dispute) and *shakla ve'tarya* (the back-and-forth of entertaining and exploring all angles and facets of a given question or issue), not only allowing for divergent opinions but also recognizing variant schools of thought, and even mandating their inclusion in the ongoing development of Jewish law. The Talmud—the book that makes Judaism Judaism—is inconceivable without this fundamental characteristic.

The issue of what texts mean and how (and why) we should read them is, of course, not just about Torah and the environment: it goes to the heart of what it means to interpret and therefore to be Jewish. The dialogue created between author/Author (through the text), the text itself (distinct from the author), the individual reader of today, and communities of readers in the past and present, is the meeting point of authenticity and relevance.

Reading This Book

While all the foregoing can lead to debate about the "correct" interpretation of Jewish tradition, this book does not engage traditional categories of belief, such as the nature of divine revelation, the authority of Halacha and the Rabbis, and the like. I thus sidestep denominational issues, and take aim at elucidation and inspiration, rather than at authoritative interpretation.

It should be clear, then, that the methodology of this book is emphatically not "*pasuk* mining"—that is, gathering the "greenest" verses in the tradition and making these stand in for the whole. Similarly inappropriate for our purposes here are the extremes of mechanistic cataloguing of what has already been written, and spinning highly innovative interpretations in a selective or idiosyncratic process. As leading scholar Rabbi Bradley Artson has written, the goal is to "enrich the traditional structure of Judaism with a consciousness of environmental issues rather than simply tailoring Jewish religion to fit within the procrustean bed of a dismembered ecological Judaism."

Judaism is thus neither ispo facto green, nor the opposite. Jewish language in these areas both requires and allows its own application to contemporary challenges and categories, and in so doing will enrich itself and contemporary social-environmental discourse with insights that are at one and the same time eternal and cutting edge.

A confession: this book relates primarily to what Jews have written and thought about the issues, and much less to what Jews actually have done over the ages, which has been less studied historically or sociologically. This will not prevent us, though, from relating to the crucial questions of how we should internalize and apply these ideas in our lives today. A generation ago, nobody would have written a book of this type. Not because the theoretical questions were not of intellectual interest, but because there was no sense of import, of moment, to those issues. Now, one can't write of Judaism and nature and environment without acknowledging that these are under siege in our world, and demand not only exploration but also response. In the Talmudic discussion over the relative value of study and action, the view that carried the day was the importance of study, the kind of study that leads to action. That is the goal of this book.

Concluding Reflection

I have written much of this book from the second floor of the handsome library of Oranim College, which sits on a hill in Tivon, looking out to Haifa and the Mediterranean. At times the view has been distracting—but how can one complain of a view when writing a book that has to do with nature? Actually, that view has been inspiring, though not because of the grandeur of a pristine landscape, but rather the opposite.

Close by, there are wooded hills and cultivated fields, but what truly commands the horizon is the industrial landscape of the factories in Haifa Bay. The massive scaffolding and cooling towers of the oil refineries and other petrochemical industries straddle the mouth of the heavily polluted Kishon River, put there by the British in Mandatory times, for the easy channeling of refuse.

Above it all stands "the torch": a huge tower that flares off the gaseous residue of the refining process. As it is always burning there, a veritable beacon day and night, I have come to see it as the *ner tamid*, the eternal light, of our society—proclaiming the real faith commitment of our age....

We live in a new age with new challenges. Every generation may feel that, but in our case the rate of change is unprecedented. To retain our moorings in a period of rapid change and bewildering trials, it behooves us to return to the Source, and to the sources, and to reformulate age-old guidance to meet new threats and opportunities. If God can "daily renew the work of Creation" as the morning liturgy proclaims, than surely we can be inspired to gain renewed insight into how we are to care for that creation.

A Note on the Translation

The Bible translation I have used in this book is almost entirely from the Jewish Publication Society translation of the Tanakh (1985). Except where noted otherwise, all extracts from the Talmud are taken from the Babylonian Talmud. Both the biblical translation and the Talmud text use what we today recognize as "masculine God language." This is in contrast to the language that I have used in my text throughout the book, but I leave the masculine God language intact to preserve the authenticity of the citations.

אמת ואמונות
Emet Ve'emunot

Environmentalism, Religion, and the Environmental Crisis in Context

Nature, the Environment, and Sustainability

One aspect of the "newness" of the subject matter of this book is that the basic terminology is in flux. What is meant by the words *environment* or *environmentalism*? First, the use of the term *environment* is intentional and meant to be distinct from the term *nature*. Focusing on nature circumscribes the discussion to issues of wilderness, species, trees, animals, and the like. These are fascinating and crucial issues to develop—and are some of the great *hiddushim,* innovations, of Jewish environmentalism—but they are only a part of what I would call the environmental agenda, which is best summarized by the broad term *sustainability.*

Sustainability is a big idea that can mean different things to different people, but for our purposes, a sustainable society is one that integrates social, environmental, and economic concerns of health and justice, and can both *sustain itself* over time, living up to responsibilities to future generations, as well as *sustain* and *nourish* its members, materially and spiritually, in the present and in the future. The crisis of which environmentalists speak—including everything from mass extinctions, resource depletion, and global warming to poverty, the widening social gap, unfair trade, urban issues, and loss of social capital—refers to the growing realization that we are not fulfilling either of these basic conditions, and we need to figure out what must change in order to do so.

Several things flow from this definition. First, environmentalism is about much more than just the physical environment. It has come to include issues of direct human impact, such as pollution and public health, and beyond to issues of community well-being, participatory democracy, justice, and equality. The theme of the 2002 Environmental World Summit in Johannesburg was the eradication of poverty—hardly the traditional occupational focus of ecologists. In consequence, environmentalism goes beyond the limited questions of harming nature or preventing pollution and raises the deeper questions about what it means to be human, what real progress is, and what sort of society we are striving for—questions Judaism and all religions have been struggling with since time immemorial.

Therefore, environmental questions are not technical or technological. The natural sciences can only help us grasp the *symptoms* of the problems, for the underlying *causes* of those challenges relate to human values and behavior. Thus, a discussion of Jewish perspectives on these issues is not only relevant but also necessary. It's not just about whether we as Jews love nature, and whether that love is different from secular, Christian, or pagan love. It is about the direction of society that is not only "harming nature" but also changing our cultural and spiritual horizons, the dynamic dialogue between matter and spirit, and the definition of what it means to be human.

Judaism has well-articulated visions of an ideal world, and the need for *tikkun olam* (the repair of the world). So has environmentalism: contrary to popular misconception, it is not just a litany of past, present, and future disasters; it is also an attempt to dream of a better world and bring it to fruition. And while not always identical, these visions have more in common than is often assumed.

Crises and Opportunities, Nightmares and Dreams

Since the inception of the contemporary environmental movement in the 1960s, religion, when it has been considered at all, has been a veritable battleground: are religious beliefs and practices part of the problem, or part of the solution? But first, what are these problems and solutions?

Here it would be fitting to paint a picture of the environmental crisis—a landscape in grays and blacks. Many works dealing with the environment begin with forecasts of gloom and doom to emphasize the severity of the situation, and to get people to sit up and take notice. However, while for some they may underscore the urgent need for immediate and concerted effort, for others, the more horrific the predictions, the more they engage in denial and go on with business as usual. The litany of threats feeds fatalism rather than activism, and it is ultimately disempowering.

In the end, people are more moved by a promise of fulfilling an ideal rather than averting a threat. Martin Luther King Jr. galvanized a people with his vision when he proclaimed "I Have a Dream." Environmentalists too often try to do the same thing with their version, "I Have a Nightmare"—and it doesn't quite work. Those threats, risks, menaces, hazards, problems, and challenges are indeed many, real, and serious; what will motivate us, however, is exploring positive ideals, values, and the shape of the world that could be.

As one anti-consumerist slogan has it, "More fun, less stuff." Our tone should not be suffering for the sake of some conception of environmental remediation, but rather how to recognize the different dimensions of malaise that make our lives less than what they could be, and thus heal ourselves and the world, realizing the amazing potential latent within.

Religion as Problem: Lynn White Throws Down the Gauntlet

Two generations ago, nobody thought to explore the issues of Jewish responsibilities regarding the natural world, or whether we should question our own lifestyles. Along came the worldwide environmental crisis, a growing awareness of its implications in the sixties and seventies, and fast on its heels, connections to religious traditions. The historian Lynn White Jr. catalyzed the debate with his well-known 1967 article, "The Historic Roots of Our Ecologic Crisis,"[1] published in the prestigious journal *Science,* in which he claims that those historic roots are religious, in general, and (Western) Christian, in particular. The article has been reprinted numerous times and has spawned an entire literature on religion and the environment. Many have criticized the specifics of his conclusions, but his framing of the issues has been seminal:

> What people do about their ecology depends on what they think about themselves in relation to things around them. Human ecology is deeply conditioned by beliefs about our nature and destiny—that is, by religion…. Since the roots of our trouble are so largely religious, the remedy must also be essentially religious, whether we call it that or not. We must rethink and refeel our nature and destiny.

This passage sets the question of the environment squarely in the realm of values, and rightly notes that the challenge of the growing degradation of the Earth is at the heart of religious thought as well: in our identity and roles as human beings and in our relation to the rest of creation. To quote the great farmer-philosopher (and man of Christian faith) Wendell Berry, the entire term *environmental crisis* is a misnomer, because it is not a crisis of the environment, but rather of ourselves. Whereas most technical approaches focus on managing the environment, this understanding emphasizes the need to "manage" ourselves. The crisis is of spiritual values, hence the importance of bringing religious perspectives to bear.

Why are "the roots of our trouble ... religious," according to White? His main claim is that the Creation story as told in Genesis describes a role and destiny for human beings that conceives of nature as nothing more than the raw materials for our purposes:

> Christianity inherited from Judaism not only a concept of time as non-repetitive and linear but also a striking story of creation. By gradual stages a loving and all-powerful God had created light and darkness, the heavenly bodies, the Earth and all its plants, animals, birds, and fishes. Finally, God had created Adam and, as an afterthought, Eve to keep man from being lonely. Man named all the animals, thus establishing his dominance over them. God planned all of this explicitly for man's benefit and rule: no item in the physical creation had any purpose save to serve man's purposes. And, although man's body is made of clay, he is not simply part of nature: he is made in God's image.

Critics have rightly taken White to task on the simplistic reading of the complex and multilayered Creation stories in the first chapters of Genesis, which ignores at the very least, the mission expressed in verse 2:15—"to work and to watch" (or till and tend, serve and preserve). But White is correct to focus on the account(s) of Creation as a crucial part of our religious teachings about the environment. The following chapter is an extended analysis of precisely this question: what does our own religious "myth of origins" teach us about who we are and what nature is and should be for us?

It's not just the story, or the texts, though. White points an accusing finger at Western Christianity in toto as embodying values that are inimical to environmental care and concern. White claimed that Western Christianity "is the most anthropocentric religion the world has seen," with both man and God transcendently above nature. Christianity, according to White, is the opposite of ancient paganism, because it posits a duality of man and nature, and that it is God's will that man exploit this dispirited nature. Christianity thus "bears a huge burden of guilt" for the eco-degradation wrought by the scientific revolution, because it is the Christian axiom that "nature has no reason for existence save to serve man" that led to this revolution and its consequences.

White is aware that the immediate or proximate cause of our environmental woes lies in the advances of the scientific and industrial revolutions; his point is that while technological sophistication has given us the firepower to do all sorts of bad (and good) in the world, in essence, our current skills are simply the implementation of long-held values and beliefs. Whether or not the phrase "nature has no reason for existence save to serve man" is a Christian or religious axiom, it does seem to be an article of faith in the technological sciences, and surely it is implicated in the way our society treats the natural world, its resources, and its ecosystems.

White rejects science and technology as the panacea for curing environmental ills. His conclusion? "Find a new religion or rethink our old one." Some ardent environmentalists took his appeal to "find a new religion" very seriously and called for scuttling the monotheistic faiths altogether, in favor of more sympathetic Eastern or indigenous nature-worshiping traditions. In some quarters, environmentalism did acquire the trappings of a sort of eco-religion, which raised specters of paganism in the eyes of

Christian and Jewish traditionalists, who were already on the defensive trying to respond to White's claims.

It should be noted that White chose "rethinking the old" religion over "finding a new" one: despite great sympathy for Zen Buddhism, and its popularity in the American counterculture, he felt that it could not be a widespread option. In the final analysis, he is a believing Presbyterian, and his is a prophetic rebuke from within, not a rejection from outside the fold. He proposed St. Francis, with his virtue of human humility and the democracy of all creatures, as the patron saint for ecology (an idea that was later formally adopted by the Catholic Church). In a later essay, he reiterates his belief that religious traditions have alternate schools and philosophical undercurrents that act as "recessive genes" to be accessed, interpreted, and brought to the fore to respond to contemporary concerns. This is true no less of Judaism than it is of Christianity and other religions.

Re-evaluating Religion in Light of Environmental Concerns

Many of White's assumptions are unwarranted, such as the "ecological nobility" of pagan traditions. While there are certainly inspiring examples of nature-worshiping beliefs reflected in sustainable tribal practices, often the lack of environmental damage in lands inhabited by indigenous cultures is more a function of low population density and meager levels of subsistence than some inherent values that rule out over-exploitation. More important, monotheistic religion, despite assigning a special status to the human being in its ability to use creation—or perhaps precisely because of it—has its own set of "inhibitors" of environmental destruction.

In addition, White implies that it is anthropocentrism that is the root cause of the eco-crisis, and thus the sole remedy is some form of the opposite philosophical stance, known as bio- or eco-centrism. This approach focuses on the health and well-being of nature as a whole, and the human as only a part of that whole: nature as community in which we are a plain citizen, or as a larger super-organism of which we are (but) an organ. But not only are there many difficulties in adopting a bio-centric ethic, there is also a range of possible interpretations of anthropocentric reasoning that can indeed be quite "green."

The first responses to White's accusations were either apologias or mea culpas, or both: celebrating all the positive environmental values and practices that were overlooked by White, and admitting, while contextualizing, the negative sides. This led to a more honest appraisal of religious heritage in the environmental context, and now we have largely moved beyond White to constructive appraisals and initiatives regarding the role of religion in inculcating a vision of sustainability.

Many have claimed that White was dead wrong on his substantive claims about the role of religion in environmental degradation: either that the Bible never served as prooftext in the way he implies,[2] or that it was actually the rise of secular humanism in early modern Europe that brought the sea change in the way humans saw themselves and their relation to nature and its resources, resulting in Western industrial dominion over the natural world and our current crisis.[3] Biblical religion, regardless of the exalted position it assigned man (indeed usually the male), always said God reigned supreme, and God's eternal laws stood above earthbound mortals. Thus, rather than being heavily anthropocentric, as White and others have argued, Western religion is more *theocentric,* with the search for God and the desire to establish God's kingdom on earth paramount.[4]

From antiquity all the way through modernity a central metaphor held sway, sometimes called the Great Chain of Being, which imagined the spiritual structure of creation as a linear, hierarchical order, with the more spiritual or noble at the top, and the more material or base, below. Thus, God and the celestial retinue are at the peak, followed by humans, animals, vegetables, and minerals. Indeed, in each category there are higher and lower elements: kings above slaves, lions above snakes, roses above weeds, and gold above lead. It was the Enlightenment and humanism, this argument goes, that accepted the basic structure of this Great Chain, but then "decapitated" it, leaving "man" at the top, removing the divine limiting factor on science and progress, and making the sky literally the limit. Arguably, the materialization of nature occurred despite, not because of, religious ideals. It is thus secularism that represents the ultimate disenchantment of the world, because nature is no longer even divine creation, but now just a storehouse of raw materials for us to use with no absolute divine guidance or limitations.

Classically, religious traditions had struck some sort of balance between mystery and mastery: the divine and unknowable foundations of existence versus the terrestrial realms given over to humans for the promotion of civilization according to God's will. Modern technology, though, has given us undreamt-of mastery over creation, and secular science has transformed the religious idea of mystery (a fundamental component of spiritual life) into simple ignorance, comparable to a disease, something to be cured or eradicated.

There is, indeed, something deeply irreligious about Pico della Mirandola's famous humanist slogan "Man is the measure of all things," and also something highly anti-ecological. Ecological thought, with its guiding image of the interdependent web, is a striking alternative to the linear, hierarchical structure of the traditional Great Chain of Being. From that perspective, it would only be partly tongue in cheek to parse the term *humanist*, not as parallel to socialist or modernist, but more as sexist or racist: putting humans above other classes of organisms also worthy of concern and care. There are more commonalities between ecological and religious thought than first meet the eye, which might just be the ultimate response to White's critique.

The Humble Ruler and the Stuff of Nature

Guiding metaphors are crucial in understanding our relationship to the natural world, and secular and religious languages privilege vastly different images. Are we hurtling through the void on Spaceship Earth, and if so—are we the crew, the passengers, or just a rivet on the wing? Or is the biotic sphere (living nature) better seen as a super-organism of which we are but a part, an organ? If so, which one—the brain? Likewise, it is of ultimate significance whether we conceptualize land as a *commodity,* which we buy, sell, develop, or preserve at our whim, or as a *community,* to which we realize we belong, or from which we pretend we can remove ourselves.

White uses different metaphors and images in his essay. On the one hand, he claims that the Bible has deemed us the monarchs of the world, that we are commanded to subdue and rule the rest of creation. But he also claims that "the spirits in natural objects ... evaporated [and m]an's effective monopoly on spirit in this world was confirmed." Nature becomes "de-spirited," a collection of raw materials, a tool for the fulfillment of human needs. Environmentalism that endorses the idea of spirit in nature, and the dethronement of the human from the position of ruler, raises a specter of paganism, and so one can understand a religious assumption in which these two ideas are linked or even mutually implicative.

But the opposite is true: they almost negate each other. The image of ruler, the stand-in for God, is not the relationship of the carpenter to the hammer, or even the logger to the tree. Rulers do not reign over raw materials but over other beings. Furthermore, can it ever be said that a kingdom is created for the sake of the ruler? Is it not the opposite? It is the ruler who is fulfilling a function, a means to the end of the proper flourishing of the kingdom. It is the ruler who is "created" (appointed) for the sake of the kingdom.

Thus, it is not our conception of the human as sovereign that is the constitutive feature of environmental degradation. Rather, it is our view of nature as mere stuff, as so much raw material and replaceable parts, coupled with a belief in unlimited technological potential to invent or replace the "spare parts," that has led to the absence of moral responsibility and the enabling of ecological destruction.

Transforming this doctrine allows the return of wonder: one may appreciate the functionality of the design of a table or hammer—but we are never in absolute awe of our tools. Our ability to experience the sublime, the mystery in the inexplicable intricacy of the natural world, gives lie to the view that nature is just raw material, subject only to dictates of prudence. The converse is also true: the frequent *inability* to experience those deeply human, and deeply religious, emotions stems from the complete transformation of nature into commodities, and therefore the diminution of the self to a one-dimensional consumer, someone who uses nature but doesn't live in it. As the great scholar and activist Rabbi Abraham Joshua Heschel wrote presciently more than half a century ago:

> As civilization advances, the sense of wonder declines. Such decline is an alarming symptom of our state of mind. We will not perish for want of information, but only for want of appreciation.[5]

A fundamental religious stance regarding Creation is that of awe (what Heschel referred to as "radical amazement"), a component of environmental education that is often nonexistent or underdeveloped. Emphasizing the dream over the nightmare determines pedagogy. Most technical environmental education focuses on what we do to nature, meaning how we negatively impact the world around us, and what we should do to stop. A spiritually oriented approach will eventually get to that, but will take as crucially prior, and more fundamental, what nature does to us, what it means to us (or should), how it shapes our lives, or could. If we have no spiritual connection or response to the world around us, if we have faith that technology can replace life-support systems, why worry about destroying them?

The well-known midrash from *Kohelet Rabbah,* dating back to sometime before the ninth century CE, emphasizes this as well:

> Consider God's doing! Who can straighten what He has twisted? (Eccles. 7:13). When the Holy Blessed One created the first Adam, God showed Adam all the trees of the Garden of Eden and said: "See My works, how lovely they are, how fine they are. All I have created, I created for you. Take care not to corrupt and destroy My world, for if you ruin it, there is no one to come after you to put it right" (*Eccles. Rabbah* 7).

Although we emphasize the novelty of so many environmental challenges, clearly the sages of over a thousand years ago also had a sense of the possibility of widespread destruction of which the human being was capable. But preceding the gloom of the threat is the invitation to appreciate the beauty and joy that is part of the natural world. This is a powerful educational statement: first we are to open ourselves up to what the world does to us, for us, and only then can we confront what we do to the world in return, our responsibility for it. As Fritz Rothschild wrote in his introduction to Heschel's *Between Man and God:* "One has to be responsive before one can become responsible."

Religion and Environmentalism: Common Ground and Unique Messages

There are, in fact, more points of agreement between religion and (allegedly secular) environmentalism than may first meet the eye. For instance, ecological and Jewish perspectives dovetail in seeing the natural world as precious or purposive. Biologist Paul Ehrlich compares popular complacency in the face of species extinction to a person boarding a plane, while someone is systematically popping the rivets out of various parts of the plane. But unlike the plane, we can never truly know whether a certain rivet (species) is fastening something minor (such as the "no smoking" sign) or holding the engine in place. Similarly, the midrash (*Bereishit Rabbah* 10:7, *Vayikra Rabbah* 22:2) claims that everything in the world is an integral part of creation, and that even things that seem superfluous or purposeless are necessary for human or others' needs.

Moreover, as opposed to secular humanism, both ecological thought (with its recognition of interdependence and the trans-human complexity of ecosystems) and religion (with an all-embracing God at the center) share a crucially important perspective, which I shall call "something-else-centrism." Whether in the theocentric approach of religion or the biocentric approaches of many types of environmentalism, something other than human needs and perspectives is paramount—the upshot being some version of human humility in the face of an existence greater than ourselves. Whether the Earth belongs to God or simply to itself, it surely isn't ours.

Shared views on human humility and hubris are relevant to the environmental claim that our behavior has reached and breached limits of ecological life support, putting us in peril. We need to disavow the ingrained belief that we can "invent" ourselves out of the current crisis with technology. We must work within the limitations the world places on us, not pretend they don't exist or that we can ignore them. This requires changing our notions of progress, from mere economic growth to holistic conceptions of fundamental human welfare for current and future generations. Religion can fill this function as well, serving as a ground of meaning, as a locus of faith and connection (from *re-ligate*) to our progenitors and the wisdom of the ages on the one hand, and our progeny, our responsibilities to future generations on the other.

Modern Western liberal technological society and free-market capitalism have made an idol of the individual and the immediate gratification of her or his personal needs. Environmentalism and religion emphasize the devastating implications of that fetish, and harmonize in their belief in the importance of a greater whole.

Religion speaks in terms of eternity, emphasizing the long term, much as environmentalists emphasize how our actions today will affect the Earth and future generations. This contrasts sharply with the quarterly report and the four-year term of office, which fail to take environmental health and human well-being over the long term into account. Religion can also help promote spiritual fulfillment over materialism, helping us combat the rampant, vapid consumerism of modern life. Focusing on spiritual growth helps our reprioritization of personal and collective goals, re-envisioning the good life and what is necessary to make it a reality.

Traditional fears that concern for nature either flirts with paganism or hinders fulfilling important human needs have been, or should be, replaced by the realization that contemporary materialism and consumerism are much more idolatrous than preserving God's Creation ("their idols are silver and gold ..." [Ps. 115:4]) and that ensuring a just, sustainable society in a healthy world is the supreme fulfillment of human needs, as well as a religious imperative. Finally, the realization that we are but guests on this planet, and that we have a choice as to how we bequeath it to our posterity, is an overarching theme for both religion and environmentalism.

Addressing potential skeptics, geographer Jeanne Kay sums this up well when she writes:

> A society that explains destruction of pasturage as the result of God's anger over idolatry or insincerity in Temple sacrifices rather than as the direct outcome of climatic fluctuations or overgrazing may have little to offer modern resource management. Few environmentalists today believe that environmental deterioration results from oppression of widows and orphans.... Yet an environmentalism based upon biblical commandments can discourage coveting one's neighbor's property and exploiting the poor as stepping stones to wealth and power: greed has long been blamed as a root of the current environmental crisis. An environmentalism based in biblical poetry can encourage us to see in nature living souls who praise their Creator and shout for joy. A belief that the entire range of human actions has environmental repercussions can add a new dimension to ecological awareness.[6]

Unnatural Judaism: From Alienation to Reconnection

While there is much more to be said about the environment and religion in general, Judaism is its own special case. Regarding the immediate responses to White, in that first decade there were a handful of rabbis and scholars who took up the cudgels to defend the honor of Israel. Robert Gordis, Eric Freudenstein, Norman Lamm, and others wrote persuasively about the environmental values of biblical and rabbinic Judaism,[7] and it was relatively easy to acquit Judaism of the charge leveled at the "Judaeo-Christian" tradition of despoiling the Earth, both in principle and in historical reality: if Jews couldn't even own land in Europe and the Middle East for much of that time, how could we be blamed for ruining it?

So how much could Judaism have to say about this whole issue? When people heard the topic of this book, a common response was: "Short book, huh?" While some made this comment out of ignorance of the breadth and depth of Jewish tradition, the quip has a deeper level. After all, the connections I am trying to make are not facile or obvious. Indeed, another early publication (the first Jewish piece to be published in an environmental journal) was highly critical. The provocative essay "The Unnatural Jew," by rabbi and professor Steven Schwartzschild begins:

> In my philosophy department the graduate students organize an annual picnic. For some time past quasi-formal invitations have explicitly excluded me on the grounds that I am known to be at odds with nature. So I am. My dislike of nature goes deep: nonhuman nature, mountain ranges, wildernesses, tundra, even beautiful but unsettled landscapes strike me as opponents, which, as the Bible commands (Gen. 1:28–30), I am to fill and conquer. I really do not like the world, and I think it foolish to tell me that I had better.... One explanation of my attitude is historical. My paternal family lived in Frankfurt-on-the-Main, where I was born, since before 1500. We have been urban for well over half a millennium.... Here I want to analyze whether this is only an idiosyncratic or mainly historical attitude, or whether more important, even philosophical, factors are significantly involved. Might it be that Judaism and nature are at odds? Richard Popkin once put this "Zen" problem to me: who was the last famous Jewish mountain climber? Indeed, most Jews in remembered history are unnatural persons.[8]

This text never fails to trigger a heated discussion in groups. Most people are offended by his claims. Schwartzschild meant it as highest praise, but in this day and age, who wants to be classed as "an unnatural person"? When asked for responses, examples are usually given from biblical sources: psalmic paeans to the natural world, sabbatical restrictions, in general the vision of an agrarian people living in harmony with the land. While these go back twenty-five hundred years and more, they do serve both to widen his horizon from the period of the Diaspora to which he refers and also to critique implicitly his notion of un/natural persons. Is a connection to nature only through picnics and extreme sports? What about the day-to-day productive relationship involved in agriculture?

Schwartzschild's claim boils down to a radically transcendental theology, which essentially takes no account of other theological strains in Judaism. Or rather, he acknowledges them and labels them heretical: anything remotely immanental, such as Kabbalah, Spinoza, and even Zionism, are beyond the pale for him. In his view, both God and human are radically separated from nature. Furthermore, he claims that too much admiration or even appreciation of nature may indeed be ultimately heretical: we are commanded to combat nature and emerge victorious. Critics of this position claim that that would be the ultimate Pyrrhic victory. But is his view Jewishly justifiable?

Indeed, the typical or normal historical situation of Jews in the Diaspora and their environment, or natural surroundings, was more one of alienation or non-engagement, and much work needs to be done to reconnect Judaism and Jewish sources to questions of nature and the environment. There are several reasons for this historical disconnect, which are important to raise and evaluate. They are presented here in somewhat telegraphic form and discussed in greater length at relevant places in the coming chapters. As another illustration of the plural voices in our history and sources, the "point" (the reasons for alienation or neglect) is presented here, along with the "counterpoint," the features in Jewish tradition or belief that negate or offer an alternative narrative to the ecologically or environmentally unsympathetic tendency:

- *Anti-paganism:* An oft-cited factor regarding monotheistic religions and their attitudes to the natural world is deeply rooted anti-pagan polemics, stemming from a strong belief in a transcendent God, which implies a chasm between Creator and Creation, and therefore a desacralization of the natural world. Once nature ceased to be an object of worship, it is claimed, it was just stuff, raw materials awaiting exploitation.

  This is countered both by kabbalistic beliefs that posit a more immanental spirituality (divine sparks within the animal and inanimate worlds), as well as a stewardship ethic that is fundamentally different from a more biocentric (nature-centric, or nature-sanctifying) paganism. That is, the natural world does not have to be holy or worshiped in order to be nurtured or protected as God's creation and our own source of sustenance, physical and otherwise. See more on this in chapters 2 and 3.

- *Exile from the Land:* Two thousand years of exile from the Land, leading to Diasporic Jewish life without an organic and autonomous relationship to the immediate environment, or social responsibility for it, have taken their toll. The book replaced the world in many senses, becoming a virtual reality that took the place of the real one outside the window. The only natural environment that was related to seriously in the liturgy and celebrations of traditional Jewish culture was the Land of Israel, and so the local one—whether Europe, North Africa, or Asia—was deemed insignificant.

  Here, Zionism and the return to the Land of Israel suggest a profound redefinition of the relationship between

Judaism and the natural world, and of our responsibilities toward our environment, that have implications for Jews the world over. Moreover, not everything is place-dependent: there are a host of values and practices that have universal validity, or *could* have much wider application, given changing consciousness and identities. The "at-homeness" of Jews in the United States, and their involvement with leading social issues of all types, together with the rise of global environmental challenges, have created an opening for a new type of Jewish engagement with the environment. See chapters 3, 5, and 6 for an exploration of these claims.

- *Eternal Truth vs. Temporal Reality:* A dominant strain of traditional belief dichotomizes and prioritizes between body and soul (*guf* and *nefesh*), matter and spirit (*gashmi* and *ruchani*), transient existence and eternal life (*chayei sha'ah* and *chayei netzach*), paralleling this world and the next (*olam hazeh* and *olam haba*). The strong emphasis on the spiritual, with the nearly exclusive value placed on Torah study as the key to eternal life, makes a deep relationship with nature and environmental concern seem inconsequential (or even spiritually dangerous) by comparison.

  Again, Kabbalistic and Hasidic approaches to *avoda begashmi'ut* (material work), focusing on the physical world, as well as other, no less classical ideas of the relative importance of this world versus the next, and the essential goodness of the body and of nature being God's handiwork, stand in contrast. See chapter 3 for further discussion of this point.

Beyond the historical question of Judaism and the natural world is the contemporary question of the range of Jewish attitudes to the loosely defined movement and collection of ideologies and worldviews known as "environmentalism." Here, too, there have been some misgivings:

- Environmentalism is a social-political ideology that encourages a global perspective. Might the cosmopolitanism of environmentalism be a threat to traditional Judaism? Being a universal concern, it should in this view be secondary to the focus on ensuring continued Jewish existence. Moreover, it seems to imply commonality with humanity at the expense of uniqueness and distinctiveness. Connecting to Torah makes us Jewish—what does connecting to nature (even when viewed as Creation) make us? If our survival is paramount, how can our engaging with a global, physical issue be of help?

  Responses to this range from the ethical *"Im ani rak le'atzmi, ma ani?"*—"If I am only for myself, what am I?" (the second half of Hillel's famous dictum), to the more strategic "Kids today are concerned about ecology, and to keep youth committed we need to speak their language," to the spiritual response that connecting to creation and caring for the environment (through traditional teachings) are indeed Jewish acts that can deepen Jewish identity and expression.

- Some traditional Jews, already heavily involved in more familiar acts of *tzedakah* and *gemilut chasadim* (acts of charity and lovingkindness), see environmentalism as competing with all those other more traditional claims on their *chesed* energies and resources. So while they might not actively oppose the support of environmental causes, those would have a distinctly low priority.

  Here an appropriate rejoinder would be that environmentalism concerns a lot more than just support of a cause; lifestyle and public-policy issues are paramount, in areas where one has to make fateful decisions no matter what organizations one contributes to.

- Among some circles of Jews with deep belief in divine *hash-gacha* (providence), too much worry can be a sign of not enough faith. In other words, we should be able to fulfill *mitzvot*, commandments, without worrying about the consequences. For instance, when an Ultra-Orthodox colleague of mine was asked about her family of eight, in a discussion about population increase, including crowding and environmental stress, her response was simply: "God brings the children into the world, He'll [*sic*] find a place for them."

  In contrast, though, we are bidden not to depend on miracles to solve problems *(ein somchin al ha-nes)*, and in the midrash quoted on page 22, God takes Adam around the garden, and makes it clear that there will be no one to clean up after us, and solve our problems for us.

בראשית ברא
Bereishit Bara'

Creator, Creating, Creation, Creatures, and Us

Biblical Beginnings: Readers, Reading, Readings, How to Read—and Us

If the Bible were meant to be exclusively the law book of a particular tradition, or just the historical narrative of one people, it could have dispensed with the opening chapters of the Book of Genesis. These chapters tell a cosmic tale, beyond any legislation and beyond the particularistic story of any one nation, which puts those laws and narratives of later sections into a universal context of all creation. This tale paints a complex portrait of creation and of humanity, a single family (eventually split into distinct branches) inhabiting that world. Moreover, it presents, both descriptively and prescriptively, the intricate, at times contradictory, relationships between the two.

These relations, between humanity and creation, between people and the world *(adam* and *adamah)*[1], are quintessential religious issues, even as they are the overarching categories of environmental discourse. A central thesis underlying this work is that religious values and worldviews meet up with environmental critiques of modern society in many more places than we might think, and the broad human-world nexus of the beginning of the Beginning, with all its problematic commandments, ambivalent blessings, and mythic pronouncements, is the first and perhaps foremost such encounter.

In opening the Bible and reading Genesis, what exactly are we reading? What type of text is it, and what can we realistically hope to gain from our encounter with it? An academic approach finds mainly historical interest in these ancient texts, seeing them as myths that have informed the development of Western civilization, artifacts of intellectual history to be held at arm's length and scrutinized. My purpose is the opposite: to look at them as a living tradition, a spiritual language in which we can grapple with current issues. Although it is important to assess claims such as White's, that certain texts and traditions have functioned in a certain way in society throughout the ages, that is background to the more central question of how they can contribute to us, in our society, in our age.

Readers of a more fundamentalist bent often read Genesis as a type of science, that is, a source of truths (or at least incontrovertible, empirical data) about the formation of the physical world. Neither is this my purpose here: indeed, "creationism" does not hold wide currency in the Jewish world, most probably because of the strong tradition of multilayered interpretation, including midrashic approaches, that free the text from the straitjacket of a narrow or shallow literalism. Moreover, to read the magisterial chapters of Creation, which deal with some of the fundamental mysteries of existence, as a textbook of paleontology is, in traditional Jewish terms, to miss the *ikkar,* the main thing; it is to focus on trivial, temporal physical events *(sha'ah)* instead of the significant, eternal, spiritual truths *(netzach).* We are searching for values, not facts, and just as we should acknowledge that we currently possess better sources for ascertaining the facts of "how it really may have happened," we should equally allow that when it comes to guidance about how to act, "how we should make it happen," we have a great deal left to learn, and contemporary thinking has no absolute or necessary advantage over ancient sources.

Another approach states that since the Bible is a religious book, it is mainly about God, and we should read it for theological reasons. In response to this, Rabbi Abraham Joshua Heschel has written that more than human theology, what people think about God, the Bible is "divine anthropology"—a God's-eye view of people. In other words, we are not looking primarily for scientific, historical, or even theological insight—we are looking for wisdom and understanding about human existence, and guidance about understanding our place in the world.

Stories of Creations: Biblical Cubism

Our rights and responsibilities—our duties and privileges—with respect to the world that is our common home are elaborated and specified in other parts of the Bible and rabbinic literature, but their fundamental conceptual basis is here in Genesis[2] and the Creation stories. Yes, *stories,* for Genesis presents us with two distinct versions of the creation of the world, and of people, each with its own internal complexities and layered meanings. Moreover, when read together, these stories (in Genesis 1 and 2) use a sort of "literary parallax" to create a composite portrait that strives to do justice to the many sides of its subjects: the Creator, the creating, the Creation, and the creatures, including ourselves. Biblical scholar and literary critic Robert Alter likens the artistry of the biblical author/editor to that of a post-Cubist artist, able to present different perspectives of a complex and even contradictory multidimensional subject together in the same text.[3]

Lest we be sidetracked by denominational polemics, it should be noted at the outset that this insight of multiple versions of Creation has been championed by traditional commentators, such as Rabbenu Bahya, and contemporary Orthodox thinkers, such as Rabbi Joseph Soloveitchik and Rabbi Mordechai Breuer, as well as by secular critics, scholars, and others. Although it is true that those looking for proof that scripture is less than divine and stems from many (human) textual traditions have come to look upon repetition and contradiction in the biblical narrative as evidence attesting to an imperfect source, this is far from a logical imperative. As we shall see in the following discussion, the text itself may be "contradictory" in many details of the Creation stories, but like Alter's image of Cubist visual art, this stems from the contradictory nature of the subject, and the inherent impossibility of representing different perspectives and dimensions in what is essentially a linear, or two-dimensional, medium—the written word.

Genesis 1 and 2: Comparative Readings

What are these two stories? The first, in chapter 1, is probably the better known of the two, with the orderly day-by-day creations ("and there was evening, and there was morning ...") culminating in the creation of *adam*/the human (male and female together—1:27) in the divine image on the sixth day, blessed to be populous and dominant, and then the declaration of Shabbat on the seventh day. The second chapter starts right after that, and tells the whole progression quite differently, with no daily rhythm, and including the well-known scene of the creation of the companion for *adam* from that creature's side or rib. Chapter 2 also tells of the Garden of Eden, and the placement of *adam* there.

> **First Account (1:1–2:4a; excerpts)**
> When God began to create heaven and earth ... God said, "Let there be light"; and there was light. God saw the light was good, and God separated the light from the darkness....
> And there was evening and there was morning, a first day.

God said, "Let there be an expanse...." God called the expanse Sky. And there was evening and there was morning, a second day.

God said, "Let the water below the sky be gathered into one area, that the dry land may appear.... Let the earth sprout vegetation...." And God saw that this was good. And there was evening and there was morning, a third day.

God said, "Let there be lights in the expanse of the sky...." God made the two great lights.... And God saw that it was good. And there was evening and there was morning, a fourth day.

God said, "Let the waters bring forth swarms of living creatures and birds that fly...." And God saw that this was good. God blessed them, saying, "Be fertile and increase...." And there was evening and there was morning, a fifth day.

God said, "Let the earth bring forth every kind of living creature...." And God said, "Let us make man in our image, after our likeness...." Male and female He created them. God blessed them and God said to them, "Be fertile and increase, fill the earth and master it; and rule...." God said, "See, I give you every seed-bearing plant that is upon all the earth, and every tree.... they shall be yours for food...." And God saw all that He had made, and found it very good. And there was evening and there was morning, the sixth day....

On the seventh day God finished the work that he had been doing ... and God blessed the seventh day.... Such is the story of heaven and earth when they were created.

Second Account (2:4b–2:25; excerpts)

When the Lord God made earth and heaven—when no shrub of the field was yet on earth and no grasses of the field had yet sprouted, because the Lord God had not sent rain upon the earth, and there was no man to till the soil ...

the Lord God formed man *(adam)* from the dust of the earth *(adamah)*....

The Lord God planted a garden in Eden, in the east, and placed there the man whom He had formed. And from the ground the Lord God caused to grow every tree that was pleasing to the sight and good for food, with the tree of life in the middle of the garden, and the tree of knowledge of good and bad....

The Lord God took the man and placed him in the garden of Eden to till it and tend it. And the Lord God commanded the man, saying, "Of every tree of the garden you are free to eat; but as for the tree of knowledge of good and bad, you must not eat of it; for as soon as you eat of it, you shall die."

The Lord God said, "It is not good for man to be alone; I will make a fitting helper for him." And the Lord God formed out of the earth all the wild beasts and the birds of the sky, and brought them to the man to see what he would call them.... And the man gave names to all the cattle and to the birds of the sky and to all the wild beasts; but for Adam no fitting helper was found.

So the Lord God cast a deep sleep upon the man; and while he slept, He took one of his ribs ... and fashioned the rib that He had taken from the man into a woman; and He brought her to the man. Then the man said, "This one at last is bone of my bones, and flesh of my flesh. This one shall be called Woman, for from man was she taken...."

The two of them were naked, the man and his wife, yet they felt no shame.

Notice the basic difference in the simple order of Creation in the two versions of the story. The second version relates plainly that there was no vegetation, since God had not yet made it rain, and significantly, there were no people to work the ground (2:5). Then God made *adam* (v. 7), and only then did God plant a garden, and make the trees to grow (vv. 8–9). Later on (v. 19), God deems *adam's* solitary existence problematic and makes animals (including birds) as potential companions. This proves equally unsatisfactory, and the duality of the sexes comes into being as a better response to human solitude (vv. 21–23). Compare this with the well-known order of chapter 1, in which plants are created (Day 3, v. 12), then birds (Day 5, v. 21), then animals (Day 6, beginning v. 25), and only then *adam*, male and female simultaneously (Day 6, end–v. 27).

Again, rather than reading these blatant contradictions as flaws in the text,[4] we can more profitably see them as signposts to be attentive to other, more subtle differences between the retellings. For instance, the first story begins (1:1) and ends (2:4) with the ordered couplet "the heaven and the earth." The significance of the ordering becomes apparent when compared with the second half of the latter verse, deemed by many to be the beginning of the second story:[5] "When the Lord God made earth and heaven ... the Lord God formed *adam* from the dust of the earth." The first emphasizes the primacy of the heavenly member of the dyad, while the second gives precedence to the earthly element.

If this were an isolated instance, it might be of no account. But this distinction encapsulates some of the major differences between the two stories. The general perspective of the first story can be characterized as idealistic and "top down": God plans and executes the various acts of Creation, which are all deemed "good" (the whole being "very good"). There are no negatives at all, and everything seems to proceed according to plan, like an architect building from an existing blueprint.

All the various creatures are described in the most general terms, as species (with the curious exception of "the great sea monsters" of 1:21), including the human, who is seen as having an exclusively divine origin, with a divine character and mission. Indeed, were it not for chapter 2, the derivation of the name *adam* (from *adamah*) would be completely obscure. The commandment/blessing given to *adam* is a positive imperative to go forth, procreating and dominating—with no express limitations, either in their place or in their actions.

Compare these characteristics to the second story, which is more "bottom up" and realistic, more "earthly/earthy" in every respect. The story begins with a close-up of the parched and barren earth, and describes what God had *not* done (made it rain), and the fact that there was *no* human to till the earth to help the plants grow. The divine Creation seems to proceed more by trial and error than by grand design. Thus, in contrast to the multiple repetition of the "goodness" of everything in the first story, here the word *good* is used sporadically, in very different contexts. It is first contrasted with "evil" (a nonexistent concept in chapter 1) in the Tree of Knowledge of Good and Bad in the Garden (2:9). But most significantly, it is said unambiguously that it is *not good* that *adam* be alone (2:18). In other words, one of the creations is not working properly; God has created something imperfect. Then, like an artist or an inventor, trying to correct a flaw in the design, God tries one strategy—the animals as companions—and that, too, fails. Indeed, it is hard to imagine this type of failure in the Creation story of chapter 1. Only then does God hit on the "rib" idea, and the fact that the ideal type of fellowship will only be found within the human fold.

The earthiness of the world is expressed in the second story through much more specified, tangible descriptions: distinct rivers (Pishon, Gihon, Tigris, and Euphrates—vv. 11–14) flow to places with their own specific resources (Havila, with its gold and onyx; Ethiopia; Assyria). And *adam* is not "created" (*bara*, as in 1:27) but rather fashioned *(yitzer)* very explicitly out of the "dust of the ground" (2:7), and while that does include being infused with the divine breath of life, it is only in the first story that *adam* is said to be created "in the image of God" (*betzelem elohim*—1:27). *Adam* is then placed in a very particular place on the earth, a home in the Garden of Eden, which sets the stage for the possibility of exile from that home. In contrast, the entire world is home to the human race of chapter 1, and the idea of exile is inconceivable. Although chapter 2 does mention a positive mission in the Garden (*le'ovda uleshomra,* "to till it and tend it"), the divine commandment is an *issur,* a prohibition against eating from two particular trees there.

There are other stylistic and content differences between the stories. For instance, the first describes Creation as coming about primarily by separations and distinctions, while the second emphasizes mergers and combinations. Chapter 1 begins with water ("the deep"), and chapter 2 begins with the significant absence of water. God seems more distant, more transcendent in chapter 1, creating through fiat, while in chapter 2 the Divine is more present, more immanent, creating through physical formation. Of course, the relations of the sexes are radically different in their formulation: chapter 1 is essentially egalitarian (being created identically and together), while chapter 2 is more complex, certainly admitting of a more sexist reading of the story of the creation of woman from man.[6]

Orthodox scholar Rabbi Joseph Soloveitchik, in his seminal work *The Lonely Man of Faith,* elaborates a spiritual typology of two types of human existence based on these stories: Adam I, endowed with technical prowess and therefore embodying a majestic approach to the world, and Adam II, who is existentially alone, searching for connections to God and to fellow humans.[7]

Another distinction, which will lead us to the more particularly environmental implications of these narratives, is the apparent representation or conceptualization of nature. In chapter 1, the world is wilderness, with no hint of agriculture/horticulture, domestication, or human labor as such. The creation of humanity comes as the culmination of the ordered series of creations, and so the rest of Creation that preceded *adam* exists independent of humans and human needs and purposes.

Compare that with chapter 2, where the human is at the narrative center, not the climax. As mentioned, the world has differentiated places, and *adam* is placed specifically in a garden, for the express purpose of labor—cultivation and preservation. Animals come into being to fulfill a human need, although significantly it is an emotional, not an economic, one. And while Adam acquires a certain amount of control over the animals in the act of naming them (2:19–20), this also expresses intimacy and relationship.

Genesis 1: Master and Rule—The Demands of Dominion

Given the preceding elaboration of the differences between the Creation stories, we are now ready to look at them more closely, and read them, separately and together, with more specifically environmental questions in mind. Let's begin with the most ecologically notorious part of the narrative, the charge of 1:28, which states: "God blessed them and God said to them, 'Be fertile and increase, fill the earth and master it; and rule the fish of the sea, the birds of the sky, and all the living things that creep on earth.'"

There is no linguistic way to get around the central terms here. They cannot be reinterpreted to align with twenty-first-century environmental sensibilities. We humans are indeed enjoined to breed like rabbits (or more specifically, like fish and birds, for they receive the same divine blessing of fecundity—cf. 1:22),[8] but distinctive to the human *telos,* we are to "master" (or "conquer") the land *(vekivshuha)* and "rule" (or "dominate," "have dominion over"—*ur'du)* the rest of the fauna. The root *k-v-sh* means literally to trample or crush (which is done in pickling vegetables, *kevushim,* or from a different context, in paving a road, *kvish).*[9]

And dominate, *r-d-h,* implies a distinct hierarchy of who is above and who below,[10] and it gives us the modern Hebrew word for dictator *(rodan).* Medieval commentator Nachmanides, in his comment on this verse, even glosses this root as referring to the relationship between master and slave.

But the easy, superficial, and therefore mistaken reading would be one in which Genesis 1 is stereotyped as the environmentally "bad" chapter, and Genesis 2 as the "good" one—that reads 1:28 as the root of all ecological evil, effectively counterbalanced only by 2:15, the mission to "work and to guard" the Garden. A closer look at the specifics of the texts shows why this simplistic dichotomous reading is misguided. The larger narrative texts in which these lone verses are embedded are more nuanced and complex, and so we must remember also the difference in historical context. This verse, mandating conquest and dominion, is categorically a *blessing,* and an uplifting and empowering one at that. Some three thousand years ago (and two thousand and one thousand as well), this vision promised hope and dignity for a society with a short average life span and great susceptibility to natural threats (see, for instance, the very real threat of animals to humans expressed in Jer. 15:3 and 34:20 and in Isa. 34).

Moreover, as much maligned as transcendental biblical monotheism is regarding the separation of the Creator from Creation, this blessing is also an emancipation proclamation from the more oppressive nature-human relations of paganism. While it is currently fashionable to idealize nature-worshiping tribal religions, especially in environmental terms,[11] the power ascribed to deified nature, coupled with the technological inability to cope with natural threats, often led to the increased subjugation of humans to natural forces, which induced terror and required appeasement, including human sacrifice. So, a statement such as the human subjugation of nature, while difficult to interpret clearly in the affirmative, has a strong and clear referent in the negation of its opposite: humans are not to be cruelly subjugated to the natural world, or to natural forces. The promise of human mastery and dominion over the natural world—a total pipe dream at the time of its promulgation—was therefore reassuring, and even liberating.

But let's go deeper: what is the nature of this mastery and dominion? What type of behavior does it sanction? Are we truly meant to govern the wild animals—or does this just mean to domesticate some? R. Saadya Gaon (Egypt, tenth century), basing himself on the Gemara in *Sanhedrin* 59b, elaborates at length:

> the entire range of devices with which man rules over the animals: over some with fetters and bridles, over some with ropes and reins, over some with enclosures and chains, over some with weapons of the hunt, over some with cages and towers and so on ...[12]

Nachmanides as well, in his commentary on this verse, emphasizes that God gave humans "strength and authority to do whatever they wish with animals and all crawling creatures, to build and to uproot, and to mine copper from the mountains...." Yet a close reading of the verses reveals the surprising fact that whatever else dominion of the animal kingdom may have meant when the text was originally promulgated, it did not include eating animals! The very next verse, 1:29, states: "God said, 'See, I give you every seed-bearing plant that is upon all the earth, and every tree that has seed-bearing fruit; they shall be yours for food.'"

Although no ban on eating meat is explicitly stated here (there are no prohibitions of any type in chapter 1), the affirmation of those things that are permitted fare makes the limitation clear (*Sanhedrin* 59b). And as the next verse attests, this was true of all living things: there was no carnivory in Creation as originally conceived.[13] This condition also implied a deeper affinity or fellowship between humans and other animals than what might be otherwise inferred from the verses on subjugation: here, all humans and animals were on the same side of the knife and fork (and tooth and claw). This situation changed after the Flood (cf. Gen. 9:3), when overt permission to eat meat was granted, in the context of the Noahide laws of general morality. According to one interpretation, this concession was made as an outlet for humans to sublimate their aggression, the lack of which had led their antediluvian predecessors to lawlessness and violence.

Another significant aspect of the narrative of chapter 1 is the often overlooked fact that God famously deems "good" all the various creations throughout the process, crucially before the appearance of humans. Although it is clear that the human is no afterthought in Creation, there is no hint that light, earth, water, vegetation, stars, planets, and other animals are good for their eventual functional value to humans. They are proclaimed good on their own terms, for their own, or general divine, purposes. This is emphasized by Maimonides in his *Guide for the Perplexed*: "all beings should not be believed to exist for the sake of man's existence. Rather, all other beings too were intended to exist for their own sakes, not for the sake of something else" (3:13).

No less noteworthy is the fact that neither of the two mentions of "good" on the sixth day is applied to the human.[14] It is the whole of Creation, including the human, that is declared "very good" (1:31). And so, while it could be claimed that Creation comes to its fruition with the presence of humans, each part of that whole clearly has its own intrinsic value.

So even in the context of the Creation story of chapter 1, dominion and conquest are not as rapacious as they have been made out to be. Likewise, throughout the ages this verse was rarely used as a mandate to engage in acts connected to "subduing nature": much more attention was given to the first half of the verse, and questions surrounding the demands of procreation.[15]

Looking at the relationship between the two halves of this verse, a number of connections can be pointed out. One is that there seems to be a certain dissonance here: abundant reproduction is usually seen as a reflection of our animal selves, mastery of the world as an expression of the divine image. Another is that under certain interpretations, procreating and mastering or subduing nature are connected as activities incumbent upon males. In Jewish law, the commandment to procreate devolves, rather counterintuitively, only upon men (see the last mishnah of tractate *Yevamot,* ch. 6). When the Talmud asks why this should be so (*B. Yevamot* 65b), the answer is given: "it is written 'fill the earth and master it,' it is the nature of a man to master but it is not the nature of a woman to master." And so not only is procreation identified with mastery (making it a male commandment), but mastery also becomes associated with procreation, implying the womb to be a tool in the hands of men for populating and controlling the world.

But we need not let certain contemporary sensibilities cast such a cynical pall on our explication of these two fundamental human qualities and their connections. As mentioned above, the promise of mastery can be uplifting, and the blessing of fertility sheer joy, and the two together not far off from the psychological sources of meaning and fulfillment that we refer to as "work" and "love." Both are creative, both imply connecting to divine abundance, and as opposed to the previous androcentric interpretation, both can be seen to combine masculine and feminine principles and forces.

So as we have seen, the general context of chapter 1 is more nuanced and layered than a superficial reading might suggest, and even the call to mastery and dominion is not as irrevocably damning as imagined. Indeed, the common vegetarian diet, the joint blessing of fecundity (vv. 22 and 28), even the creation of humans on the same day with all other mammals, bespeak a fellowship, a continuity with the rest of the created world that is a powerful counterpoint to the usual assumption of the uniqueness of the human being implied in having been the only creature to be explicitly created in the image of God. So much so that perhaps a new interpretation of this central facet of the human creature in the biblical context is necessary—but that can only be explored after a discussion of chapter 2, the complementary completion of the Creation narrative.

Genesis 2: Serve and Preserve—The Stipulations of Stewardship

And what of the second story? Here, too, there are nuances and complexities. On the one hand the human, formed from the dust of the earth, is placed in the Garden with a much gentler charge, not to rule but, in effect, to serve, and the animals are seen as candidates for companionship. This seems to imply deep affinity and connectedness. But on the other hand, the human is still set apart as having uniquely received the divine breath of life, and no less important, the animals in the final analysis are ruled out as soul mates for the human. So this dynamic of the human as simultaneously a part of the created order but also apart from it, is central here as well, being a feature common to both stories and therefore a deep feature of the existential dilemma of being human. This will be expanded upon at some length below, but first, this central charge of "to work and to guard," *leovda uleshomra* (2:15), bears some unpacking.

Avoda is work or labor (and in the context of land, cultivation), and *shemira* is guarding or protecting. Interestingly, in translating the pair of terms here, alliteration has been favored: as in *to work and to watch* or *to till and to tend*. Along these lines, one of my favorites is *to serve and to preserve*. One can add to that *observe* (as in commandments, such as *shemirat Shabbat,* the observance of the Sabbath), for it is surely no accident that both these terms have such cultic associations. Cultivating the soil and worshiping God are the same word in Hebrew *(avoda)*; indeed, the English word *worship* comes from *work*, just as *cult* is the root of *cultivate*.[16]

If we try to divine the meaning of these terms from their referents in other contexts, our relationship to the Garden and, by implication, the world, is homologous to our relationship with God: we are enjoined to do to the Garden what we do for God *(avoda*—service), and also what God does for or to us, as in the priestly blessing of Numbers 6:24: *"yevarechecha ... veyishmerecha,"* "May God bless you, and watch over you."

These strongly religious connotations of the central phrase of *leovda uleshomra* raise some troubling questions: if there is indeed a religious component to our relationship to the soil, to nature, to the world-as-garden, then how can we express that in our lives today, which are in general so cut off from the soil and its life? This certainly applies to the urban among us—the vast majority of Western society—but in many ways it is no less true about farmers. Ecologists attest that the land is a community, yet we treat it solely as a commodity, and our highly technologized agriculture, with its fertilizers and pesticides, hardly expresses a reverent attitude to the object of its endeavors. Work and worship, tilling and tending, could not be further apart.

This observation leads us to dig deeper into the dynamic of *leovda uleshomra* and uncover further layers. For instance, from what exactly are we meant to protect or guard the Garden? Some say from wild animals, or the less ordered, more chaotic world of nature outside the Garden. This doesn't ring true, though, because animals are clearly included in the Garden, the entire world has already been deemed "very good," and there is no implication of a radical dichotomy between the Garden and the world. I would suggest that the main threat to the Garden, and by extension, the world, is precisely the other pair of the dyad—the cultivation, the human work.

The mission is to work, to produce, to develop—but at the same time to preserve, to guard, to be vigilant that the work doesn't get out of hand. It must remain, in a word, sustainable. Indeed, perhaps the best translation of the biblical phrase *leovda uleshomra* is "sustainable development." Working the land is crucial for human flourishing, but guarding the earth is the critical complement. We need to guard the world precisely from our *avoda,* the effects of our own work. In our struggle for the earth's fruits, we sow the seeds of our own, and the world's, destruction, unless we temper our toil with responsibility and concern for posterity. This responsibility is at the root of the very important contemporary notion of stewardship. Classically, to be a steward is to be in the middle: above is the lord of the manor, who has entrusted his domain to the charge of the servant-steward, below is the realm of responsibility. Notice the duality here in the notion of responsibility: the steward is responsible *to* the one who is really in charge and at the same time responsible *for* the things entrusted. There is no traditional Hebrew term for the idea of stewardship, but it seems clear that this is another good translation of the biblical ideal of *leovda uleshomra.*

The image is developed in the mystical text *Zohar Hadash* (5a), where Creation is likened to a king who ruled a city, who built and maintained it, and then decided to appoint one of the residents as ruler over it in his stead. Everything would be handed over to the appointee, his job being *melechet olam,* the work, or craft, of the world—to provide for the needs of the world and its perpetuation. Here we see a synthesis of Genesis 1 and 2: preserving, sustaining, and developing the world as an expression of dominion. Human dominion can only be stewardship, because we are not autonomous or sovereign rulers in a world that is not ours. This is as valid a claim from a secular Darwinian point of view as it is from a religious perspective: in neither case is the human being nature's transcendent lord and master.

Stewardship, though, as an environmental ethical ideal, has been criticized from different quarters. More extreme "greens" note its effectively anthropocentric stance, and the strong role it assigns to humans in the natural world. It is indeed different from a Jainist, or a deep-ecological radical ideal of absolute nonintervention, but for that very reason, it may be a more realistic model for the world today. Others say that behind the noble idea of stewardship lurks the much more problematic, more technocratic concept of management. Is nature something to be managed? A few years ago, *Scientific American* put out an issue titled "Towards A Managed Earth." Note the acronym (TAME)—is that the ideal that we strive for? What about wildness, and wilderness? What happens to the world, and to the human being, if everything comes under our (now well-meaning, hopefully greener) thumb?

Moreover, are we capable of managing the world? Will we ever know enough to perform that task wisely? The Earth is infinitely more complicated than a module of our own design. What about human humility? These two critiques dovetail: one of the phenomena in the world that inspires, or even enforces humility, is awe-inspiring wild nature. It is interesting to note that contemporary Hebrew has no simple translation for the idea of wilderness. The most common colloquial term that is used is *Eretz Bereishit* (lit. "the land of Creation," or "Genesis-country").

The most cogent response to these criticisms is that while we always need to temper our attempts at understanding and administering the environment with healthy doses of humility, we no longer really have a choice regarding our role as stewards (if we ever did). True, we cannot totally manage the earth—nor should we strive to— but our impact on it is so great that we have to take responsibility for shaping policy for our actions, which determine a great deal of the course of the planet. In other words, if there is anything that we need to manage, it is ourselves, first and foremost. Stewardship, then, is more of a stance, an attitude about service and discipline than a scientific vision of a type of control. And it may be an unavoidable part of the human condition. As with freedom, in the words of Sartre, it could be that we are doomed to stewardship.

The issues of human humility and responsibility are explored in a well-known midrash from the Talmud on the meaning of the Creation stories. In tractate *Sanhedrin* (38a), the Rabbis ask the seemingly straightforward question: Why was the first human created on the very eve of Shabbat, last in the order of Creation? What can we learn from this detail of the narrative of chapter 1? As in many midrashic contexts, there isn't one (correct) answer, but a plurality of interpretations. Here are four different answers, each of which undercuts an easy or superficial reading:

> The Rabbis taught: *Adam* (the human) was created on the eve of the Sabbath (i.e., last). And why (what can we learn from the order of Creation in chapter 1)?
>
> a. So that heretics would not be able to claim that God had a partner in the act of Creation;
> b. *Another answer:* so that the human could enter into a mitzvah immediately (Shabbat);
> c. *Another answer:* so that if he becomes too haughty, he can be told: the gnat preceded you in the order of Creation;
> d. *Another answer:* so that he could enter into a banquet immediately. This is similar to a flesh-and-blood king who built a palace, furnished it, laid a banquet, and then invited in the honored guests. (Talmud *Sanhedrin* 38a).

The first answer (a) points out that if humans had appeared earlier on the stage of Creation, it might be claimed that they participated with God in creating the other creatures. Although we are created in God's image, and charged with imitating God, we are not God, and must not appropriate for ourselves Godlike powers of creation. Being last, while perhaps not least, emphasizes the chasm between the human and the Divine.

Why, though, specifically on the eve of Shabbat? The second answer (b) emphasizes that the first human action is to observe Shabbat—that is, celebrate Creation—and not intervene in it, thus crucially postponing the immediate fulfillment of the commandment to conquer and dominate.

So much momentousness is ascribed to the creation of humans that it is taken as a given that the human being is the crowning glory and completion of the Creation process. But that would be a mistaken reading of the text: the human is the *penultimate* creation in the first Creation story, not the ultimate one. If there is any implication at all in the ordering of Creation (simple to complex, lower to higher level), it is the Shabbat that is the crowning glory. The best way to understand the significance of the myriad Shabbat restrictions and limitations is as a limit to human creativity and a reinforcement of human creatureliness one full day a week.

The message of humility is more caustic in the third answer (c). This is the most radically decentering reading of a story that is otherwise a paean to the human being as the crowning glory of Creation. Last, and therefore least, there is little meaning to the vigor associated with conquest if it takes no account of the precedence of other "lower" creatures.

The Talmud's last answer (d) finally plays up human centrality: God is the king, and we are the guests of honor at the feast. Here, finally, is the standard reading of the Creation story, with the human at the very top and everything else created to serve human need.

Or is it? If I could choose one text from all of Jewish tradition to represent the essence of environmental values, this would be a strong contender. Guests, even honored ones, are not the lords of the manor; indeed, most of environmental ethics and sustainable development policy could be based precisely on the viewpoint of the guest. Just think of what you would and wouldn't do as a guest in someone else's home. How much would you eat from another's table—even if you felt it were a banquet laid for you? Would you chop up the furniture for kindling? Kill the pets? Deny other guests their share of the host's bounty? Whether we base this sensibility on belief in God as the ultimate landlord or not, we are indeed guests, here for a twinkling in the cosmic long haul. This ties in directly with stewardship, for even if we are guests, or tenants, maybe even the "main tenants," we are still responsible for the maintenance that is within our power.

Between Apes and Angels: On Being a Part of, and Apart From

> What is the question now placed before society with a glib assurance the most astounding? The question is this: Is man an ape or an angel? My Lord, I am on the side of the angels!
>
> —Benjamin Disraeli

> The Torah inculcates in us a sense of our modesty and lowliness, that we should ever be cognizant of the fact that we are of the same stuff as the ass and mule, the cabbage and pomegranate, and even the lifeless stone.
>
> —Ibn Kaspi, *Adnei Kesef,* commentary on Deuteronomy 22:6

The image of the steward, or of the (honored) guest, is still troubling to some eco-critics, concerned that any belief in the centrality of the human in the natural world is infected with the hubris that has brought on our current environmental crisis. They would deny any uniqueness to the human species, arguing that only a radical egalitarianism among all creatures will achieve the requisite sea change in values and behavior. Yet the very existence of a human-caused environmental crisis argues for exceptional human capabilities, which bestow upon us an exclusive status with concomitant responsibilities. This is partly analogous to the traditional Jewish doctrine of chosenness, which implies a certain mission or role to play, defining duty rather than conferring privilege and making no claims to intrinsic superiority. A certain element of chosenness of the human species is virtually inescapable. Again, this is not a claim to some absolute supremacy, but rather to some pivotal function in the ongoing development of the world that implies both obligation and accountability.

We can also temper this rather grandiose view of human significance for all of creation with a modicum of modesty and even a sense of humor. For is it not understandable that we have an anthropocentric view of the world—that we see ourselves somehow at the center of our environment (i.e., that which surrounds)? Wouldn't a fish have a pisco-centric view of the world (in its case, probably just the ocean), and the horse an equo-centric philosophy? Anyone who knows cats understands that they absolutely have a felino-centric ideology. Seeing the world as surrounding us, with us at a special place in the center, may be the most common, *natural* point of view.

But therein lies a paradoxical implication, because a religious conviction that affirms the divine character of the human spirit should actually require us to transcend that natural species-centric perspective and assume a God's-eye view of the world and its ongoing functioning. In environmental terms, this is very close to environmental philosopher Aldo Leopold's well-known call to "think like a mountain," to assume the point of view of the whole system, which may demand different conclusions than those concerned solely with the benefit of a single species.

This debate centers on that most basic of religious questions: what is *adam*, the human? That exact phrasing appears first in the

Book of Psalms, where the classic dual answer is formulated quite sharply:

> When I behold Your heavens, the work of Your fingers,
> the moon and the stars that You set in place,
> what is man that You have been mindful of him,
> mortal man that You have taken note of him,
> that You have made him little less than the angels
> and adorned him with glory and majesty;
> You have made him master over Your handiwork,
> laying the world at his feet. (Ps. 8:4–7)

A unique combination of humility and grandeur, Godlike, yet dwarfed by God and some of the divine creations, man is still meant to be master in some sense over the rest. It is interesting to note that Benjamin Disraeli in the quote above was insulted by Darwin's implication that there is a continuum among animals of which we are a part. He felt this necessarily denied the divine image in humanity. But Genesis 2 proclaims that we come from the dust of the earth—can one get more lowly than that?! Indeed, as medieval commentator Ibn Kaspi emphasizes so poetically, we are connected to much more than just the other higher primates.[17]

In grappling with this question, of the divine and earthly sides of the human being, the Rabbis had no problem affirming that we are indeed both. Like animals, we eat, defecate, and procreate, whereas our powers of understanding, speech, and upright posture are like the angels, in the rabbinic conception (Talmud *Chagiga* 16a).

This connects with a startling interpretation of that difficult verse from Genesis 1:26: "And God said: 'Let *us* make man in *our* image, after *our* likeness.'" Who was God addressing? The possibility of plural deities is of course theologically ruled out. The most sensible, yet also most radical, interpretation is presented in a different midrash (*Genesis Rabbah* 8:3), which says plainly that God consulted with heaven and earth, with all the creations of each and every day. Similarly, the commentator R. David Kimchi (the RaDaK) on this verse quotes his father, R. Joseph Kimchi, who said that God proposed to all the elements *(yesodot)*, "Let us, you and I, make the human together in partnership *(beshituf)*."

Disraeli's choice is a false one, because as we see from biblical and later Jewish thought, we are surely both apes and angels. The mediation of these two sides of humanity, one of our greatest existential and moral challenges, is raised in the Book of Ecclesiastes. Environmentalists critical of religious doctrines of human superiority often quote relevant verses approvingly from this worldly-wise book, that affirm the connection, even the identity, of people and animals. For instance, 3:18–21:

> So I decided, as regards men, to dissociate them [from] the divine beings, and to face the fact that they are beasts. For in respect of the fate of man and the fate of beast, they have one and the same fate: as the one dies so dies the other, and both have the same life breath; man has no superiority over beast, since both amount to nothing. Both go to the same place; both came from dust and return to dust.

Yet, though occasionally salubrious as a slap in the face to human arrogance, isn't this cynicism or despair exactly what fuels the materialism and even hedonism of mass consumerism? The very next verse states:

> I saw that there is nothing better for man than to enjoy his possessions, since that is his portion. For who can enable him to see what will happen afterward?

Here, the "reduction" of the human to mere beast can lead to a preoccupation with the gratification of those animal qualities surrounding matters of consumption. The opposite, a spirituality that translates into an extreme otherworldliness, is problematic for different reasons, which are discussed in the next chapter. We need to stay on the tightrope, balancing the different sides of being human: overemphasize either side, and we fall to our doom.

The view of the human as uniting heaven and earth has deep significance for our understanding of the fundamental belief in the creation of the human in the divine image *(betzelem elohim)*. So far, we have assumed that God's image refers to the eternal or spiritual side of the human being, supplemented or balanced by the earthly component of the human being. The question of the extent to which the human being is apart from nature, or a part of it, exactly mirrors the theological discussion surrounding the nature of God as both transcendent (over, above, apart from the created order) and immanent (residing within, the divine presence being a part of Creation).

If that is so, then the idea of the divine image in which the human was created is not just one, spiritualized side of the equation—it represents both sides at one and the same time. Our being of the earth is no less Godlike than our creative intellectual and spiritual faculties. While being created in the image of God doesn't mean that we physically look like God, our divine *tzelem* is a physical-intellectual-spiritual unity. As Rabbi Lawrence Troster has written, "The immanence of God in the world is to be found in the physical presence of human beings."[18]

Precisely because humans are created with the capacity to transcend nature, we are commanded by God to protect nature. In the words of ecologist and author Michal Smart Fox we must "acknowledge our separateness in order to take responsibility, and to recognize our creatureliness in order to apprehend our limits." It would be a repudiation of our divine nature and our appointed task in the world to be merely anthropocentric; we must take a God's-eye view of the whole (of which we are a dependent part) and the conditions for its flourishing.

So, if it is moral agency and responsibility that is the crux of *imago dei,* the divine image (and not, say, shrewdness or technological know-how), then we best fulfill our divine image/destiny through acknowledging our moral responsibility for the world, rather than playing out the material possibilities of civilization and its development. Part of that responsibility, again mimicking behavior attributed to the Divine, may best be described by the kabbalistic concept of *tzimtzum,* contraction. According to Lurianic Kabbalah, the world could only come into being if God, whose presence was the totality of all being, "made room" for Creation. We, too, have a strong presence, filling up spaces and places that were once not humanly affected or defined, no longer leaving much room for what was once a vast, nonhuman creation. Even if we see this as an expression of our Godlike inclinations to replenish the earth and express our dominion, it may now be time to fulfill that other divine precedent, and undertake a willful contraction of our impact, for the sake of all of which we are also a part.

Again, this is not to downplay the awe-inspiring achievements of human civilization through the ages or the manifold blessings we enjoy today. This eternal dance of human empowerment and restraint, grandeur and humility, is expressed well in the Hasidic maxim of Reb Simcha Bunim: We should all walk around with two notes in our pockets. On one is written "the world was made for me" and on the other "I am but dust and ashes." The better part of wisdom is simply knowing when to take out which note.

The Rest of the Story: Where Does Creation Stop and History Begin ...

Where does the Creation story end? As we have seen, though the first chapter of Genesis reaches a climax and a culmination of sorts, Creation is clearly re-presented in the second chapter, which then continues seamlessly into the story of the expulsion from the

Garden, and then on to life on "the outside." Yet there we continue with the paradigmatic story of Cain and Abel, and as long as we are in the context of the primal family, and not really a human race, we have not yet entered the realm of history. I would claim that it makes sense to see all the following chapters, about Noah, the Flood, and the Tower of Babel, as rounding out the Creation narrative and determining, or filling in, essential details of the human relationship with the rest of the earth. We shall look at each of these stories in turn, though even before Cain and Abel and the rather shocking story of sacrifice and fratricide, we should briefly explore the changes that occur in response to the expulsion.

One of the main changes is in the notion and function of work. In the Garden, work was a basic assignment predicated of the human, because the human was responsible for the Garden. Although clearly not a curse, as such, it was not exactly a blessing, either—perhaps it should be considered a holy task. In the expulsion speech of Genesis 3:14–19, work was not presented as a punishment but, clearly, the pain and difficulty later required in procuring food was an unpleasant consequence of leaving the Garden: "In sadness *(itzavon)* shall you eat of (the ground) all the days of your life.... By the sweat of your brow shall you get bread to eat until you return to the ground" (Gen. 3:17–19). Bread is mentioned for the first time, and behind this single word may lie the entire Neolithic revolution that represents the transition from gathering, hunting, and nomadic herding to settled agriculture, crop domestication, and cultivation, with the possibilities for accumulating food surpluses and therefore building larger settlements, professional diversification, and so forth.

Like responsibility, human work in the world is also a dual concept. It connects us to the world, its cycles and abundance, though in many ways, even in primitive forms of plowing and cultivation, it is an aggressive intervention, and so separates us from it. This can be seen as both a blessing and a curse of sorts, though the latter term, a common one in reference to the expulsion from the Garden and its aftermath, is misleading here. The serpent and the ground are each "cursed" in some way, but the woman and the man receive the trappings of adulthood, pain in childbirth, and hard-won sustenance. Like some of the other consequences of leaving the Garden, these are better viewed as a process of becoming fully human, of growing up and living in the real world. Birth and death are central to the transformation that takes place as a result of the expulsion, and they both come into being with the first children of the world.

These children, Cain and Abel, exist on two distinct planes. As the first brothers, they embody the very individual psychology of jealousy and sibling rivalry. But they also represent prototypes for entire cultures. It is no accident that Cain is a farmer and Abel a shepherd: the tension between the settled tiller and the nomadic herdsman dates from the beginning of agriculture and continues to our day.

Regarding work and death, it was the much-maligned Cain who was doing the good work in tilling the ground by the sweat of his brow, fulfilling God's decree. Abel, shepherd and sympathetic victim, was the one who introduced the taking of life. And though the first slaughter was apparently for sublime ends—worship, not appetite—the first human murder was not long in coming. It has been suggested[19] that Cain's ability to murder Abel came from his not making distinctions between humans and animals. Initially he killed neither. But once he saw that Abel's sacrifice of lambs was not only acceptable but also preferred to his own, he concluded that all was permitted, even slaughtering (offering?) his own baby brother.

Ironically, Cain's punishment for knocking off the competition is to join it, becoming a nomad, banished from the soil. He experiences the second expulsion—this time not from the bounded Garden, but from the soil itself. Quickly, he ceases his supposedly endless wandering, founding the first city (Gen. 4:17), though urban life might be seen as remaining exiled from the life of the soil. So the first city was founded by a murderer, and the strongly anti-urban cast of the Book of Genesis (continuing with the city of Babel and later Sodom and Gomorrah) is set.

As far as human behavior goes, there was that first murder, and it was downhill from there. Perhaps it was that precedent, directly leading to urban immorality and a sense of lawlessness, that laid the groundwork for Noah and the Flood. In the Flood story, the entire human race, save a family of eight, was deemed irredeemably evil and wiped out. Significantly, all but a saving remnant of the animal kingdom is annihilated as well—the slate is wiped clean. All of God's glorious Creation gets "rebooted."

For reasons that are not made explicit, Noah found favor with God, and is described as the first *tzaddik,* righteous one. Whatever the justification, he is judged worthy to become a new Adam—the progenitor of postdiluvian humanity. So not only are we all *b'nei Adam,* the physical descendants of that primal *adam,* human, but we are also all *b'nei Noach.* This term, interestingly, adds a moral layer to our common humanity. Augmenting our shared genetic heritage is an ethical one, stemming both from Noah's personal example of compassion (at least for the animals for whom he cared) and from the explicit commandments following the Flood, known as the seven commandments of *b'nei Noach* ("Noahide laws"). These include prohibitions of idolatry, blasphemy, murder, incest, theft, and eating a limb of a live animal, and the injunction to establish a judicial system, which are seen as basic moral imperatives for human society.

This is the human side to the covenant established after the Flood among God, humanity, and the world. God's side, the divine part of the bargain, is simply never to destroy the world again: "I will never again destroy every living being as I have done.... So long as the earth endures, seedtime and harvest, cold and heat, summer and winter, day and night shall not cease" (Gen. 8:21–22).

This is all very comforting. Indeed, the simple, child-friendly reading of the Flood story is quite rosy and optimistic: virtue triumphs, evil is punished, the menagerie is saved, and a colorful rainbow appears to seal the bargain. But between the lines lies a much darker tale: Noah and his family must have been witness to inconceivable carnage. Everyone they knew died (how many must have screamed and pounded on the ark hatch as the waters rose?), and they drifted aimlessly for more than a year, presumably amid floating corpses and other horrors. The world was a wasteland that they had to rebuild with the nightmarish memories of survivors. It's no wonder that Noah's first act on dry land was to plant a vineyard and drown his sorrows (see Gen. 9:20–21).

One theme in the narrative is clear: the complete interdependence between humans and the natural world. Human behavior pollutes and then dooms the entire world. God orders Noah to build an ark to save not only himself and his family, but also significantly, exemplars of all the animals. There is a radical egalitarianism here, too, for all the passengers on the ark are merely representatives of their species, whose job is to replenish the world after its devastation. They—we—are all literally in the same boat.

In the same boat, but in a new relationship. One change that occurred in the aftermath of the Flood was the permission to eat animals, which expresses a new and different connection. Embedding the human as a "predator" with the appropriate trophic niche in the food web created distance—for now the animals had reason to fear humans:

> The fear and the dread of you shall be upon all the beasts of the earth, and upon all the birds of the sky, everything with which the earth is astir, and upon all the fish of the sea.... every creature that lives shall be yours to eat. (Gen. 9:2–3)

Once again, humans are a part of and apart from. God's covenant, though, significantly reinforces the commonality of all beings, because it is uniquely with all of Creation:

> And God said to Noah and to his sons with him, "I now establish My covenant with you and your offspring to come, and with every living thing that is with you—birds, cattle, and every wild beast as well—all that have come out of the ark, every living thing on earth." (Gen. 9:8–10)

This, together with the promise of 8:21–22 ("Never again will I doom the earth because of man.... So long as the earth endures, seedtime and harvest, cold and heat, summer and winter, day and night shall not cease"), is a strikingly beautiful and comforting statement. But regarding our own day and age, with the attendant challenges of widespread environmental degradation that endanger life on the planet, our ancestors did not imagine a human race that would break the promise to refrain from destruction. From their perspective, this was the exclusive province of God; when God promised that He would never bring another Flood, they could rest easy.

But whether we like it or not, we have acquired the Godlike powers to influence the continued existence of the human race and the world in which we live. In the quotation above, it is promised that the natural order will continue. But now we are the ones altering basic earth systems: from global warming that threatens "cold and heat, summer and winter" as we know them, to chemicals such as endocrine disrupters that blur the distinctions between the sexes in animals, upsetting the procreation of species. A human race that is "progressing" in one direction, yet leaves the animals, or all of nature, behind, or outside, the human project, isn't riding on Noah's ark, but rather on the *Titanic*.

That is probably the closest image that we have in our modern context for the symbolism of the Tower of Babel. The rabbinic name for the Tower of Babel story (Gen. 11:1–9) is the Generation of Division *(dor ha-pelaga)*. The outcome of this nine-sentence micro-novella is initial confusion, dispersion, and hence division of the human family into otherness and ethnicity. Before this incident, the whole earth was unified and of one speech (11:1). If the Flood represented a second Creation of sorts, with Noah and his family as the unique progenitors of humanity, Babel replaces Eden, and the humanly constructed city-cum-tower supersedes the divine Garden in a story that is both a continuation and a strange retelling of the Edenic narrative. Babel is, in effect, the virtual-reality version of Eden.

Both are tales of humans (apparently) subverting divine intent, resulting in exile and dispersion into the world. The confounding of tongues leading to social division, an abandoned city, and a stunted tower are often read as punishment. But if so, what was the crime? Herein lies a tension between tower and city. Tower-building signifies hubris: storming heaven, idolatrously desiring to "make a Name for ourselves" (11:4). The tower, and the power it can bestow, can itself become a god. In Rabbi Joseph Soloveitchik's prototypical terms, this is the Adam of Genesis 1, commanded to dominate the world, here wildly out of control. They were unified, but they turned their unity to acts of domination. They pulled out the stops: "nothing that they may propose to do will be out of their reach" (11:6). So of course they need to be confounded, reined in, redirected.

The building of the city, though, represents something else: fear, not brashness, the need for a sheltering center, "else we shall be scattered all over the world" (11:4). This is the anxious voice of the Adam 2, created alone, and lonely, seeking companionship, desiring the cohesion of a centralized civilization, and fearing the potential isolation of dispersal.

Ironically, there is a causal connection between the two: the hubris and need to dominate, "Adam 1 out of control," is caused by the fears of Adam 2—loneliness, isolation, and lack of intimacy. Rather than truly addressing those needs and fulfilling them, the aggressive stance of building and conquering only reinforces them, deepening them and making them more intractable. It's lonely at the top, perhaps most for those who have crushed others underfoot on the way there.

The expulsion from Eden was an exile into the world; Babel—tower and city—was a last-ditch effort on the part of the renewed human family to dominate land, landscape, and one another, and avoid truly living in that world. "The top" is clearly where these anxious, primordial tower-builders wanted to be. Since antiquity, towers have been built for command and control. From the ancient Babylonian ziggurat to prison watchtowers to modern skyscrapers—people controlling people, either directly and literally or symbolically, by cowing them—these structures are "trans-human," and not on a human scale. People in towers can control others' movements, gather information, survey, and supervise.

The vertical metaphor is at the core of our stratified society: being of high rank, "climbing the corporate ladder," the allure of the penthouse, the upper echelons. The narrative represents God as imprisoned in this vertical metaphor as well. He (*sic*) is in heaven, and heaven is, well, in the heavens, up there. Mystics and renewalists rightly reframe God talk with images of depth and interiority: the Divine is in here, not up there; truth wells up out of the depths, it is not handed down from on high. But in Babel, architecture, theology, and sociology all speak the language of hierarchy.

Existentially, the vertical tower—here the ziggurat (from a root meaning "to build high"), but any tower—such as the urge to climb high, fly high, and see things from above, is an expression of the desire to separate, deny our embeddedness in the earth, and soar free of earthly and bodily constraints. In response, God disperses: across plains and prairies, through forests and tundras, to the edges of oceans and seas, and beyond. The message is that we are to live on the earth, not above it; to gain a view from within, not from without.

Significantly, it was the mosaic of languages and cultures that was the antidote to that first hierarchical technocracy, shattering the vertical with wider horizons for people and their place in the world. The dispersion returns humanity to themselves, and to the world. The tower was not only a vertical reality but a virtual one as well, perhaps the first in history. Ancient Mesopotamians built ziggurats—cultic towers—on the flat flood plain, as a replacement for an actual mountain, a mountain of God. Even their building materials were artificial substitutes for more natural stones and mortar (see Gen. 11:3).

Real mountains and vast natural phenomena also dwarf people, but they do not oppress them socially. Those truly *are* transhuman—we should feel humble in the face of the cosmos, or even local representations of it. Perhaps there is a built-in "humility gene," evolutionarily acquired to engender wonder, to give us a healthy respect for things we cannot fathom, much less control. But when towers—or technology, or other products of human ingenuity—begin to mimic that effect, to co-opt that feeling, we begin to lose sight of reality, we subjugate ourselves to our own tools, and we experience wonderment only at the work of our own hands.

After Babel and the adumbration of the extended and now-diverse human family, Abram and Sarai, and thus a specific branch of that family, now assume center stage for the rest of the Torah and the Book of Prophets. Arguably, Creation has ended and history has begun.

Concluding Thoughts: On Goodness, Settlement, and Chaos

In the final analysis, after all our *hitpalpelut* (mental gyrations or argumentation) about the paradoxical and contradictory nature of the human being and our complex relationship with the rest of the natural world, one of the most significant components of the Creation stories is also one of the most basic and most easily overlooked: the pronouncement that Creation is good. Notice what this says, and also what it does not say. First of all—good is good, and not evil. Contrary to other doctrines at the time, which saw matter as bad, or evil, in certain natural forces, the biblical account affirms the basic goodness of nature. The world was not created by a demiurge; it is not a snare or a distraction. It is not malevolent: it is good.

Second, good is good—and not holy, that is, untouchable. There are not a few religious environmentalists out there who seem to feel that for nature or the environment to be taken seriously, it has to be deemed holy, and nothing less will do. It's true that there is a land that the Jewish tradition considers holy, though that is not without its questions and problems. And one can even make the case that certain lands outside Israel can be imbued with holiness, given the right conditions.[20] But that is a far cry from declaring that the entire Earth is holy, with all that that would entail. Nature is not the *mysterium tremendum*, nor is it cultically set aside, revered, or off-limits for daily use.

And finally, good is good—and not perfect, that is, representative of some unchanging ideal. We are to somehow partner with God in Creation, and we have work to do in the world. Perhaps we should adopt the Hippocratic norm, *primum non nocere*, that, first and foremost, we need to make sure we do no harm—but after that, there is still much to be done.

A key phrase from the prophet Isaiah (45:18) that ties into the basic thrust of Genesis is quoted by the *Sefer Hachinuch* (*The Book of Education*, a late medieval explanation of the 613 commandments) in its explication of the first mitzvah of Genesis:

> The purpose of this commandment is this—that the earth should be settled, for God desires its settlement, as it is written (Isa. 45:18): "He did not create it a waste *(tohu)* but formed it for habitation." This is an important commandment, on the basis of which exist all the other

commandments in the world, for they were given to men and not the angels of god.

There are several ways to interpret this claim. If we see *tohu* as wilderness and settlement as a sort of primal sprawl, then this is a mandate for the anthropocentric eradication of nature. But, in point of fact, *tohu* as mentioned at the beginning of Genesis is not wilderness as we know it; it is the void that preceded the nature of the Creation. Without getting overly scientific, it is possible to translate *tohu* as entropy, the formlessness and disorder that characterizes both the pre-Creation state that was inhospitable to life and to habitation and the state we ourselves are creating through pollution, making disorder out of natural order. And so the declaration is that the world was created for habitation and therefore we are forbidden to make it less so by our destructive acts. Even if that *drasha* (interpretive sermon) does not win over the unconvinced, when coupled with the green-belt ordinances of the Book of Numbers, the mandate to settle (like the blessing to have dominion) can't be a license for obliterating wilderness and green space, or as a blanket call for sprawl.

In sum, we can look back and embrace a plurality of models of human-nature relations from within the texts themselves, and in true midrashic style, affirm that they are all facets of the same complex reality. Israeli environmentalist and educator Eilon Schwartz enumerates four archetypes.[21] The first two, what he calls "little lower than the angels" (mastery) and stewardship, correspond closely to what I have identified with Genesis 1 and 2, and they are potentially complementary. The Book of Job represents a third model, more grounded in mystery and awe, with a strong emphasis on human humility in the face of ultimate transcendence.[22] A fourth model is the mystically inspired vision of the world as filled with the holy sparks of divinity, and so acting in the world can lead to actual communion with the Divine. While clearly stemming from different traditions, with different emphases and priorities, they are non-exclusive. On the contrary: we need to find a way to help humility and grandeur, mystery and mastery, awe and empowerment, reside together in the same individual and in the same society, and mutually nourish and guide one another.

Traditional Sources and Resources

In terms of the "bridge in two directions," the preceding chapter has firmly established the "bulkhead" of the tradition, the perspective that begins in the Bible, exploring how one of the most significant texts in our sacred bibliography grapples with the most timeless and timely question of the meaning of being human, and the relationship with the rest of the created world. In this chapter, I will further explore ideas and values from Jewish sources and traditions that can be brought to bear on how we see the world and act in it. More specifically, the Creation stories dealt with what it means to be human in general; here, the focus will be on specifically Jewish beliefs and practices in areas of environmental import.

Regarding this project, a preliminary question we need to ask is: in expending so much energy in trying to develop a Jewishly informed environmental ethos, are we not attaching too much importance to this transient, material world as opposed to the traditional, overriding spiritual importance of God, Torah, and the quest for eternal life beyond the confines of nature or history?

The elements that seemingly stand in contrast to an involvement or concern with the natural world, including the ultimate, often exclusive value of Torah study, and a focus on *olam haba,* the world-to-come (or afterlife), can be grouped under the rubric of *chayei netzach* (the eternal) versus *chayei sha'ah* (the temporal), or *ruchani* (the spiritual) versus *gashmi* (the physical, material). The roots of these last terms are highly significant for our work here: *ru'ach* means spirit, but also wind, and *geshem* means quite literally rain. Thus, the most basic metaphors for our inner life are elements of the natural world around us.

When these couplets are seen as dichotomies, or opposites, they both distinguish and prioritize, which has several implications. First, positing a radical rupture between the spiritual and the physical means that spirituality is de-physicalized, with no bodily expression, and physicality is de-spiritualized, lifeless and inert. Furthermore, this implies that the former is the ends, with the latter but a means, often base or corrupt, and even dispensable. In short, regarding the natural world: if it's really just matter, then it really doesn't matter, in any real way.[1]

Nature: Is It and Does It Matter?
(I)—Heaven v. Earth

Some may be surprised at the mention of heaven or otherworldly concerns in a Jewish context. We tell ourselves that Judaism, especially as compared with Christianity, is a very this-worldly tradition, that dogmas concerning the afterlife play a comparatively minor role in our faith. That is not completely false, but since post-biblical times, there has always been a central strain that has emphasized the other or next world over and against this one.

The belief in an afterlife[2] or eternal life has always been an effective and satisfying strategy when confronted with questions of theodicy: how is it that in this world, this "vale of tears," the wicked may prosper and the righteous often suffer? If one doesn't want to come to the conclusion that the world is random and therefore a- or immoral, or that God is uncaring or malicious, then it is but a short leap to conceive of another, better world where the suffering righteous will get their ultimate and eternal rewards, and the unpunished wicked their just and also eternal desserts.

The centrality of the belief in the hereafter, together with other eschatological doctrines such as *techiyat hameitim,* bodily resurrection,[3] appear in central texts such as the Talmudic tractate *Sanhedrin* (chapter 10). Likewise, *Pirkei Avot* (Ethics of the Sages) includes quite unambiguous statements, such as:

> This world is like a vestibule to the world to come; prepare yourself in the vestibule that you may enter into the (banqueting-) hall.... Better is one hour of bliss of spirit in the world to come than all the life of this world. (4:16–17)

However, in addition to statements such as these, which denigrate the temporal concerns of this world (including the environment), there is another, positive side to a strong belief in heaven. Arguably, emphasis on the hereafter represents the ultimate in delayed gratification. The belief in an eternal reward was a mega-incentive, in the longest of long terms, against wrongdoing, ill-gotten gain and its enjoyment, and short-term materialism. One can accept suffering or hardship or a humble material life now, if one believes one will eventually live the truly good life in the hereafter.[4] Indeed, the belief in "the truly good life" as one that is essentially a spiritual endeavor has the power to shape our values and how we live our lives here and now. If heaven is something to emulate in our lives now and not only to wait for after them, then it could have positive repercussions for the society we strive to build in this world.

Regarding the eternal dyad of heaven and earth, overemphasis on this-worldly mortality can lead to a preoccupation with immediate gratification and material pleasures: eat, drink, and be merry for tomorrow we die.... But likewise, an exclusive focus on the otherworldly can denigrate this world and its needs—why care about a mere tree? Thus, "over-presentism," or lack of faith in the future and a commitment to the well-being of coming generations, is inherently unsustainable, but the other extreme— complete inattention to the here and now—can be no less destructive. It is a balancing act of appreciating and nurturing the gifts of this world, in gratitude and awe, but without fetishizing them and detaching them from the larger picture. Nature needs history, a sense of past and future; or more accurately, we need a deep understanding of our place in the chain of generations, and our responsibility with them, to ensure the basic context of our continued existence.

Nature: Is It and Does It Matter (II)—Torah v. *Teva* (Nature)

Beyond this world and the next, the other great eternal dyad is Torah, that is, God's words (revelation), as compared with *teva,* nature, or God's deeds (creation). A lovely saying, also from *Pirkei Avot,* seems to deny that the natural world has anything at all of value to offer: *"Hafoch bah vehafoch bah, dechula bah"*—"Study it [the Torah], and review it, for *everything* is contained within it" (5:24, attributed to Ben Bag-Bag). Like other maxims in *Pirkei Avot,* this is the opinion of the sage who uttered it, but its very inclusion in the collection endows it with a certain air of canonized authority. And it is indeed indicative of a prevalent school of thought, which has contributed to a widespread blindness to all those things that are not contained in the books—as wide and deep and rich as our vast sacred bibliography is.

An even more significant teaching in this regard, also from *Pirkei Avot,* is the one brought in the name of Rabbi Ya'akov or Rabbi Shimon (versions differ) in 3:7:

One, who while walking along the way, reviewing his studies, breaks off from his study and says, "How beautiful is that tree! How beautiful is that plowed field!" Scripture regards him as if he has forfeited his soul.

This *mishnah* has been a lightning rod for comments about Torah (and therefore Judaism) and nature throughout the ages, and I will use it to focus the discussion here.[5]

First is the question of the identity of the sage in whose name this is taught, which will return us briefly to questions of eternal life. The Rabbi Shimon in question is none other than Rabbi Shimon bar Yochai (RaShBY), reputed author of the mystical commentary on the Torah called the Zohar. He was one of the five remaining students of Rabbi Akiva who survived the failure of the Bar Kochba revolt, and he had to flee the Romans, eventually hiding out in a cave. According to the Talmudic account (*Shabbat* 33b), he secluded himself, together with his son, for thirteen years, studying Torah day and night. When they finally emerged, they saw people going about their daily affairs, plowing and sowing, and not devoting themselves to Torah. They exclaimed: *"Menichin chayei olam ve-oskim be-chayei sha'ah?"*—"They forsake eternal life (i.e., Torah study and its rewards), and devote themselves to temporal life?"[6]

When their fiery gazes destroyed all they looked upon, God rebuked them: "Have you emerged only to destroy My World? Return to your cave!" RaShBY eventually reconciled with the Jewish people and the world when, as Shabbat eve approached, he saw an old man running with two myrtle *(hadas)* branches in his hand. He asked the man what they were for, and the man told him that they were in honor of the Shabbat, one symbolizing *zachor* ("remember") and the other representing *shamor* ("observe"), the different aspects of Shabbat mentioned in the two versions of the Ten Commandments in Exodus and Deuteronomy. In other words, the ritual use of a natural element, the leafy branches, in the context of Shabbat put his mind at ease about the fate of the Jewish people and Torah, embodying a synthesis between divine teachings and the material world.

The other purported author, Rabbi Ya'akov, refers to Rabbi Ya'akov Korshai, a contemporary of Shimon bar Yochai. Significantly, he is the author of the sayings quoted previously from chapter 4 of *Pirkei Avot,* which denigrate this world and praise the next. Here is an intriguing story about the person behind the teaching, which deepens the parallels in the oppositions between nature and Torah, and this world as opposed to heaven.

Rabbi Ya'akov was the grandson of the (in)famous apostate Elisha ben Abuya, known as *Acher*—"the other." The Talmud (*Kiddushin* 39b, also *Hullin* 142a) tells how Acher, the rabbi-turned-heretic, might have lost his faith. It presents a scene in which a father instructs his son to gather some eggs from a nest, but to be careful first to let the mother bird go. Performing his father's request, the boy should be doubly rewarded with a long life: he is honoring his parents and fulfilling the divine command of sending off the mother bird (both of which are commandments whose reward for fulfilling them is "length of days").[7] The boy falls from the tree and dies. How could this be? It is suggested that Elisha ben Abuya may have witnessed just such a scene and, presuming that the biblical promise referred to the length of life of the individual in this world, concluded that the promise was false, and thus there is neither Judge nor justice in the world.

In contrast, Rabbi Ya'akov believed firmly that the poor child who died, though fulfilling two *mitzvot* that should have guaranteed him long life, would receive his length of days and just rewards in the world-to-come. He states there that: "There is no reward for observing commandments in this world"—all rewards for fulfilling

God's will are heavenly rewards. A Rabbi Joseph is quoted there as saying that "if Acher had interpreted as did his daughter's son, Rabbi Ya'akov, he would not have come to sin."

By either author, Shimon or Ya'akov, this passage of "one, walking by the way" has frequently been understood to teach a rejection of the (natural) world and any appreciation of it in the face of the supreme—and ultimately, exclusive—value of Torah study.[8] As such, it serves as a central prooftext for the claim that Judaism, at its core, is spiritually alienated from nature—that Jewish tradition stands squarely behind revelation (Torah) as its central religious category of experience and source of Truth, while creation (nature) is seen as a potentially dangerous competitor, an alternative and therefore heretical source of inspiration, or experience of the Divine, whose seductive charms must be contained, or in this case, vehemently censured.

Most interpretations of this mishnah[9] work from an unspoken assumption of the dichotomization between nature and Torah—the breaking off of Torah study in order to experience nature. This assumption results in a black-and-white, either-or world view: choose one or the other, for you can't have both. But what if we don't accept this assumption and reject a radical rupture between Creation and Revelation?

A key phrase in this text is *"mafsik mi-mishnato"*—"ceases, breaks off from his study." Yes, if in order to relate to the world you have to cease your learning, then your soul is in grave danger. What previously was a working assumption is here the crux of the sin, the unbridgeable rift between Torah and nature. What is needed then is *synthesis,* a supreme effort to mend that gap, to forge a common language for our disparate forms of spiritual experience.

One who perpetuates this dichotomy, this spiritual feud, is in truth risking great spiritual and physical harm. But one engaged in study, in developing Jewish identity and commitments, and who "*mamshikh be-mishnato*"—"continues that study," those Jewish values, and sees the beautiful tree and field, the world they represent and our relationship to it, as an extension, as an expansion, of that study, that person will have performed a great act of *tikkun* (repair): *tikkun ha'olam*, of the world, and *tikkun hanefesh*, of our (previously distorted) souls.

The Zohar apparently agrees with this interpretation as well:

> Rabbi Shimon, Rabbi Elazar, Rabbi Abba, and Rabbi Yossi were sitting under the trees in the valley of the Sea of Ginnosar (Kinneret). Rabbi Shimon said: "How beautiful *(na'eh)* is the shade with which these trees protects us; Let us crown them with words of Torah!"[10]

Ironically, this is the same Rabbi Shimon, but here he teaches of the mystical oneness of all, and of the need to merge physical and spiritual beauty, deepening both.[11]

My conclusion regarding this mishnah, then, is really the message of this book as a whole: true *tikkun* will only be possible when we can overcome that alienation, strengthen the bridge in both directions, and deepen the relationship between Judaism and the world. Both Torah and the environment will profit from a renewed engagement and dialogue between them. This cuts the Gordian knot of the question of ends and means, *ikkar* and *tafel* (primary and secondary importance), because previously dichotomized realms of experience or sources of wisdom—the *ruchani* and the *gashmi*—will be revealed to be aspects of a larger whole: complementary, interconnected, and interdependent.

Having put this question in perspective, we can now return to furthering our understanding of the natural world and its different manifestations.

More on the Nature of Nature

According to the texts we have looked at, the world is God's creation, and as such, has received the divine stamp of approval: it is very good. We are also part of that created world, but whether or not the human creation was successful in God's eyes is still to be determined. Free will, it seems, precludes an a priori heavenly imprimatur of excellence. That may make us inherently different from other created beings, *apart from* them, but we are nonetheless still also a *part of* overall creation and embedded in it. Here, then, is one paradox of sorts regarding the biblical perception of nature: we are a part of it and it is the context and ground of our existence; it is also the object of our care and attention; at the same time, it forms the raw material for our civilizational development. Those are three vectors, as it were, that define the stewardship/dominion dynamic of the Creation stories.

But nature is so much more than that, even in the confines of the classical sources. In chapter 3 of Genesis, nature was the medium of divine punishment, when that vaunted human free will seemingly went awry. That same earth that humans were to conquer, and over which were supposed to have dominion, was painfully recalcitrant in what it deigned to give them. A continuation and sharpening of that theme is evident in Deuteronomy (e.g., chapters 11 and 28) and later in Prophets (Amos, Isaiah 24), where the natural world—rainfall and drought, fertility and crop failure, health and pestilence, wild beasts—became the prime instrument of divine favor and wrath. But how can that possibly square with a world we are supposed to rule and/or take care of? Put another way, the ongoing connection of the natural to God reduces human claims to both dominion and stewardship to absurdist illusions—or at the very least, puts them in their proper perspective of a very circumscribed influence.

Precisely because of this connection—the origin of the essentially transient natural world in transcendent and eternal divinity—nature can serve an additional, different function entirely. The natural world is also an independent source of wisdom and even morality. Sources such as Proverbs 6:6–9, exhorting us to learn diligence from the ant, and one of Job's diatribes emphasize a nature that is neither raw material nor object of care:

But ask now the beasts and they shall teach you;
And the fowls of the air, they shall teach you;
Or speak to the earth, and it shall teach you;
And the fishes of the sea shall declare unto you.
    (Job 12:7–8)[12]

Similarly, the Talmud takes off on a different verse from Job (35:11), which can be understood to say that God teaches us wisdom from animals and birds[13] and gives us the following midrash:

R. Yohanan observed: If the Torah had not been given we could have learnt modesty from the cat [who evacuates in private and covers its feces], honesty from the ant [who will not take a kernel of grain from another ant], chastity from the dove [who mates for life], and good manners from the cock, who first coaxes and then mates [whose elaborate mating moves are interpreted to mean that he does not force himself on the hen]. (Eruvin 100b)

Here, moral virtues are not only present in other species, but they can also be sources of wisdom, theoretically on a par with the Torah. That certainly is a different sort of nature than the one we associate with mainstream Jewish views, which remain on the dominion/stewardship axis.

It is particularly surprising as well, for it is common to contrast our traditional Revelation-based morality, which includes values such as the pursuit of justice and the protection of the weak, with what is perceived to be the patently amoral character of the natural world, where the weak perish and there is no pretense of equity or fairness. Here we see a different view entirely, that the truth about nature is not summed up in the famous but misplaced slogans of "the survival of the fittest" and "red in tooth and claw." Although the above examples are highly anthropomorphized, they actually dovetail with recent insights from the field of ecology that show that symbiosis, altruism, and cooperation (behavior that we would deem morally positive) have a much more central place in the workings of the natural world than previously imagined.

Even further afield, as it were, are traditional texts that are highly evocative of the contemporary "Gaia hypothesis" of scientist James Lovelock. This theory conceives of the Earth as a self-regulating mechanism that has the characteristics of a single organism. Fully explicating that theory is beyond the scope of this work,[14] but its basic tenet—and its iconoclastic nature—can be seen from Lovelock's presentation: the Earth as a living being symbolized by Gaia, the ancient Greek Earth goddess. Thus by implication, the theory allegedly resurrects pagan beliefs in scientific garb.

But the idea that the universe itself is alive, even sentient, is not a belief restricted to pagan cultures. The great rationalist philosopher Maimonides understood the universe to be a living being: "Know that this whole of being is one individual and nothing else."[15] In other words, the universe is an individual like a person—and its constituent parts are like the limbs or organs of a person. This being is endowed with life, apprehension, even a soul: it is not a dead body like fire or dirt.[16] This has ethical implications as well: it subordinates the existence of the individual (whether an individual person or the human race as part of the whole) to the health, well-being, and continued existence of the entirety of the created world:

> [A]ll the existent individuals of the human species and, all the more, those of the other species, are things of no value at all in comparison with the whole that exists and endures. (Maimonides, *Guide for the Perplexed,* III:12, p. 442)

This conception is very close to what I have called "biocentrism" (or eco-centrism), and though not the dominant view in Jewish tradition, it is expressed in a variety of sources, from God's speech to Job "out of the whirlwind" (Job 38–41) to certain interpretations of Shabbat and rationales for the mitzvah of *bal tashchit* (see below). As stated, it is identical to the central tenet of the radical environmental movement known as "deep ecology,"[17] and though environmentally inspiring, it is not unproblematic, potentially leading to a different moral calculus than the one we're used to, regarding the value and rights of individuals compared with "the whole" (whether the community, the state, or the biosphere in general).

Also indicative of the sentience of the world and its constituent parts are numerous scriptural passages, which emphasize that natural entities are also spiritual beings, and praise God. "The heavens declare the glory of God" says Psalm 19 (v. 2), and all of Psalm 148, recited every day in the liturgy, is a paean of nature worshiping God:

> Halleluya! Praise the Lord from the heavens ...
> Praise Him, sun and moon, praise Him all bright stars ...
> Praise the Lord, O you who are on earth,
> all sea monsters and ocean depths ...
> all mountains and hills, all fruit trees and cedars,
> all wild and tamed beasts, creeping things and winged birds,
> all kings and peoples of the earth ...

Other texts in Psalms (96:11–12, 98:7–9), Isaiah (44:23, 55:12), and parts of God's response to Job (38:7) emphasize this. This theme is ably explored by biblical scholar Rabbi Everett Gendler,[18] who makes the very cogent point: How can the idea of a *brit,* a covenant with the Earth, such as expressed in Genesis 9:8–17, between God and all of nature after the Flood, make any sense if the Earth and its inhabitants do not have some sort of standing or sentience?

Much of prevalent contemporary Judaism is the heir to Western European Enlightenment and philosophical rationalism,[19] and so we have learned to ignore the *peshat,* the clear straightforward contextual understanding of these many texts, that Jews from the Bible onward have believed that nature is alive and deeply spiritual. We must acknowledge that if we reject the sentience of nature, we are not rejecting paganism for the sake of Jewish belief; rather, we are rejecting some deeply rooted Jewish values in the name of a hyper-rationalist scientific world view.

It is important to touch upon these examples in order to contradict the prevalent notion that nature is a rather uncomplicated idea, and that we substantially know what it is about. The dominant scientific world view, with its sharp scalpel of rational analysis and positivistic probability focusing on demonstrable causality, is an important part of the story, an angle, a dimension. But it simply can't be the whole picture. As noted historian of science Seyyed Hussein Nasr has remarked:

> The secular, exploitative side of science must correspond to something in nature, otherwise it wouldn't be so efficacious in destroying the world. But at the same time, it must be missing something essential, for precisely the same reason.[20]

Divine reward and punishment through the medium of the natural world may seem primitive to many, but recurrent tsunamis, earthquakes, hurricanes, and asteroids reinforce for us the awesome, completely trans-human power of the world—something we can neither rule or manage nor naively care for. Likewise, acknowledgment of the morally exemplary character of elements in nature, and their spiritual merit and import, can break down the strict dichotomy many of us hold between our responsibilities to humans and to the nonhuman world.

Extending our human and humane consideration to other animals, species, and places, is one direction for the development of an environmental sensibility. The idea of the integrity of the biosphere, the world-as-organism, holds a potentially different message for us. It calls upon us to transcend our focus on individuals, and recognize that it is impossible to speak of our well-being apart from the well-being of the whole. Therefore, the very particular human perspective—including the limitations of a human-centered morality—is quite circumscribed and even provincial, given this new cosmic context. Rather than extending and thereby reinforcing a human-based view, we should take a God's-eye view of the good of the whole. Again, a religious approach such as this is not so different from a secular, more ecological understanding. To use environmental philosopher Aldo Leopold's evocative formulation, we shouldn't think like a deer, a wolf, grass, a hunter, or a conservationist—we should think like a mountain, the context of the whole.[21]

Wind, Rain, Mountains, and Fields

As mentioned above, the terms for the overarching concepts of "spiritual" and "material" come from the natural world: *ru'ach*, *ruchani* (spirit and spiritual, from "wind") and *gashmi*, *gashmiut* (material, materiality, from *geshem*, "rain"). When a people's spiritual language is so anchored in meteorology, it demands elaboration.

The cultural-historical background of this is clear: the great formative period of Jewish culture, from patriarchal, through biblical, and up to Mishnaic times (over a millenium and a half) was spent physically in, or in close relation to, the Land of Israel and its environmental reality. Although there are definitely many environmental values and practices that are not tied to place, much of their original context comes from the very specific place of the Land of Israel, with its particular conditions.

This natural context was formative of Jewish culture in a variety of ways. For instance, classic Hebrew boasts of at least six different words for liquid precipitation *(geshem, matar, yoreh, malkosh, revivim, se'irim),* denoting different times and intensities of rainfall. This is indicative of the fact that, unlike Egypt or Iraq, riverine countries, Israel is dependent exclusively on rain. Israel's mightiest streams are tiny trickles compared to the Nile, the Tigris, and the Euphrates. Whether it takes water from the perennially depleted Sea of Galilee or from rain-nourished underground aquifers, Israel's ecology and economy is rain-based.

Rain then becomes far more than precipitation. The Torah emphasizes the theological significance of rain when it observes:

For the land ... is not like the land of Egypt from which you have come. There the grain you sowed had to be watered by your own labors ... [here] a land of hills and valleys soaks up its water from the rains of heaven. It is a land which the Lord your God looks after, on which the Lord your God keeps His eye. (Deut. 11:10–13)

Both symbolically and literally, rain expresses the physical connection between heaven and Earth, and thus becomes the most direct expression of the divine abundance that we experience in the natural world. Rain in the reality of semi-arid Israel is a life-giving event, equated with the ultimate of spiritual landmarks: "Rav

Yehudah said: 'The day when rain falls is as great as the day when the Torah was given ...' Raba said: 'It is even greater than the day when the Torah was given ...'" (*Ta'anit* 7a). Here, Creation trumps Revelation, *geshem* takes precedence over *ru'ach*. Or rather, it too breaks this dichotomy, for what is more spiritual than the recognition that life is dependent on divine gifts such as rain?

The Talmudic tractate of *Ta'anit*, from which these quotations came, takes its name from the public fast days, one of the acts of prayer and repentance that is called in response to catastrophes, chief among them drought. These are meant to represent the submission of the people of Israel to God's commandments, and their desire to renew divine favor, whose lapse has led to the withholding of the rains, as described graphically in Deuteronomy 11:13–17 and 28:23 and 1 Kings 8:35–6.

However, a different kind of theological significance of rain is elucidated in the first chapter of this tractate, one connected to prayer and the natural world. The question is asked (*Ta'anit* 2a): "When do we make mention of 'the power of rain'?" That is to say, when do we add the sentence referring to *geshem* (and *ru'ach*) in the second paragraph of the *Amidah* prayer (the central silent prayer, also known as the prayer of 18 Benedictions)? As it says further on, "we ask for rain only close to the rainy season," but exactly when do we include the prayer? Rabbi Eliezer says on the first day of Sukkot, while Rabbi Joshua says on the last day. This is one of those Talmudic disagreements that seems hopelessly esoteric at first glance, but constitutes a fascinating window onto divergent world views.

The reason for R. Joshua's opinion is quite logical: rain during Sukkot, when Jews eat and sleep outdoors in the holiday huts, is not only unpleasant, it is also seen as a curse! We should only ask for rain, according to him, after the holiday is over. What is R. Eliezer's response then? He makes the interesting distinction that he is not talking about *praying for* rain, just mentioning that causing the rain to fall is indeed one of God's attributes. And indeed, the prayer under discussion says: "[God] causes the wind to blow and the rain to fall" (i.e., it is not an explicit request for rain to fall now). R. Joshua retorts that if that is the case, then that sentence should be part of the year-round liturgy, because it is always true, whether there is rain or not.

So why the difference of opinion? Further on (*Ta'anit* 9b), we get more insight into these sages' hydrology and thus their theology. R. Eliezer teaches that the world's water comes from the ocean, and via evaporation, it comes down in the form of rain (to evaporate again). R. Joshua, on the other hand, says that "the whole world drinks of the upper waters," a view that seems to imply that there is a storehouse of water above the clouds (cf. Gen. 1:7) that God directly controls. Beyond the fact that we would identify these views with more scientific and mythical approaches, respectively, the difference in their attitude to prayer becomes clear. R. Joshua has a transcendental theology—both God and rain are above the Earth, and can respond to human initiative such as prayer. God can and does turn on and off the spigot, in response to human action. On the other hand, R. Eliezer takes a more cyclical and possibly even immanental view: rain is part of a cyclical mechanism, and therefore God makes the rain fall and the wind blow via this cycle. That is, God has established the cycle, and perhaps even should be seen as part of it. We don't pray "for" rain; we praise God by acknowledging the working of the cycle (i.e., natural forces and elements).

Thus we see that the most basic conceptions of God's role in the world, and the efficacy of prayer, are expressed in the most naturalistic terms. Judaism speaks the language of rain in the most profound sense, both metaphorically and literally—which is another form of answer to Schwartzschild's claim that Jews are "unnatural persons."

Another example of deep connections between prayer and natural elements is the way the midrash (*Pesachim* 88a) associates the patriarchs with representative archetypal landscapes. Abraham's worship, because of his sacrificial trek to Moriah (Gen. 22:2, 14), is seen as tied to *har* (mountain); Isaac, who went outdoors to the fields to meditate (Gen. 24:63), or pray, with *sadeh* (field); and Jacob, both a homebody (compared with Esau) and the progenitor of the House of Jacob/Israel, named his place of contact with God *Beit El*, the House of God, and so is linked with *bayit* (house or home).

This triad is suggestive of ways of thinking of the natural world around us: the wild *(har)* and the domestic *(bayit),* mediated by the agricultural seamline *(sadeh),* each with its own ecological and spiritual sensibility. Likewise, the historical sequence is indicative of a generational progression of the successive domestication of nature and humanity.[22]

Bein Adam Le'olam? Jewish Legal and Moral Categories Regarding Nature

This chapter brings together sources, values, and ideas that were never grouped together as forming a coherent category before the rise of the environmental movement. While "creation" is of course a central theological archetype, nature or the environment was not an overarching organizing principle, legal or otherwise. For instance, there is no tractate in the Talmud whose theme is the environment—though the orders of *Zera'im,* Seeds, dealing with agricultural issues, and *Nezikin,* Torts and Damages, have much relevant material.

Moreover, if one of the core concepts of Jewish life is the *mitzvot,* the commandments and their interpretation and observance, here, too, is a seeming lack of basic vocabulary. The dominant classical understanding of the *mitzvot* divides them into *mitzvot bein adam la-makom* (obligations of people to God, literally, "between human and the Place")[23] and *mitzvot bein adam le'chavero* (obligations between people, literally, "between human and 'his' fellow"). The former are seen usually as ritual or cultic observances, while the latter are ethical and social responsibilities. Environmental issues, neither ritual/cultic nor ethical in a classical sense, fall between the cracks.

Today we need a new category. This is not to suggest inventing new *mitzvot* or *halachot* out of whole cloth, but rather regrouping and refocusing existing concepts and values to facilitate our engagement with them. We need to begin speaking in Jewish language of our moral and ethical obligations to the Earth—these actions that have never been grouped together before—as *mitzvot bein adam le-olam,* "between people and the world."

Although the main explicit traditional values that outline our relationship to the inanimate and animate parts of nature, *bal tashchit* and *tza'ar ba'alei chayim* (literally, "the suffering of living things," referring to the prevention of cruelty to animals), go a fair way in filling in the blanks of a Jewish environmental ethic, there is still something missing in the big picture. Traditional *mitzvot* such as these delineate how to be prudent or compassionate in environmental terms. But with the changing reality of modern industrialized society, mere prudence is often not enough, and it does not sufficiently express our capacity for great damage as well as great *tikkun.* Where is the consciousness that we have a larger task, a mission for humanity regarding the world? Given the global challenges facing us, we need a framework, a guiding vision, a purpose.

The idea of stewardship, the unique human responsibility in safeguarding the fate of the Earth, is just such a mission. There is criticism of this approach from both sides. Green detractors worry that the centrality this affords humanity in "running the world" is easily distorted into a weak version of minor reforms that in the end will afford little protection and long-term remediation. From the other side, non–environmentally minded critics claim that narrow notions of stewardship (i.e., serving nature's needs) cannot and should not trump human well-being and the fulfillment of the idea of dominion by subduing nature for our purposes.

There is seeming support for this latter idea in Psalms 115:16, which says, "The heavens belong to the Lord, but the earth He gave over to humanity." Here is the same dominion motif, sometimes quoted as a basis for the total human use of creation. But according to twelfth-century Spanish biblical exegete Abraham ibn Ezra, that would be the view of the stupid, or uneducated:

> The ignorant have compared humanity's rule over the earth with God's rule over the heavens. This is not right, for God rules over everything. The meaning of "but the earth He gave over to humanity" [Psalm 115:16] is that humanity is God's officer (or steward, *pakeed*) over the earth and must do everything according to God's word (ad loc.).

In other words, humanity is not free to do as it pleases with God's creation. Ibn Ezra's use of the term *pakeed* is richly suggestive. The root *p-k-d* has a variety of meanings, including command, count, appoint, remember, and deposit. If humanity is the *pakeed*, the agent in whose care a pledge has been placed, the Earth is the *pikadon*, the deposit itself, and God is the *mafkeed*, the lessor or depositor. God, too, is the *po'ked*, the one who commands, inspects, and remembers, both for punishment, negative consequences (*po'ked avon*, "visiting the sin upon"), and for positive ones, for grace (as when God "remembered," *pakad*, Sarah, and caused her to conceive). As outlined before, the notion of stewardship embodies a sense of responsibility in two directions: "downward" *for* the Earth, the deposit, that thing that is held in trust for the sake of the owner, and "upward" *to* God, *koneh shamayim va'aretz*, the Creator and possessor of the universe, the Place of all.

These phraseologies may seem highly metaphysical, yet they tie in directly to traditional categories of legal responsibility in which to frame the demands of stewardship of the world. For instance, the Torah discusses the conditions of accountability for possessions of others under the laws of bailment, *dinei shomrim*. These are outlined in Exodus 22:6–14, and expanded upon in the Talmud, tractate *Bava Metzia*, chapter 3. Mishnah *Bava Metzia* 7:8 denotes four types of "bailees," or guardians, which include the paid and unpaid watchers, borrowers, and lessors.

Although the distinctions among these classes (including different levels of use, and legal and financial liability for damage) are important for civil law, they are less relevant here, in our context of God, humanity, and the world, because we were indeed commanded *leshomra*, to be in the role of a *shomer* (guardian). In every case, the bailee *(shomer, sho'el, socher—*all types of *pakeed*) has total responsibility in cases of gross negligence. Even in cases where the guardian is permitted to use the object in question, it is forbidden to diminish its value.[24]

Another interesting Halachic category that could be relevant here is the idea of *hatzala*: rescuing innocent persons from injury or death (Lev. 19:16) and not standing idly by when harmful acts are occurring. Rabbi Saul Berman[25] writes that this is a powerful metaphor for environmental responsibility. In his opinion, this is not an expression of our direct debt to the Earth and our relationship to it, but rather to God and to humanity. Of God he writes in exactly the same vein as the laws *of shemira*:

> In Jewish law, the duty to rescue persons is extended to the rescue of their property. The mitzvah of the return of lost property is one manifestation of this responsibility. Our duty to the beloved neighbor is to keep him whole in both body and property. But ... an essential Jewish teaching is that the entire world belongs to God. If then we love God, we are duty-bound to protect and preserve God's property—this entire Earth.

Our love of humanity is the other great reason to work to sustain the world. According to Berman, who differs from more radical Jewish environmentalists in claiming that "there is, in Jewish law, no duty to love nature or God's world," it is the essential and irreplaceable role the Earth plays in our continued survival that makes it imperative to become environmentally active. Even more generally, the whole idea of *brit*, covenant, which exists between God and the Jewish people, but also among God, humanity, and the world (see the aftermath of the Flood in Gen. 9:8–17) is relevant in defining our role in the continuation of Creation. According to Jewish historian Hava Tirosh-Samuelson:

> The obligation to respond to the needs of the other is at the core of the covenantal model, the foundation of Judaism. The covenantal model establishes the everlasting relationship between God, Israel, and the Land of Israel. If extended to the earth as a whole, a covenantal model would spell out the obligations of humanity toward the earth and its inhabitants as one manifestation of humanity's obligations to God.[26]

The full manifestation and fulfillment of this three-fold covenant may have to wait for messianic times,[27] but the covenantal responsibilities are relevant now: we have our role to play in bringing about that idyllic period. And a particularly important common attribute of the covenantal idea and the vision of sustainability is the centrality of our responsibilities to future generations. As Rabbi Soloveitchik has written:

> Within the covenantal community, not only contemporary individuals but generations are engaged in a colloquy and each single experience of time is three-dimensional, manifesting itself in memory, actuality and anticipatory tension.

> This ... results in an awesome awareness of responsibility
> to a great past which handed down the divine imperative to
> the present generation in trust and confidence and to a
> mute future expecting this generation to discharge its
> covenantal duty conscientiously and honorably.[28]

We do indeed take on commitments in the name of future generations, and responsibilities to them, as it says in Deuteronomy 29:13–14: "I make this covenant not with you alone, but ... [also] with those who are not with us here this day." The world, like the Torah, is both a bequest that we have inherited from those that have come before, and a birthright we are holding in safekeeping for those that will come after us.

Bal Tashchit I: From Battlefield Forestry to Environmental Values

Probably the best-known Jewish value concept and collection of *halachot* regarding environmental responsibility are those grouped under the heading of *bal tashchit* (literally, "do not destroy"), which prohibits many forms of waste, destruction, vandalism, and the like. The career of this mitzvah begins in the Book of Deuteronomy, develops in Tannaitic literature, expands in the Talmud, is refracted through medieval commentaries and codes, and is applied in early and late Halachic responsa.

For anyone familiar with this value from references in contemporary environmental literature, it may be surprising to discover that the original context (Deut. 20:19–20) refers exclusively to fruit trees and their use, and that in a time of war! While other texts deal with proper treatment of the enemy, and terms of peace agreements, the verses in question here focus on the treatment of nature during the waging of war. This may seem esoteric at first, but the fact is that from the ancient Romans' sowing salt in enemy fields, to the scorched-earth policy of the Russians in their desperate war against Napoleon, to devastating American chemical defoliation with napalm and agent orange in Vietnam to Saddam Hussein's burning of oil wells in Kuwait, armies have used environmental destruction as a tactic in warfare. Why cavil at the loss of a few trees (or farmland, or air and water) when military victory and human lives are at stake?

And yet, the Torah, which calls us to dominion, and generally justifies various uses of nature, says here that there are strict limitations: acts of destruction with dire long-term consequences are inadmissible even for pressing short-term goals. Moreover, a strict distinction must be preserved between human conflicts and our relationship with the natural world, which must be kept out of the fray. Nature must not become a pawn on a human chessboard.

Let us remember the context, which is essentially one of life and death: shortening a war means saving lives and reducing suffering. Given the supreme value of human life in the Jewish tradition, one would think that nearly anything that would lead to the end of a conflict would therefore be justifiable. In particular, actions that would provide the means for a speedy victory should be encouraged, provided they are neither blatantly immoral, violating precepts between humans and their fellows, nor heretical, violating laws pertaining to humans' relationship to God.

Thus it is surprising to find that what the Torah is concerned about is how the Israelite army treats the trees. Our text forbids the chopping down of fruit trees in order to construct siegeworks, however necessary those may be for the conduct of a siege. Given the nature of siege warfare, the potential suffering that an extended siege may cause, and the need for construction material to get through the city's defenses, limiting the use of those trees was a serious restriction.

That much, what is forbidden, is clear. The *reason* for the prohibition, however, is not, and the ambiguities in these verses relate to some of the most contemporary controversies in current environmental thought. Here is the text:

> When in your war against a city, you have to besiege it a long time in order to capture it, you must not destroy its trees, wielding the ax against them. You may eat of them but you must not cut them down. *(Ki ha'adam etz ha'sadeh lavo' mipanecha bamatzor.)* Only trees that you know do not yield food may be destroyed; you may cut them down for constructing siegeworks against the city that is waging war on you, until it has been reduced. (Based on New JPS translation)

The line left in Hebrew above is highly ambiguous and admits to two very different interpretations:

1. "… (for the tree of the field is man's life) to employ them in the siege" (King James version).
2. "Are trees of the field human to withdraw before you into the besieged city?" (New JPS).

Translation 1 interprets the relationship between people and trees as one of connection, even need, or reliance. As the medieval Jewish commentator Ibn Ezra explains, we are not to cut down fruit trees because our lives are dependent on them and the food they produce. The reasoning here can justifiably be termed "anthropocentric": destroying fruit-bearing trees is forbidden because it harms human beings. Scorched earth is immoral, for though you may need the wood of the fruit trees to secure immediate victory, you will need their fruit even more in the peaceful years to come.

This imperative reveals the stark difference between what it means to fight over one's home (or what would be one's home) versus fighting someone else in his home. For example, the Americans could lay waste to great swaths of North Vietnam because it was halfway across the world—they wouldn't have to live with the consequences. If you're going to live in a land after the smoke clears and the fighting is over, you had better not destroy exactly that for which you are fighting.[29]

Translation 2 offers a very different rendering of the same verse. What the King James version and Ibn Ezra read as a simple assertion is parsed here as a question, and a rhetorical one at that: "Are trees of the field human to withdraw before you under siege?" (Because the traditional text has no punctuation, the reader must decide whether a statement is declarative, interrogative, and the like.) As the great medieval French commentator Rashi reads the verse: Are trees like people, that they can run away from an advancing army, and take refuge in the town? The answer being clearly: Of course not! They are innocent bystanders. Therefore, don't involve them in your conflicts, and don't cut them down. This approach makes no reference to human needs. The trees have a life of their own; they are not (only) a means to human ends. Though perhaps we may not speak of absolute rights for trees, this understanding argues for their *intrinsic value,* which is in line with the approach today termed *biocentrism.*

It should be emphasized that each translation/interpretation has strong and weak points. Translation 1 and Ibn Ezra are logical in that they help us understand the distinction the commandment makes between fruit-bearing and non-fruit-bearing trees, the latter's use being permitted (apparently precisely because they are not a long-term source of human sustenance). Grammatically, however, theirs is the weaker interpretation, as evidenced by the convoluted parenthetical phrase that doesn't quite square with the syntax of the entire verse.

Translation 2 and Rashi are better formulated grammatically, accounting well for all parts of the sentence, but they raise a philosophical question: if the trees have intrinsic value, and should be protected for their own sake, surely this holds for the non-fruit-bearing trees as well? Yet cutting them down is permitted! On what, then, can we base a differentiation between the two types of trees? Rashi doesn't address this challenging question, but I can suggest here a possible distinction between an almost utopian, spiritual ideal and the uncompromising needs of the real world.[30] Ideally, we should live without harming nature at all, and even the non-fruit-bearing trees shouldn't be used for the sordid purpose of waging war.[31] But when we translate that absolute norm into the life-and-death demands of the here and now, we are forced to revert to the anthropocentric distinctions based on human survival, though they fall short of the biocentric ideal.

The four words of the original encapsulate in their ambiguity the two main schools of thought on issues of preservation and development. First is the view that nature has value in and of itself, that it exists apart from us and our needs, that we should refrain from destroying what we cannot create. Second is the equally legitimate anthropocentric approach, which speaks to "the bottom line," what we get out of the deal. It also implies a generational perspective—we harm not only ourselves but generations to come when we selfishly exploit resources for our short-term gain.

Some claim that we can arrive at a pragmatic synthesis of the two positions because it is impossible to conceive of human survival outside the boundaries of healthy and stable ecosystems: doing what is best for humanity over the longest of long terms will necessarily dovetail with what is in the best interest of nature. Nevertheless, just as we need both interpretations of the biblical verses to do full justice to the richness of the original, neither by itself accounting for all the manifest and latent meanings, we need to worry about nature and about humanity, and about the ongoing connection and interdependence between them.

Bal Taschchit II: Negotiating Needs and Wants

Despite its somewhat esoteric context—battlefield forestry rules—
the Rabbis rightly perceived the wide-ranging implications of such
a regulation for daily life. One can apply the reasoning known as
kal va'homer (a fortiori): if in the most extreme case of wartime, a
life-and-death situation, it is forbidden to harm irrevocably the natural environment, then how much more so regarding day-to-day
situations of personal comfort and economic profit and loss? The
Mishnah (*Bava Kamma* 8:6) categorically states that while one
who cuts down plants belonging to another is criminally liable, it
is likewise unlawful to cut down one's own plants (*neti'ot*, apparently not even limited to fruit trees). Here is a clear limitation on
what we modern Westerners would take as basic property rights;
what is ours is not really ours.

In confronting real-life situations, the Rabbis widened the
scope of this principle but also limited its applicability. As framed
in Maimonides' classic legal code, the *Mishneh Torah* ("Laws of
Kings" 6:10), it becomes forbidden to "smash household goods,
tear clothes, demolish a building, stop up a spring, or destroy arti-
cles of food" (cf. *Shabbat* 129a). Even human-made elements are
protected against wanton destruction.

As in many instances in Jewish law, the strict ideal is
expressed, but softened in practice to allow for the needs of everyday life. Halacha stipulates when and what type of trees may in fact
be cut down, mainly according to quantity and value of the fruit
produced. Rabina (a fourth-century Talmudic sage) is quoted as
saying: "If its value for other purposes exceeds that for fruit, it is
permitted (to cut it down)" (*Bava Kamma* 91b). This is a very
rationalized, economic reading of the commandment that takes it
out of the realm of the biblical categorical imperative, and into the
cold calculations of cost and benefits.

But despite these legal leniencies (or maybe because of them) others reemphasize the spiritual principle: Rabbi Haninah states that his son Shibhat died only for having cut down a fig tree before its time. It is important to pause and dwell for a moment on the idea of a bereaved father ascribing the death of his son to divine punishment for cutting down a fig tree. How far is Haninah from Rabina! And Haninah was not alone: in *Bava Batra* 26a, Raba refuses to cut down date trees that are damaging the vines of his neighbor, Rabbi Joseph (even though, apparently, it is halachically required), because of what happened to Shibhat.

Other sources, too, give voice to the almost mystical understanding of the life and worth of trees, one that contrasts starkly with economic reasoning. A mystical medieval midrash reinforces both the inner life of trees and the similarity between a tree being cut down and a person:

> When people cut down the wood of a tree that yields fruit, its cry goes from one end of the world to the other, and the sound is inaudible.... When the soul departs from the body, the cry goes forth from one end of the world to the other, and the sound is inaudible. (*Pirkei de Rabbi Eliezer*, 34)

And in the tractate of *Pesachim* (50b), it is claimed that one who cuts down good trees, even non-fruit-bearing trees that give shade or add beauty, will never see blessing in his life.

These two views—those who see economic justification and human need as paramount and those who will go to great lengths to protect the integrity of natural objects[32]—persist in the extensive responsa literature down through the ages. Real-life dilemmas (Can I cut down the tree in my yard to expand my house? Can communal monies be used for events or public works that may be deemed extravagant?) are addressed by *poskim* (rabbinic decisors), and they show a continual effort to finesse the fine line between needs and wants, between valid acts of use and those that cross the line into misuse or abuse. The rabbinic expansion of the jurisdiction of *bal tashchit* encompasses a variety of areas that are quite environmentally salient. For instance, the question of energy conservation is addressed in the tractate of *Shabbat* (67b):

> Rabbi Zutra said, "One who covers an oil lamp, or uncovers a naphtha lamp, transgresses the prohibition of *bal tashchit,* since these acts cause the lamp to burn with unnecessary speed."

It is not at all a far cry to ask what this value has to say about gas-guzzling cars or energy-intensive appliances, and the rate at which we are consuming resources for energy. If it is possible to be more efficient, to slow down, to conserve—than we are violating a mitzvah by not doing so.

We can contemplate similar extensions in our own day. For instance, *bal tashchit* can be defined as forbidding the wanton destruction of anything of value. But value is relative: for instance, recycling technologies mean that garbage now has value. Therefore, not recycling should be declared a flagrant violation of this biblical injunction. Similarly, the Talmudic sages Rav Hisda and Rav Papa (*Shabbat* 140b) even ruled that conspicuous consumption is a violation of *bal tashchit*. Others claim that this is going too far, but this is exactly the debate we need to have: what are the limits, what "uses" are actually abuses, and what demands do holiness and sustainability make on our lives and lifestyles?

The *Sefer Hachinuch,* a thirteenth-century elucidation of the Commandments, saw in this mitzvah a very general principle, a *midda,* a virtue, to be cultivated:

... to love that which is good and worthwhile and to cling to it, so that good becomes a part of us and we will avoid all that is evil and destructive. This is the way of the righteous and those who improve society ... that nothing, not even a grain of mustard, should be lost.... if possible they will prevent any destruction that they can. Not so are the wicked, who rejoice in the destruction of the world, and they are destroying themselves. (#530)

Given the role of our economy and consumer culture in the creation of environmental problems ranging from global warming to species extinction, our society indeed rejoices in acts whose end results are the destruction of the world. Both public and private sectors have difficulty in articulating and protecting the long-term public good. Religious tradition, though, is used to thinking in terms of eternity, and that concern with posterity, with the ongoing well-being of Creation, is exactly one of the strong messages that religious environmentalism can bring to the fast-paced (and short-sighted) industrial world.

Empathy and Ethics: The Pain of Living Things

While *bal tashchit* relates primarily to inanimate nature, such as plants and resources, the central value that informs relationships with animals is *tza'ar ba'alei chayim,* the prevention of cruelty to animals. The fact that we use animals in our lives and derive benefit from them is a fact of our "animal" nature—it's how the world works. But the ways in which we use them, the choices we make, express our humanity.

Laws pertaining to *tza'ar ba'alei chayim* in the Torah assume a rural community, where animals and their use are part of life. Our highly urbanized, mechanized lives seem less intertwined with animals by contrast. Nowadays, we are shielded from the economic processes that make from animals food, clothing, and other goods. As a result, whatever cruelty is done in our names happens far away, in labs, factories, or on factory farms, where of necessity we feel less compassion and have less direct control.

The biblical and rabbinic imperatives were immediate responses to everyday situations: is that a donkey struggling or fallen under a heavy load? Go help it (Deut. 22:4). And although that beast of burden is somebody's property, it doesn't matter whose, for as Exodus 23:5 states, you are obliged to do this even for your enemy's animals. As in the prohibition on cutting down fruit trees in wartime, here, too, we are to keep enmity between people, and not involve in our conflicts nature and other creatures, which have their own existence and concerns.

Should we desecrate Shabbat to save an injured animal? Yes, *pikuach nefesh,* the mandate to save lives, extends to the lives *(nefashot)* of animals (*Shabbat* 128b). Furthermore, when you plow, don't yoke an ass and an ox together (Deut. 22:10)—the weaker one will suffer. And when it comes time to thresh, don't muzzle that ox (Deut. 25:4), preventing it from eating the grain always before its eyes. These regulations, along with others, such as the obligation to allow one's animals to rest on Shabbat (as stated in the Decalogue, Deut. 5:14), are like labor laws, protecting the conditions of the workers (who here happen to have four legs).[33]

Yet the question is asked: are not animals merely property, and taking care of one's possessions simply good sense, not weighty moral responsibility? Indeed, the return of a straying animal to its master, mandated in Deuteronomy 22:1–3, is likened to returning any lost property to its rightful owner, and it seems that animal welfare is not paramount here.

Likewise, in the next verse, we are bidden to help those whose pack animals are straining under their burdens. Is this for the sake of the animal or (just) to aid the person? The Talmud (*Bava Metzia* 31–32) makes a distinction between helping the driver unload an animal who might be carrying too heavy a load and loading the goods back onto an animal that has fallen. The latter is indeed of benefit mainly to the owner, and so one can legitimately demand remuneration for the help proffered. The former, however, is a direct response to the suffering of the animal, and should be done for the animal's sake, with no monetary compensation.

The debate over whether kindness to animals is for the sake of the animal (Maimonides) or in order to inculcate kindness in humans (Nachmanides) does not bear on the question of whether the Torah cares about cruelty to animals: clearly we couldn't inculcate kindness in human beings by requiring kindness to random, unfeeling bodies. Even if the animals are a means here, they are an appropriate one, because they feel pain, and we can be edified by our behavior toward them by refraining from causing them pain. When Maimonides (in his *Guide,* 3:48) writes of the emotional capabilities and the compassion of the mother animal for her young, he is presaging philosopher Jeremy Bentham, who wrote passionately that regarding animal welfare, the question is not: can they reason, can they talk? It is: can they suffer?[34]

The Torah affirms three central propositions regarding animals and their treatment: that although they are "ownable," they are more than chattel, that they do indeed suffer, and that it is incumbent upon us to minimize that suffering in our dealings with them. And what seemed like a few isolated examples becomes a whole subclass of ethical imperatives, incorporating some eighteen different laws, including those mentioned, as well as the laws of the separation of milk and meat (the life of the animal and its death), feeding domestic animals before oneself (Talmud, *Berachot* 40a), and critical attitudes to hunting, among others.

In speaking of our relationships with animals, we are primarily referring to animals within the sphere of direct human influence, animals we use in various ways, and that have been domesticated. The phenomenon of domestication creates what philosopher Mary

Midgely calls "the mixed community," where there are indeed mutual relationships and obligations. Domestication and the mixed community are predicated upon kinship, empathy, and emotional communication—and so moral consideration is a result of common membership in that community. The idea of animals and human beings being part of the same moral community was clear to Jews in antiquity in ways that are difficult for us to conceive. For instance, Jonah 3:5–8 describes Nineveh making atonement, with the cattle joining in the fasting and wearing of sackcloths. Likewise, Mishnah *Sanhedrin* (1:4) speaks of animals tried in capital cases (like humans, and not like property), based on Exodus 21:28–9, where oxen are held responsible for their goring.

This is not obvious: after all, is there not a metaphysical chasm between us and the rest of the animal world, since we are uniquely created in God's image? Criticism of animal-welfare activists often comes from those who feel that when we expand the moral consideration we give to animals, we contract that which we give our fellow humans—the boundaries blur, and human welfare is liable to suffer.

Yet care for animal well-being does not debase the divine image in humanity—it expresses and ennobles it. God's mercy extends to all creatures (Pss. 145:9,16; 36:7), demonstrated in scenarios such as God's concern for the cattle, at the end of the Book of Jonah, and in reprimanding Balaam for treating his donkey violently (Num. 22:32). We are bidden to imitate that: "My people Israel! Just as our Father in heaven is merciful, may you too on earth be merciful, and don't slaughter an animal and its young on one day" (*Targum Yonathan* to Leviticus 22:28).

Thus we are obligated to treat animals with compassion, not because of our similarity to them, but because of our difference. We are bidden to bridge that difference in empathy and understanding. We don't think of righteousness as knowing the needs and wants of animals. Yet that is exactly what Proverbs 12:10 asserts, that the righteous, the *tzaddik,* knows the *nefesh* (soul or life) of his animal.

Being righteous necessitates not only providing for animals, as one would for any property, but also acquiring intimate knowledge of the animal's self. This is neither abstract nor instrumental knowledge; it is part of a relationship, and as anybody who has had a pet will attest, the knowledge, and resultant obligation, is mutual.

Likewise, the two people referred to in the Torah as *tzadikkim,* Noah and Joseph, both acquired this title for having saved animals in their efforts to preserve the world from natural disaster (*Tanhuma Noah* 5).[35] Moses and David proved or acquired their capabilities from shepherding—in particular, kindness to the flocks. And let's not forget the *tzaddeket* Rebecca who was deemed a worthy wife for Isaac because of the character she revealed in her treatment of Eliezer's camels (Gen. 24:14–20).

Critics of animal rights are right about one thing: we should not allow concern for animals to degenerate into misanthropy, opposing the legitimate needs of human society. It is easier to be at one end of the spectrum—either "no holds barred" on exploitation of animals—or the opposite—don't do anything to an animal that you wouldn't do to a human. The tough choices are in the middle: we may see medical experimentation to save lives as unavoidable. But what about experimentation just to improve the quality of life? Or massive social transformations, such as overhauling our agro-industrial system, to reduce cruelty? Although it may be hard to agree all the time on exactly what absolute needs are, it's hard to believe that they would include common practices such as perennially new brands of mascara, requiring continued animal testing, or unnaturally fat goose livers, which entail extensive suffering.

Moreover, while certain uses are condoned, callousness is not.[36] The great Rabbi Yehudah HaNasi was afflicted with severe pain for speaking insensitively to a calf destined for slaughter:

A calf en route to slaughter passed before Rabbi Yehudah HaNasi. It broke away, hid its head under Rabbi's skirt and lowed. "Go," he said. "What can I do for you? For this you were created." Thereupon they said [in heaven], "Since he has no pity, let us bring suffering upon him." Rabbi was afflicted for thirteen years. One day, his daughter sought to kill an animal which crossed her path. He said to her, "Let it be, as it is written, 'His tender mercy is over all His creatures.'" At that moment he was cured. (*Bava Metzia* 85a, *Genesis Rabbah* 33:3)

His grandson, R. Gamliel, perhaps inspired precisely by this incident, remarked: "Whoever has compassion upon his fellow creatures, upon him will God have compassion" (*Tosefta Bava Kamma* 9:30, *Sifrei Deuteronomy* 96).

The sages emphasized that animals raised for food must experience a painless *death* because they couldn't imagine the type or quantity of pain and suffering involved in the merchandized *lives* of farm animals today. Are we sufficiently aware of that? Does it reflect the righteousness we seek? Are we doing enough to create and implement alternatives?

What the Torah mandates regarding animal welfare—and more to the point, what it *doesn't* require—may not be enough for some. That's okay—there is and always has been room for more righteous approaches. The question of our duties to animals may indeed be a case wherein tradition requires a certain minimum of the average person, but those who feel compelled should adhere to a higher standard—which may be the Torah's own ideal, but which is hard for the general public to attain.

True concern for animal welfare is a lesson in humility, both in learning the deep connections we have with the nonhuman, animate world and in confronting its ultimate otherness. We expand our moral universe when we break out of the shell of the self to include others in relationship, when we develop a multicultural sensibility to appreciate the contributions of other peoples.

Insensitive "species-centrism" is a similar blinder, and we need animals to help put ourselves in perspective.

In addition to rubrics such as *bein adam lechavero,* we may need a new category of *mitzvot,* such as *bein adam le'olam,* for environmental issues. Regarding animals and their treatment, *chaver* (friend, fellow) could be just the right term. Why must our fellows be limited to members of our own species? It's true that animals failed the test to become the sole human companion (Gen. 2:19–20), but the fact that they were considered at all for the job says a lot about the actual and potential connections between us.

Not inflicting suffering on creatures that feel is a moral and ethical imperative, and it certainly should trump considerations of convenience or luxury. As Abraham Lincoln once said: "I care not for a man's religion whose dog and cat are not the better for it." Shouldn't commercial animals also be included in that now? It's time we reevaluate whom we include among those worthy of moral consideration, our circle of friends.

Tikkun and Partnership, Flax and Foreskins

This chapter makes eminently clear what the Jewish engagement with the environment and environmentalism is, and what it is not. It is not a cut-and-dried, rigid catechism of dos and don'ts that we can apply automatically, and that we must either accept or reject in toto. One reason for this is, of course, rapidly changing historical situations and new global and local challenges, which make the application of traditional categories anything but straightforward. But even more significant are the sources themselves, which delineate a range of values and a gamut of opinions concerning the nature of nature and the role of the human creature in Creation, where our horizons of action rightfully lie, and what the limits are to those horizons.

The previous two sections, in explicating the value clusters of *bal tashchit* and *tza'ar ba'alei chayim,* have presented the scope of our possible actions and behaviors, and the dilemmas and uncertainties involved in committing to right action. The dialogue consists in the wide latitude of opinion regarding what constitutes legitimate use, and what becomes inadmissible abuse. Regarding *bal tashchit* in particular, the context is one of exploring restraints on human action, where we need to reign ourselves in.

Beyond what we are bidden to refrain from doing, however, the question remains: what is the positive ideal of our interaction with the world? That we need to learn to avoid destruction is clear. But what about how and when and where and what to build?

These questions are answered, in part, by the concepts of *tikkun* (repair or mending) and of being God's partner in the act of Creation. Both of these ideas are based on the belief that nature is imperfect, or incomplete. Remember, the created world was pronounced "very good" at the end of the six days of Creation, which is different from "holy" or "perfect." The act of creation is ongoing, and we have a role to play in developing and improving the raw materials God provides. This is the fundamentally activist stance that is at the root of the dynamic of dominion and stewardship, and which requires channeling and guidance in order to avoid degenerating into self-serving pillage.

The idea that the natural world in all its wonder and glory is somehow imperfect and requires active human intervention to be brought to completion sounds strange to the modern ecological ear, which perceives human impact on nature as generally diminishing its inherent goodness or wholeness. But while it is common to stereotype and stigmatize environmental sensibilities as being opposed to all development, there are fruitful points of contact between these Jewish and environmental attitudes, in the enterprise of remediation (actively intervening to improve conditions) and the whole idea of sustainable development, growth, and progress that does not entail systematic destruction.

The meaning of this activist stance of *tikkun* is highlighted in Jewish texts from a period when Judaism clashed with its surrounding cultures. The idea of the aesthetic and formal perfection of the natural world and the human body characterized ancient Hellenic culture, and the Greco-Romans who occupied the Land of Israel at the beginning of the common era were very critical of a number of Jewish practices in this regard. The Jewish value of *tikkun* and the requisite stance regarding the natural world is clarified in a story, described picturesquely in Midrash *Tanhuma*, about circumcision (of all things).

The time was the early second century CE. The place was Roman Palestine, the Land of Israel. The powerful Roman governor Tinneius Rufus was beginning to familiarize himself with the strange habits of his new subjects. First, they were lazy: they refused to do any work one day out of seven. How different this was from the ceaseless activity that made his own Imperial Rome so accomplished (and feared)! Stranger yet, they insisted on maiming the natural perfection of their bodies by circumcising their male infants. Tinneius[37] Rufus looked around at the Greco-Roman statuary he had brought to this remote outpost. Like the nude sporting events he enjoyed, it glorified and reveled in the flawless human body. "What's with these Jews?" he thought. "Enforced inactivity, ritual disfigurement—they're such 'unnatural' people! They even give charity to the poor, whose lot is so clearly foreordained."

Rufus decided to summon Akiva, a rabbi known for his wisdom, less to learn from him than to outwit him and prove the superiority of his own values:

> "Akiva," challenged the Roman, "whose deeds are finer? God's or those of flesh-and-blood humans?"
>
> Rufus assumed the rabbi would say that God's deeds are finer. But, sensing the gambit, Rabbi Akiva replied, "The deeds of humans are finer."

"Behold the heavens and the earth!" Rufus countered. "Can man create the likes of them?"

"Don't speak to me of things over which we have no control," Akiva responded. "Speak rather in terms of a human scale."

"Well, then, why are you circumcised?" Tinneius Rufus then asked the rabbi.

"I knew this was really what you wanted to know," said Akiva. "Hence my previous response: that human deeds are finer than God's."

Rabbi Akiva brought Tinneius Rufus wheat stalks and cakes, flax and fine linen. "The wheat and the flax are God's handiwork," he said, "and the cakes and the linen are man's. Are not the cakes and the linen, the finished product, finer than the plain stalks, the raw material? Even you, Tinneius Rufus, cannot miss the clear analogy: We are born incomplete and perfect ourselves through following God's law."

"But if God had intended man to be circumcised," Rufus argued, "why wasn't Adam created circumcised? Why doesn't every newborn male emerge from the womb that way?"

"You see," Akiva explained, "everything created during the six days of Creation needs perfecting (tikkun): mustard needs sweetening, wheat needs grinding, and even man needs perfecting. This 'perfection' or purification is achieved not according to our whims but by following divinely ordained commandments."

Adapted (with only slight embellishment) from Midrash *Tanhuma* (*Tazria* 5, cf. also *Pesikta Rabbati* 23:4), the imagined dialogue above presents the Greco-Roman pagan world view, which sees nature and the human body as perfect, because there is no external, transcendent scale or source of value. What is, is ideal.

In contrast, Akiva espouses the religious view that there is an ideal beyond the present reality toward which we should strive.

Akiva's explanation of circumcision embeds the human—both body and soul—in nature. It claims that both humanity and nature are imperfect, or unfinished, and can be the objects of transformation—when guided by a spiritual objective, not a selfish profit motive. This proactive approach to nature is not, however, an anti-wilderness or even a "wise-use" statement; Akiva's realm of dominion is a domesticated one. The vast world, like the heavens, is beyond us in more ways than one; it is not for us to create, re-create, or control. To want to do so is more a result of Roman-style hubris than of the biblical mandate of care.

My mention of Shabbat here together with circumcision is similarly no coincidence. They symbolically complement each other. Both have their origins in the pre-Sinaitic Genesis narratives, and both are described as an *ot* (sign) and a *brit* (covenant). Together, they represent a balanced praxis: an activist stance focused on knowing when and how to perfect aspects of the natural world (including ourselves), punctuated by a weekly lesson in how and when to stop.

The negative—limiting ourselves and refraining from action—and the positive—pushing ourselves and embarking on initiatives—need to go together and inform each other. Although the model is conceptually clear, its application in real life is far from uncomplicated: one person's *tikkun* may be another's *kilkul* (rupture or breakdown). The idea of completing or improving nature doesn't obviate the need for exploring and defining the limits; rather, the opposite is the case—it makes that need all the more urgent.

עולם ומלואו

Olam Umelo'o

4

Contemporary Topics and Issues

This chapter starts out from the opposite direction of the previous one, namely from the "life" pole, the "current events" side of the bridge, and moving from there to the "book" side, the sources and traditions. Its organizing categories are the issues and components of our lives today, from population growth and consumerism to urban planning, biodiversity, and vegetarianism. Although there are sometimes new things under the sun, little is completely unprecedented, and there are insights to be had in approaching the most contemporary of challenges in the language of classical ideas and values.

The sections in this chapter do not cover all the significant issues we face, nor do they say all there is to be said about the ones that are mentioned. As an esteemed teacher of mine once said: the goal of education should not be to *cover* the material, but to *uncover* it. Hopefully, beyond the specific content it includes, this discussion will be suggestive of a type of learning, or a mode of dialogue, that we should be developing in grappling with any issue of this type. Again, I'm not trying to come up with easy answers, but to help enrich and enliven the questioning. Sometimes this means jump-starting a conversation that hasn't begun yet.

The conclusion? *Zil g'mor:* let us continue the discussion ...

Multiply and Fill Up the Earth: Are We There Yet?

The population explosion used to be *the* top-rung environmental issue. In the 1960s, overcrowding, famine, and resource depletion were the dire predictions of the day. There's no question that the Earth has experienced nothing short of a population explosion in the last three generations—from approximately 2 billion in 1930 to over 6 billion today—and the curves reveal a situation that is certainly not sustainable ad infinitum:[1]

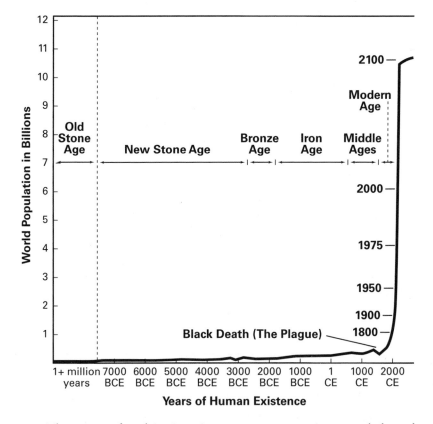

The causes for this situation are not mysterious, and though the resultant numbers are problematic, many of them stem from positive developments. Life-saving progress such as improved sanitation and health care led to reduced infant mortality and increased longevity, which translated into more people living longer and having more children.

Clearly, the situation is more complex than that: family size and reproduction rates are a function of many factors beyond the biological, including cultural norms and religious values, education and employment (especially of women), the nature of that employment, and economic realities such as stability and secure pensions. A major reason for large families and increased population is poverty, and the resultant need for more working hands to ensure a minimal family income. Defining the population question as a problem to be solved (abstracted from those complexities) has often led to quite draconian policies (such as China's one-child law), which can lead to other brutalities, including infanticide.

Today, the issue is seen in a more complex light. First is the question of which populations do indeed have high rates of growth, and which do not, which often translates into which kinds of people "we have too many of." Most European countries reproduce at or below replacement levels, while Africa, South America, and Asia still have relatively high birthrates. The discourse around population issues has thus acquired undeniable colonialist or racist overtones, often resulting in white Western technocrats preaching to developing countries about the virtues of family planning or more stringent methods of population control.

Moreover, we don't have a single uniform standard of living, which we can use to calculate how many people the Earth can support. Ecologists speak of the "carrying capacity" of a certain area for a given species: the size of a herd that can be sustained in a forest, based on the area, the quantity of food that can be produced, and so on. But people are rich and poor, ostentatious and modest, wasteful and thrifty. In ascertaining the carrying capacity of a given area, we have to ask not only how many people, but also at what standard of living, with what sorts of technologies, and with how much foresight and planning. The question of consumption levels (the "ecological footprint")[2] is at least as significant as population statistics.

But population size cannot grow forever, and certainly not at the rates it has been growing in our lifetimes. At even the most meager or efficient of lifestyles, there is still an upper limit to how many people can survive together on Earth. And the question of maximal quantity doesn't begin to touch on the question of optimum level: what is the size of the population for which we can realistically ensure a sustainable quality of life for all?

Although many general religious values have suffered or been embattled in the modern era, here we see one that we have fulfilled, and in spades. As Genesis 1:28 states, we are to be fruitful, multiply, and fill up the earth. The phrasing *mil'u et ha'aretz,* "fill up the earth," seems to imply that it can indeed be full, that there is a limit, that we can be *yotze'*—we can fulfill our requirement of this mitzvah, and stop. What this and no other text tells us is: how will we know when we get there? Are we done yet?

This mitzvah has always been applied on the individual level: how many children are required to fulfill the commandment of being fruitful? The answers are either just two, no matter which sex (Beit Shammai), or at least one boy and one girl (Beit Hillel—see *Yevamot* 6:6, 61b). These are the minima; is there an upper limit? From a second mitzvah, "settling the earth" (Isa. 45:18, "the world was created for habitation"), we learn that more is better.[3] No attention is paid to the larger picture, to local or global limits. That question arises in times of limitations, when there are not enough resources to support everyone, such as during a famine or severe overcrowding (as in Noah's ark). The conclusion is the same: non-reproduction, or limiting family size, is permissible, even praiseworthy.

Genesis 41:50 casually relates that two sons were born to Joseph before the onset of the famine that was to beset Egypt, which Joseph had foreseen via Pharaoh's dream. This is hardly trivial: Joseph, one of thirteen siblings, had only two children himself, and he stopped procreating before the famine he knew lay ahead. The Talmud uses this example to state: "It is forbidden to engage in marital relations in time of famine" (*Ta'anit* 11a). What is the reason for this invasion of the bedroom? Rashi interprets this as an admonition to avoid selfish indulgence (i.e., sexual pleasure) out of sympathy for others in distress. But the parallel passage in the Jerusalem Talmud sees the prohibition as a call to population control, stating bluntly: "When you see great deprivation entering the world, keep your wife childless" (J. T. *Ta'anit* 1:6). The very personal is suddenly *very* political.

A different precedent for the same position is educed by the midrash (*Bereishit Rabba* 31:7 to Genesis 6:18) from the story of Noah and the ark. When Noah and crew went into the ark, God said: "... you shall enter the ark, with your sons, your wife, and your sons' wives" (Gen. 6:18). Later, when the Flood was over, God instructed them to disembark: "Come out of the ark, together with your wife, your sons, and your sons' wives" (Gen. 8:16). R. Yehuda b. R. Shimon says that this difference in word order, the separation of the men from the women and then their reunification, hints that they were instructed not to procreate in the difficult conditions of the ark. Given contemporary threats to biodiversity and living systems, our world is often compared to the ark, and our own mission to that of Noah.

How should we relate to this issue as Jews? For our part, we're still recovering from the massacre generations ago of a third of the world's Jews. To top it off, North American and European Jews are like their non-Jewish compatriots—only more so. The world Jewish population (outside of Israel) has actually been falling in recent years, due to intermarriage, assimilation, and low fertility rates. Like other decimated tribal peoples, world Jewry needs to regroup and replenish, and the meaning of six billion should rightfully take a backseat to the six million. If environmental concerns motivate us, we should be focusing on unsustainable levels of consumption, reducing net impact per family, and not necessarily family size.

Joseph is an interesting example regarding consumption and judicious planning as well. Thanks to him, during the seven years of starvation, Egypt had more than enough grain for all. Besides having just two children, his response to the environmental catastrophe of his day was central planning. In contrast to ancient Egypt, our age's major problem is not famine. Other environmental problems, such as global warming and pollution, are more grave than food shortages. The same Talmudic discussion from *Ta'anit* (11a) offers direction on those issues as well, stating: "When the public experiences calamity, let no one say, 'I shall eat and drink and let peace be upon my own soul.'" Given the global implications, personal apathy and high consumption levels are not neutral positions.

But individual awareness is not enough; collective action is critical. For that, Joseph is both a positive and a negative example. He began wisely and compassionately, stockpiling food for the years of scarcity to come. But then he carried out a complete nationalization of the land, subjugation of the all-too-servile people, and mass population transfers (see Gen. 47:13–27)—probably sowing the seeds of Israel's later enslavement. When it comes to the basic challenges of sustainability, not only is the personal highly political, but the environmental is very social as well, and what is required to address the challenges is an involved populace and visionary leadership.

Eat and Be Satisfied: How Much Is Enough?

The other side of the population coin is consumption. From 1900 to 2000, the population grew by a whopping factor of four. The twentieth century was the first, and almost certainly will be the last, to experience such massive growth of the human race. But this growth, while contributing greatly to our increasing environmental impact, is not the main driving force. Expanding consumption levels dwarf population growth and put it into perspective. In that same period, when the population quadrupled, energy use grew eleven times, and overall economic activity in 2000 was an astounding seventeen times its level in 1900 as measured in GNP!

Lifestyles and levels of material consumption that were once the province of the very wealthy have become the birthright of the middle class: this is the success of the "affluent society." But the achievements and relative prosperity of Western production and consumption, which have led to perceived comfort for millions of individuals, are becoming increasingly problematic for us as a society.

Consumption used to be a disease (tuberculosis); now it's an ideology. Consumerism, though, is simply a different type of disease, dubbed by some "affluenza" (or "stuffocation"). Let there be no mistake, there is nothing wrong with consuming things: all organisms consume air, water, and food; we humans add to that list shelter, clothing, entertainment, and the like. The important change from mere consuming to consumerism (or consumer culture) is not just the quantitative increase in levels of consumption, but also the qualitative transformation from consumption as a means to existence to being an end in itself, a focus of greater and greater amounts of energy and resources, a purported solution to too many of life's problems.

Over and against the Zeitgeist of wanting more and better things, and seeing nothing wrong with that, come religious pronouncements that seem downright primitive, if not anti-humanist: "Who is rich? One who is satisfied with one's portion" (*Pirkei Avot* 4:1). Although no one can argue with inner peace, many of us unconsciously equate contentment with complacency, and from there it is but a small step to stagnation. Western society, it is claimed, has succeeded because of *dissatisfaction,* the struggling and striving for more. But there are two nagging problems with this otherwise rosy picture. One is ecological, or material: the continually increasing through-put of the consumer society is leading to resource depletion and increased waste and pollution. The other is psychological, or spiritual: perennial dissatisfaction is not a great recipe for satisfaction.

Anti-consumerism is often wrongly perceived as a simplistic call for belt-tightening and doing without, when so many others seem to be doing so much with. But, as environmental scholar Alan Durning points out, most environmental damage or degradation is caused either by people who have too much (and therefore are unconcerned about efficiency or waste) or by people who don't have enough, who, in the struggle for daily existence, are unable to take into account long-term considerations. Likewise, there are human prices to pay at both extremes of excessive want and privilege. Thus the main question, which few ask, and even fewer attempt to answer, is: "How much is enough?"[4] What is a decent standard of living, for one and for all, and for once and for all?

The Rabbis had extensive discussions regarding what is justifiable use and what it wasteful or extravagant. These were usually under the rubric of *bal tashchit,* the prohibition against needless destruction. For instance, one exchange suggests that conspicuous consumption is a direct violation of this precept:

> Rav Hisda said: "If you can eat barley bread and you choose to eat wheat bread, you are guilty of violating *bal tashchit."* Rav Papa said: "If you can drink beer and drink wine instead, you are guilty of violating *bal tashchit."* (*Shabbat* 140b)

In other words, if you can get by on cheaper food or drink, but you insist on spending more money for luxury items, you are being wasteful and therefore destructive (and violating Halacha). Contemporary examples include everything from types of cars to fancy electronics and brand-name clothing. If the text ended there, we would have an unambiguous statement in favor of simplicity, or at least simply doing with less. But the text continues, and ends with an unattributed "bottom line," which states:

> But that is incorrect: for bal tashchit *"degufa,"* "not destroying," as applied to one's person [body], is more important. (Ibid.)

Here we find the surprising idea that *bal tashchit* is applicable not only to natural objects such as trees, or even to money or possessions, but also to one's own body! The implicit message is that the more expensive items might be more healthful, and therefore the expense would be justified. Put another way, our own bodies are also part of the natural world and demand safeguarding, and both sides need to be taken into account. Again, the contemporary examples are rife: Should we spend more for health food? Is that luxury car safer or more dependable than the economy model? Are expensive brand-name shoes a better value because they are better for your feet?

The whole *sugya,* Talmudic textual unit, helps us frame the difficult questions: What is a sufficient level of material life? How do we define our well-being and what contributes to it? What is legitimate use, and what is abuse, or waste? We are invited to explore the shifting middle ground between the castigated extremist poles of hedonism and asceticism, between too much and too little, where each of us separately and all of us together can decide when we say *"dayenu,"* it is enough for us.

There are other teachings, though, that are unequivocal about what is too much. When ostentatious practice got out of hand, the Rabbis had no problem legislating sumptuary laws limiting conspicuous consumption. For example, traditional Jewish burial practice requires only *tachrichin*, a simple shroud, and eschews fancy coffins. Why should this be so, and when did this become the practice? The Talmud recalls this turning point:

> At first the carrying out of the dead was harder for his relatives than his death [because of the great expense involved in customary burial], so much so that they would leave him [the corpse] and run away. Until Rabban Gamliel came and demanded less deference to himself, and they carried him out in [inexpensive] linen garments, thereupon all the people followed his example of carrying out the dead in linen garments. (*Ketubot* 8b)

The difficult image of Jews abandoning a corpse because they couldn't afford the expense expected of them should be a warning about social pressures of this sort. Perhaps we need a Rabban Gamliel of our own day to take a personal stand on things such as excessive wedding and bar/bat mitzvah celebrations.

Similarly, Maimonides legislates against eating or drinking to excess, wearing ostentatious clothing, or leading an extravagant lifestyle that requires going into debt or living off the largesse of others (*Mishneh Torah*, "Laws of Opinions," ch. 5). Again, this is a spiritual issue of character improvement for the individual, but in our day and age, it has become a basic issue of survival in a planet of limits. It has a theological side as well: if we are commanded not to take God's name in vain, then how much more so should we not waste, taking God's creations, literally, in vain?

This religious contribution is important, not only because there is precious little helpful guidance in these areas from our surrounding culture but also because the question of what is enough is even subversive in mainstream environmental circles. The standard call for sustainability generally seeks to ascertain the *maxi-*

mum resource flows that are sustainable over time. Moreover, popular practices, such as recycling, allow us to avoid challenging our love affair with consumption by claiming to mitigate the physical dimension of too much garbage, while ignoring these deeper issues.

Asking not how much is possible, though, but how much (or how little) is enough, refocuses the discourse on *sufficiency*. Although this may sound grim to some, no one is speaking of suffering—for that would be insufficiency, trying to get by with not enough. The value of sufficiency reemphasizes the fact that too much may be as harmful as too little.

There are many problems in our society, many sources of suffering, that stem not from lack, but from excess: obesity and many other health-related problems, pandemic credit card debt, and a widening social gap between those who can afford to indulge and those who can't. Durning presents this elegantly in the following table:[5]

Consumer Class/ Consumption Category	Consumers (1.1 billion)	Intermediate (3.5 billion)	Poor (1.5 billion)
Diet	Meat; processed food; soft drinks	Grains; clean water	Undernourished; unsafe water
Transportation	Private cars	Mass transit; bicycles	Walking
Material Culture	Disposable	Consumer durables	Bio-mass; local organic

Nearly all readers of this book will fall into the upper "consumer" class. Clearly, members of the lower impoverished division need to be able to expand their options upward. But we, too, need to adopt more of the behavior of the middle category, not only for the health and well-being of the planet but also for our own individual welfare. We are not constraining our options or painfully cutting back when we make lifestyle choices that are healthier for us as individuals and for the world. We delude ourselves if we do not see the implications for our own survival and thriving—again, individual as well as collective—from overconsumption. Based on the idea of *bal taschchit degufa*, not destroying one's body, we can appreciate the statement of the moral tract *Orach Meisharim* that overeating (and by extension, overconsumption in general) is actually a double sin, twice violating *bal tashchit:* wasting food *and* hurting your own body (6:29).

What is required is not frugality and self-denial, but a different model altogether of happiness and fulfillment, a radical *decoupling* of personal satisfaction and happiness from the need for ever-increasing material goods. The tone of the standard religious discourse on this point is admittedly antiquated. But it is exactly "stuffocation" that we need to avoid, as in the hipper slogan: "more fun, less stuff." A picture of how this is supposed to work is presented in the following graph, called the "Fulfillment Curve":[6]

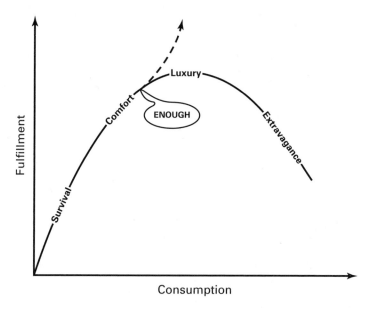

Of course, satisfaction improves with material advancement that fulfills basic needs. But after a point, what's the point? We should rephrase the *Pirkei Avot* question and answer: "Who is wealthy? One whose personal fulfillment and happiness is not tied to material affluence and consumption; where the good life is not a function of a life of goods."

Our ability to decouple inner peace or personal fulfillment from outer possessions is increasingly embattled. The bombardment in the form of consumption hype comes at us from one pervasive medium: advertising. Whereas psychotherapy, religion, and education all try to cultivate some sense of stable self-worth in the individual, consumer culture, via advertising, fosters the opposite, a deep sense of inadequacy and deficiency. This would be seen for the pernicious message that it is were it not for the chimerical hope that we can overcome the lacks and needs that advertising creates and feeds on by buying the products it proffers.

Put it this way: if there were a multibillion-dollar industry in our society whose sole purpose were to get you to murder, commit adultery, steal, or perjure yourself, then we might wonder about its legitimacy. These are commandments 6, 7, 8, and 9. For commandment 10, though, "thou shalt not covet," there is just such an industry—advertising. This industry is designed to make you want things you don't have, to covet. And yet the captains of this industry are not put behind bars; instead, they are handsomely rewarded. The "products" of this industry (ads) do not reach their target audiences in brown paper wrappers: they are trumpeted in broad daylight, and are evident in every nook and cranny of our social, cultural, and even private spaces.

"Coveting" is an old-fashioned, even Puritan, word, but the psychic state of continually wanting more, of perennial dissatisfaction with what we have, and therefore with who we are (for the two have become pathologically connected), is the driving force of our consumer society. Once, greed was bad—avarice, cupidity, rapacity, lust: these were vices to be rooted out. They threatened social relations, the common good, and the spiritual well-being of the individual. But the advance of the free market economy, based on the profit motive coupled with a belief in "the invisible hand," marked a sea change: act solely for your own material betterment, and the mechanisms of supply and demand will ensure benefit for all. Greed has been rehabilitated, and in the guise of "enlightened" self-interest, it is now quite respectable. Consumptive culture cultivates covetousness. And what of spiritual well-being? Oh, don't be so New Agey!

To be sure, the tenth commandment is not a societal one: it is an individual precept condemning coveting the property of one's neighbor. But what does that mean? There is a two-thousand-year-old argument among commentators, both Christians and Jews, about whether this mandate concerns inner feelings or outward behavior. On the one hand, it seems unreasonable to legislate desire or its avoidance. On the other hand, the improper actions that stem from covetousness, theft, and adultery, have already been proscribed in previous commandments. Maimonides explains that there is an intermediary state between abstract thought and concrete action—the active scheming to get the desired object, putting undue pressure on the owner of some good to sell. The actual act need not be illegal, but the intention and the method of its implementation are flagged as immoral and destructive.

It's not a far cry to see this in advertising. Now, though, it's not a buyer coercing someone to sell a possession, but merchandisers using all sorts of techniques to entice, induce, inveigle, and persuade consumers to want their products.

Social historians note a change in American advertising after World War I, from the conveying of product information to the manufacturing of desire. The public, it was feared, was too frugal; they weren't consuming enough. To rev up the engines of the economy, people had to start buying more. Products were associated with images, glamour, and personal identity, and not just the functions they performed. Marketing moved from fulfilling needs to creating them. In our consumer society, coveting goods and keeping up with the Joneses doesn't mean robbing them, just buying as much as them.

The great Greco-Jewish philosopher of antiquity, Philo, in fact generalizes "do not covet" to apply to all forms of covetousness, including greed for money, hunger for honor, sexual lust, hedonism, and gluttony. In this, he reemphasizes the emotional states associated with insatiable desires and the importance of spiritual work, which brings us back to the key question of having enough, and knowing that it is. This inner work is a necessary first step toward the ultimate goal of transforming society, from its obsession with quantity to striving for quality, from outer acquisition to inner disposition, and from merely having to truly being.

Of Pits and Piety, or Torah and Toxics

One of the main negative impacts of our consumption is how we deal with waste—in addition to "regular" garbage, there is the growing problem of hazardous waste—the deepening realization that we are slowly poisoning ourselves and the world. Now, we don't usually think of Torah as having relevant insights into toxic-waste disposal. It certainly is not a focus in the standard Sunday, Hebrew, or day-school curriculum. So it's particularly interesting to note that according to the Talmud (*Bava Kamma* 30a), one of the distinguishing characteristics of the pious was being especially concerned about the proper disposal of dangerous waste!

> The Rabbis taught: The early pious ones *(hasidim rishonim)* would hide their thorns and broken glass three handbreaths deep in their fields, so they wouldn't hold up the plowing. Rav Sheshet would throw his in the fire, and Rava would throw his in the Euphrates River. Rav Yehudah said:

"Whoever wants to be a pious person should observe the laws of damages *(nezikin)."*

The point here is, of course, not to adopt their particular waste disposal solutions: burial, incineration, direct discharge into a river. The materials they were dealing with were nettles and shards (not dioxins or petrochemicals), but the principle—protecting life and health by keeping dangerous materials out of the public sphere—is still relevant. Personal example and education combine here in the fostering of personal commitment to recommended public norms.

What are the laws to which Rav Yehudah is referring? As outlined in the legally rich portion of *Mishpatim,* "Rulings" (Exod. 21–24, esp. 21:28–22:5, and developed in the Talmudic order of *Nezikin,* "Damages," particularly the first tractate *Bava Kamma),* they regulate not only injury or harm inflicted by people or their livestock on other people or their property, but also the use of the environment as a medium for damage to others. If I dig or uncover a pit in the public domain, I am liable for damages that ensue. Similarly, if I place a jug or barrel (or thorns or broken glass) in a communal place, and someone is injured—again, I must make restitution. Even activities initiated on my property that spread and do damage elsewhere—a fire that gets out of control, an animal that gets away—are my complete responsibility.

The Mishnah (*Bava Kamma,* ch. 1) enumerates different classes of damages *(avot nezikin),* differentiating between animate and inanimate, mobile and stationary, but the underlying principle is the same: the total liability rests on the individual. This may seem like simple common sense, yet how far are we in our society from these basic guidelines? Industries create hazardous waste all the time, polluting the commons and harming individuals through the air and water, and the legal system has great difficulty in reining in the perpetrators or making them pay.

Standard economic theory sees the commons, whether the resources of commercial input or the sink for the industrial outputs, as just so much unowned raw material—first come, first served. It belongs to no one, and so can be appropriated by anyone for essentially any purpose. As biologist Garrett Hardin pointed out in his seminal article "The Tragedy of the Commons,"[7] in situations of private profit at public cost (such as being able to dump waste in the public sphere), there is a built-in incentive to pollute: the polluter gets all the profit or convenience, while the cost of the damage is shared by everyone. This is equally applicable to the factory owner, to the fisherman tempted to overfish, and to the private car owner whose exhausts go out the back into everyone's air, and not into the driver's compartment.

Environmental concern then becomes irrationally altruistic, and anybody voluntarily solving problems becomes a sucker. Hence the need for compulsory legislation ("mutual coercion," in Hardin's pointed phrase). Yet precisely this sort of legislation is difficult to pass in the context of prevailing individualistic liberal philosophy, which sees the individual and his/her property rights as inviolable—a conception that has been extended to corporations with disastrous effects.

Traditionally, using the commons inappropriately, through expropriating resources for private benefit or through disposing of unwanted goods or waste, was seen as out-and-out theft of a possession that belonged to all:

(2:6) Rabban Shimon Ben Gamliel said: Anyone who causes any sort of damage or harm in the public domain, (his damaging goods) are permitted for all to take, on account of robbery.

(10:8) Whosoever robs the public must make restitution to the public. Robbing the public is a graver offense than robbing an individual, for one who robs an individual can appease that person and return what he stole, but one who robs the public cannot appease the public and return to all of them what was stolen from them (*Tosefta Bava Kamma*).

The underlying question is one of individual convenience or advancement versus the collective good. Traditional societies, Judaism included, held to a different level of private responsibilities for public welfare. The environmentalist emphasis on the need for strong personal commitment and clear legislation protecting public welfare—even at the expense of curtailing certain primitive free-market notions of commercial liberty—speaks a common language of concern with the Torah.

Similar concern is expressed regarding sewage treatment and water quality. Holiness and godliness are dependent on effective sewage treatment (cf. Deut. 23:13–16; *Mishneh Torah*, "Laws of Kings," 6:14), and communal leaders, the heads of the *beit din* (religious court) themselves, were to inspect the wells and their quality (*Tosefta Shekalim* 1:2). Moreover, as *Sefer Hasidim* (161) notes, causing health threats such as contaminating water with (unseen) contagions is a violation of the prohibition of putting a stumbling block before the blind (Lev. 19:14), as well as not loving your neighbor as you would yourself, and standing idly by when your neighbor is at risk (Lev. 19:18, 16). Applying these general moral precepts to situations such as these is relevant to all invisible health threats, including air pollution and radiation, to name just two.

The same Talmudic tractate tells a story about a person who is taught a key lesson about how we should relate to the commons beyond our own backyard:

Once there was a man who was removing stones from his field to the public thoroughfare, when a *hasid,* one of the pious ones, said to him: "Hey, you foolish man, why are you removing the stones from property that isn't yours, to that which is?" The man laughed at the *hasid*. Later, when the man was forced to sell his field, he was walking along the thoroughfare, and tripped over his old stones. "That *hasid* spoke well about removing the stones from property that was not immutably mine to that which is." (*Bava Kamma* 50b)

Behind that simple parable is a body of legislation that enforces the profound value concept of the commons as a sphere that is not nobody's, but everybody's. Indeed, it also expresses the very non-Western notion that it is private property that is transient, and therefore not possessible in a deep way. Economic activity that leads to damage or depletion of the commons—whether a polluted stream or global warming—should be as illegal as it is impious. Without a strong ethic of the public good, and legal responsibility for the effects on that which is all of ours, privatization and economic globalization are pure plunder.

Tzedek and the City: Justice, Land Use, and Urban Life

There are two divergent views of the environmental challenges that confront us. One is that we are all "in the same boat," that we all breathe the same air, drink the same water, and suffer from the same hardships. This view has much to recommend it, especially strategically and pedagogically: it is important to clarify to all that the monumental issues with which we grapple are not sectoral or limited, but concern everyone.

But this isn't the whole story, for in the same sense that we are not all equal perpetrators of environmental wrongs, neither are we equal victims of the problems that arise. Disadvantaged groups in a population generally have less access to important resources, more exposure to agents of risk, and less power to initiate or participate in processes that can change their situation. The same poor quality water may flow to our taps, but some can afford bottled water and home filtration alternatives, while many others can't. Thus, the other side of the universal, we're-all-in-this-together story is the aspect of environmental (in)justice, systemic inequality, grinding poverty, and economic exploitation by the privileged few of the many, including the natural world.

The realization of the relevance of justice in the environmental movement is one of the big developments of the last decade. Initially, environmentalism focused on wilderness, endangered species, and other aspects of nature preservation, which appealed only to limited sectors of society. With the overarching vision of sustainability, the purview has been expanded to include issues of race, class, and equality, especially in the setting of the quality of urban life. The expanding ranks and changing identities of activists reflect this shift in emphasis.

Justice is one of Judaism's core ethical values, taking pride of place both in prophetic exhortations and in halachic strictures. It is not an incidental characteristic of the legal system, but rather a societal goal, to be actively and doggedly sought: *Tzedek, tzedek tirdof*—"Justice, justice shall you pursue" (Deut. 16:20). What are the environmental ramifications of this fundamental belief?

Although there are many aspects of the environmental justice movement,[8] the central concerns can be summarized by three *R*s: *resources* (environmental goods) and access to them, *risks* (corresponding "bads") and protection from them, and *representation* (access to power that enables participation in decision making and some form of influence over the first two areas).

An important distinction needs to be made here between things that are ours as a matter of right and those that we have the ability to acquire through the workings of the market economy. In a free-market society, there is no promise of equal access to products or services designated as commodities—that's what it means to be poor, unable to afford certain things. But regarding products and services defined as rights rather than goods, it is incumbent upon the political system to ensure basic access for all.

For instance, water is certainly something that requires infrastructure and other investments in order to be brought in sufficient quantity and quality from natural sources to people. People cover, or help cover, the cost of those expenses, but in some basic sense they are not purchasing the water, which comes from the commons and in essence belongs to, or should belong to, all equally. Water until now has been generally seen as a right that is a nonnegotiable and fundamental necessity for people to lead basic lives of dignity and value.

This example is particularly compelling because this basic idea is threatened in many parts of the world where water sources and delivery infrastructure are being privatized, changing water from a resource we all have an equal right to, to merchandise that is bought and sold, or not—depending on one's purchasing power. This has grave implications for hundreds of millions of people. In addition, there is a clear pronouncement from classical Jewish sources about the "unownable" nature of water: "The rivers and the springs that are drawn upon belong to everyone *(kol adam)*."[9] Rich, poor, Jew, non-Jew, those close to the source and those far away, all have equal rights to equal access.

What about other resources, such as land and its fruits? This is another matter, because land is a type of property, and food, though no less essential to life than water, is a commodity. Land ownership, however, is not absolute, but rather partial and contingent (Lev. 25:23: "The land must not be sold beyond reclaim, for the land is Mine; you are but strangers resident with Me"), and the poor and the landless are guaranteed a free food supply through the laws of gleaning:

When you reap the harvest of your land, you shall not reap all the way to the edges of your field, or gather the gleanings of your harvest. You shall not pick your vineyard bare or gather the fallen fruit of your vineyard; you shall leave them for the poor and the stranger: I the Lord am your God. (Lev. 19:9–10)

When you reap the harvest in your field and overlook a sheaf in the field, do not turn back to get it.... When you beat down the fruit of your olive trees, do not go over them again [and w]hen you gather the grapes of your vineyard, do not pick it over again, they shall go to the stranger, the fatherless, and the widow. Always remember that you were a slave in the land of Egypt; therefore do I enjoin you to observe this commandment." (Deut. 24:19–22)

Freedom entails the ability to be generous, not to hoard, to be a channel for the divine abundance that comes to all through the energy that flows through the land and the plants that grow upon it. Access to a dependable food source is treated as an inalienable right. This is not some esoteric form of charity; in its larger context, it is the nexus of justice and land. Indeed, according to Hava Tirosh-Samuelson, it is precisely this link between the human treatment of the Earth and social justice that makes the Jewish approach to nature distinctive.[10]

Nowadays, this function of public support of the poor is more likely to be expressed by welfare and social services. The rights of the poor and recognition of their needs are no longer a function of communal ties, and the connection of those ties with the Earth and its fruitfulness, but instead are dependent on government policy. This is one reason why we have such a bifurcation in our society between "social" issues and (seemingly unrelated) "environmental" ones: ties that were working assumptions of our forebears have been severed and many aspects of our lives compartmentalized. It is precisely this separation that the vision of sustainability aims to mend, combining as it does ecology, economics, and society—a "three-fold cord that is not readily broken" (Eccles. 4:12).

When it comes to issues of land and its allocation, alongside the agrarian questions of food and land as a productive resource, more modern challenges are usually dealt with under the heading of "urban planning." Although it's not surprising that there are challenging and insightful values about rural life in classical Judaic sources, one might think that a similar contribution to distinctly urban thought would be unlikely, for several reasons.

First, from Genesis on, the Bible has a distinctly anti-urban cast. The first recorded city was built by the murderer Cain (Gen. 4:17), presumably as a result of his alienation from the earth, which had become cursed on his account. Then comes the ill-fated city of Babel, with its problematic urban architecture, followed by the original sin-cities, Sodom and Gomorrah. The only apparent exception to this inclination is the sanctity of Jerusalem, the city of God. Jews, in general, despite eventually acquiring the reputation of being a distinctly "urban" people, often castigated the city as a source of a host of problems and annoyances. In the Talmud, R. Yossi Bar Hanina voices an accepted opinion that "urban life is difficult" *(yesihvat krachim kasha)* as one of the reasons why a husband, though he can insist that his wife accompany him to the village from the city, is not permitted to do the opposite *(Ketubot* 110b).

Furthermore, if there's one social-environmental issue that seems uniquely modern, it is the phenomenal growth of urbanization. As recently as 1800, only 2.5 percent of humankind (20 million people) lived in cities, and there were only nine cities with populations of more than a million. By 1900, that swelled to 10 percent (160 million) and 27 megalopolises. Now, more than half the world's population, over 3 billion people, live in cities, with at least 240 cities of a million inhabitants or more.

One important contemporary environmental message needs to be that while cities have often been seen as "a problem," they are, in fact, a large part of "the solution," for two reasons. By building and maintaining attractive and thriving cities, we will not only change the basic situation of the majority of humanity (as the data above show) but we will also, in essence, be able to save the rest of the world. Mass exodus from cities is the fundamental reason for suburbanization and sprawl, the heart of unsustainable land use. Thus, robust sustainable planning becomes a major item on the environmental agenda.

So what kind of insights can Jewish sources provide on questions of planning, urban land use, and quality of life? How should cities be designed and how should they function in the landscape? What should be the relationship between urban and rural, settled and wild, private holdings and the common good?

At the end of the Book of Numbers, though the Israelites are still wandering in the wilderness, there is already talk of the boundaries and tribal shares in the land. Most tribes received large areas to afford extensive agriculture and animal husbandry. But the tribe of Levi remained essentially landless, relegated to urban areas. The Levites and their work in the Temple were supported by tithes, and therefore they received no *nachala,* no "territorial share" among the tribes (Num. 18:23–24). They were apportioned no less than 48 Levitical cities, together with guidelines for their layout (ch. 35), making this a significant prooftext for biblical and later views on urban and regional planning.

The cardinal charge is to leave a sizable *migrash* around the built area of a city. *Migrash* is variously translated as pasturage, commons, or unenclosed land. Rashi explained this to be "an empty open space for the beautification *(noi)* of the city"—a public open space that functioned both as grazing land and as a "green lung" for the city and its inhabitants. In this way, open space becomes a constituent element of urban form, and the city is fundamentally defined as embedded in its regional context.

A key component of this plan is the prohibition of rezoning. Maimonides, in his Laws of Sabbatical and Jubilee (13:4–5), based on the Talmud (*Arachin* 33b and *Bava Batra* 24b), ruled that it is forbidden to build in these open spaces, to expand the city at the expense of pastureland or fields (see also *Sefer Hachinuch* 342). Moreover, Maimonides stated categorically that Levitical cities were not a special case: these rulings applied equally to all other cities in Israel.

Rabbi Samson Raphael Hirsch (1808–1888), founder and prime expositor of modern Orthodoxy, commented on this ruling with great fervor about the responsibility of one generation to another concerning the land. Regarding Leviticus 25:34, which states that a Levitical city and its surrounding area "is their holding for all time," he wrote:

> Precisely because it [the city with its open spaces] has been given to them for all the generations, no generation is permitted to change it as it sees fit. The present generation is not the sole ruler over it, but the future generations are equal in their rights, and each is required to bequeath it to future generations in the same state in which they received it....
>
> It appears that these laws are designed to maintain an urban population with a connection to agriculture.... [They] served to prevent cities from growing into metropolises cut off from the fields [from their agrarian roots].

A century after Hirsch, the influential urban historian and theoretician, Lewis Mumford, wrote extensively of the importance of the regional setting of the city. "The hope of the city," he argued, "lies outside itself." The minimal unit of urban living is much larger than the built area; a city can't be built, conceived, or occupied apart from its ecological region. Mumford echoed Hirsch's endorsement of synthesis in his support of attempts to "build up a more exhilarating kind of environment—not as a temporary haven of refuge but as a permanent seat of life and culture, urban in its advantages, permanently rural in its situation."[11]

Ironically, the contemporary suburban model, which has come to dominate the countryside, is practically a privatized parody of the Levitical locale: a house with a lawn instead of a town and its surrounding commons. This version of development is an affront to a host of Jewish values. A system that creates rich suburbs and poor inner cities,[12] with structural gaps in education, local government, and other infrastructure, is systemically unjust. Likewise, highway subsidies and other trends that support private car dependency, with no corresponding development of adequate public transport, disadvantage the already disadvantaged, who do not own cars.

Another Jewish value that is ill served by sprawl is symbolized by the requirements of traditional Shabbat observance. Living close enough to walk to shul on Shabbat, where one's community gathers, necessitates a healthy population density (not to mention sidewalks and urban spaces that are designed for people and not just vehicles), and so inefficient land use and exclusive car dependency not only lead to the decimation of natural green space but are also bad for people—and in particular for Shabbat experience.

We all need space in our place, but when we try to fill that need in atomized units, we end up with sprawl and alienation from each other and our environment. Wise planning should re-embed the urban in the rural and the natural, with open spaces, green corridors, and a healthy agricultural sector, thus strengthening communal ties and preserving the world for ourselves, each other, and future generations.

Wilderness and Worship

As with the initial assumptions regarding urban planning, extolling the value of wilderness would also seem to be a distinctly modern sentiment. For us, the term has a host of associations, mostly positive: romantic, thrilling, sublime. But the word itself expresses fear and apprehension. The suffix –*ness* is not the abstract nominal form (as in *wildness,* which means the quality or state of being wild), but rather means "lair," as in Loch Ness, "the lake of the lair" (of the legendary sea monster). Wilderness is literally the lair of the *wilder,* the wild beasts. In premodern times, wilderness was more threatening than threatened. That contributed to those places having spiritual force, a trans-human quality that could inspire and awe; it was God's creation unadulterated by human intervention. Thus that vast pristine[13] world was also a place of hermits, pilgrimages, visions, and quests.

The fact that today we see wilderness as a place of recreation is a cultural transformation that signifies a number of changes. The same culture that has enabled human settlement to mushroom, giving us mining, drilling, clear-cutting, and other trends that threaten wild areas all over the world, has also given us weaponry and outdoor gear, which reduce anxiety in the face of wilderness experience. These are the developments that have changed the balance of fear, making (dwindling) wild places less endangering to us, and at the same time, more endangered by us.

That self-same technological and urban expansion, and the romantic backlash that it spawned, has flipped the valences of chaos and order: these days it is the concrete jungle that is a source of threat, and nature is the gentle, predictable realm to which we escape. Now we breathe that expansive sigh of relief when we get out on the trail, away from urban stress and strain, rather than hurrying to return safely inside the city walls from the great menacing unknown. For R&R, we go to nature, which may be refreshingly arduous compared with our increasingly sedentary lives, but it is rarely life-threatening.

This increasingly tamed Earth threatens more than just the ecosystems. Those awe-filled spiritual experiences are also endangered species. But do spiritual experience, wilderness, and Judaism go together? Regarding wilderness specifically, it is interesting to note that contemporary Hebrew has no exact equivalent for the positive idea of pristine nature. The most common phrase used today is the richly evocative coinage, *eretz bereishit,* land of Genesis, or "Creation country." The biblical Hebrew term *midbar* refers to the main wilderness the Israelites knew, the desert.[14] The *midbar* of the Bible was a significant formative experience of the Jewish people and an entire historical period in Jewish history. There is even one whole book of the Torah called *Bemidbar* (in the *midbar*), known in English as Numbers. Interestingly, the Hebrew title, from the chance opening word, is a more apt synopsis of the book than the topic-based English name, which refers to censuses that take up only a few chapters.

In Numbers, the narrative shifts to the nitty-gritty of what it was actually like for the Children of Israel to live in the wilderness. The Bible provides grounds for argument about the nature of that experience. In one view, it was a time of hardship and chastisement. No sooner do they set out than they start complaining: there is no meat to eat, none of that fresh Egyptian produce, seemingly never enough water (see Exod. 16, Num. 11). Later we learn of the people's terrified response to the intimidating reports of the spies. On the other hand, it is an awe-filled time of feeling God's closeness through daily divine miracles. There is manna and quail—bread and meat directly from God—water gushing forth from the rock, pillars of fire, and clouds to guide them. Later, the prophet Jeremiah (2:2) would quote God, describing this period as one of intimacy and faithfulness: "I accounted to your favor the devotion of your youth, your love as a bride; how you followed Me in the wilderness, in a land not sown."

Anybody who has ever gone camping knows it was almost surely both. Wilderness experience can be uncompromising, harsh, and lacking in creature comforts. And yet precisely those qualities can open one up to deeper encounters. Rabbenu Hanan'el, an eleventh-century North African scholar, commenting on why the Israelites were led the long way around to Canaan, through the desert (Exod. 13:17), argued that the farther they got from human settlement, the more their experience of wonders and miracles grew.

The Book of *Bemidbar*/Numbers begins, "God spoke to Moses in the wilderness of Sinai." It is interesting that well over a thousand years after the purported event of Revelation, the Rabbis asked about this seemingly mundane phrasing: why was the Torah given in the wilderness? What can we learn from the mere physical environment of Revelation? The midrashic collection of *Bemidbar Rabba* answers: "Anyone who does not throw himself open to all, make himself masterless like the wilderness *(ka-midbar hefker)*, cannot acquire wisdom and Torah." The one to acquire and preserve wisdom and Torah needs to "be like the wilderness—set apart from the world *(maflig et atzmo min ha'olam)*." Note: "wisdom" and "Torah" are not identical, but both are symbolized by the wilderness experience.

We can't answer the question of the significance of wilderness for Torah by poring over a book or staring at a screen. Wilderness is not a metaphor or a literary trope. As we say when an anecdote falls flat: "I guess you had to be there." We have lessons to learn from the wilderness itself, from being there. The wilderness is the place of Torah, contrasted with the mighty civilization of Egypt and its corruption that the Israelites left behind. God can speak *(med-abber)* better in the desert *(midbar)*. Or maybe we can just hear better. Elijah the prophet too heard the *kol demamah dakah,* the "still small voice" (more literally, "the sound of a thin silence"), on a mountaintop in the desert, only after leaving civilization and its trials (see 1 Kings 19). In this vein, Elie Wiesel relates:

> When the Holy Seer of Lublin was a little boy, he was known to skip school for hours or even days. Once, his teacher followed the young boy to see what became of these free moments. The Seer walked to the edge of the town, into the deep woods, and there, in a small, green circle of trees, he began to pray. The next day the teacher asked the boy what drew him to those woods. The Seer of Lublin replied, "I can find God there." "But," said the teacher, "surely God is the same in the town as in the woods." "That is true," replied the Seer, "but I am not the same."[15]

Periodically leaving our bustling habitations for places of simplicity, solitude, and silence provides badly needed perspective and spiritual insight. Yet how many of us view wilderness experience as indispensable for Torah learning? Or being in nature as important for forming Jewish identity? Hiking and camping are seen as mere leisure choices, not as a quest crucial for self-discovery and holiness.[16]

Like many other issues in this book, the reason for urgently emphasizing these connections is that our society is increasingly encroaching on the places in the world that can afford us these experiences. There are few forests not threatened by logging, deserts not at risk of being "bloomed." As Yehuda ben Teima taught: "Be bold as the leopard, swift as the eagle, fleet as the gazelle, and brave as the lion to perform the will of your Father in Heaven" (*Pirkei Avot* 5:22). Our children may live in a world where leopards and eagles have no habitats, and they and our experience of them, and their homes, will disappear. How can we be like them when they aren't there anymore? We aren't just losing ecology—we are losing the ground of meaning, the basic referents for human spiritual life. How will we learn Torah then?

Without wildness, and wilderness, and our direct experience of them, our spiritual and psychological horizons contract, and we shrink into boxes of our own making. We become calculating creatures, our lives dominated by numbers. And numbers can be numbing. We must learn at least occasionally to leave Numbers behind, and go out in the Wilderness, where revelations can still happen.

Melo' Kol Ha'aretz Kevodo—The Fullness of the Earth Is God's Glory

One of the most sweeping conclusions of ecological thought is that everything is connected to everything else. This is doubly true of the topics of wilderness and biodiversity: the distinction between these two sections is illusory. Wilderness, or open space, is not just the scenery or the backdrop for the unfolding drama of life; it includes that life as one if its constitutive elements. And biodiversity, the mind-boggling variety of species, is inconceivable without the functioning ecosystems that provide the essential life-supporting conditions and circumstances.

Even more than wilderness, though, biodiversity is a recent concept. The term itself was coined by renowned ecologist E. O. Wilson in 1986 and is short for "biological diversity" (itself a neologism of Thomas Lovejoy's in 1980), which refers to the variety of species and communities that should be the focus of research and preservation efforts. In premodern, and certainly pre-Darwinian, times, the idea of an entire species disappearing was difficult to conceive. Species were pretty much fixed at Creation, and theoretically at least, were neither added to nor significantly diminished from the world. Or so it would seem.

Note that the questions of biodiversity and its preservation are fundamentally different ones from those that arose in the context of *tza'ar ba'alei chayim,* prevention of cruelty to animals, which was explored in the previous chapter. There, the issue focused on the pain of the individual animal and its treatment by humans. Biodiversity relates to the perpetuation (or not) of entire species, and the effect of society as a whole on biotic communities.

Given the recent coinage of biodiversity, and the fact that *tza-'ar ba'alei chayim* is a mitzvah from the Torah while preventing extinctions does not seem to be, we may ask: Do species have significance in Jewish tradition? To what extent is the idea of biodiversity and its preservation an important Jewish value?

The chronicle of Noah and the Flood has become a much-quoted prooftext for this contemporary challenge: we look back to a time that similarly threatened continued existence, trying to draw relevant lessons for our day. That narrative takes great pains to stress the supreme investment of time and energy needed to save all the animals along with one small human family. There are many midrashic embellishments of this episode, underscoring the importance of the animals and their continual care, but the one most relevant to the issue of biodiversity and its importance has the raven berating Noah for sending him out after the Flood:

> The raven said to Noah, "You must hate me! ... You leave species of which there are seven, but send [me] from a species of which there are two. If the power of heat or cold overwhelms me, would not the world be lacking a species?" (*Sanhedrin* 108b)

In the story that immediately follows Noah, the Tower of Babel, *biodiversity* is a subcategory of the broader value of *diversity* in general, which has cultural ramifications as well. The unity and uniformity that the people were striving for in that story were seen as undesirable, even sinful, and so they were spread out, both geographically and linguistically. Different languages and language families are part of the world's cultural richness, and they are also threatened in our day by similar forces: development and consumer culture driven by economic globalization, which frequently homogenize and erase difference. Biodiversity hotspots are also often host to great cultural diversity, and so many smaller, tribal cultures and their languages are endangered, in the same ways and for the same reasons as the ecological base upon which they are dependent.[17]

Returning to flora and fauna, probably the most general view in rabbinic literature about the importance of biodiversity is the belief that nothing in creation is superfluous or expendable, every creature having a place and a purpose:

> Our Rabbis said, what is this "And the advantage [*yitron*] of the land in all things" (Eccles. 5:8)? Even things you see as superfluous [*meyutarin*] in this world—like flies, fleas, and mosquitoes—they are part of the greater scheme of the creation of the world, as it says (Gen. 1:31), "And God saw all that God had created, and behold it was very good." And Rabbi Acha bar Rabbi Chanina said, "Even things you see as superfluous in this world—like snakes and scorpions—they are part of the greater scheme of the creation of the world."[18]

It is interesting to note that sometimes the phrasing implies the general, intrinsic value of all, and sometimes the emphasis is on the purpose all creatures have specifically for human needs and well-being. This is the anthropocentric response: What benefits and treasures are we losing when we annihilate hundreds and thousands of species of plants and creatures? What medicinal properties will be lost forever? What food sources? Not everything can be synthesized in a lab, especially without live models from nature. In this regard, what we don't know *can* indeed hurt us.

The central sources for these ideas are not only *aggadic* (based in narrative and homily), but halachic (legal) as well. Both the laws of *kilayim* (Lev. 19:19), which prohibit mixing unlike kinds, and *shiluach ha'ken*, sending away the mother bird before taking the young (Deut. 22:6–7), have been interpreted as strong statements regarding species preservation. Ibn Ezra (echoing J. T. *Kilayim* 1:7) explains the obscure laws that prohibit sowing different crops and interbreeding domestic animals as directed at "preserving the natural balance of creation" (Ibn Ezra on Lev. 19:19). Likewise, Nachmanides interprets these laws as upholding the integrity and perpetuation of species:

> The reason for [not] "mixing seeds" is that God created the species in the world among all that has a soul, among plants and moving creatures, and gave them the power of reproduction by which they may sustain themselves forever—for as long as the Blessed One desires the existence of the world.

It is Nachmanides who gives one of the clearest statements applying biblical law to the question of the preservation of biodiversity. He interprets the commandment of sending away the mother bird globally to forbid categorically actions leading to species extinction: "The Torah does not allow the total destruction of a species, although it allows us to slaughter some of its kind" (commentary on Deut. 22:6). Similarly, the *Sefer Hachinuch*, which gives rationales for all the commandments, states that the mitzvah shows that "the desire of the Blessed One is for the continuation of the species" (*Sefer Hachinuch*, 545).

These are strong and unambiguous statements—yet do we take them seriously? Some do, and have tried to translate these theologically informed sentiments into public campaigns, often with impressive rhetorical suasion relevant even to government policy.

The director of the Religious Partnership for the Environment, Paul Gorman, in his testimony before Congress for the Endangered Species Act, likened Creation to Revelation, claiming that living creatures are God's words, and extinctions are like tearing out pages from the last copy of the Bible.

If this sort of rebuke is reminiscent of a prophetic tone, there is precedent. Isaiah and Job both are relevant here and bear rereading in this light. Isaiah's time was strikingly similar to our own: when he was called to prophesy in the eighth century BCE, there had been relative prosperity under King Uzziah, including territorial expansion. But Judea faced constant threats from without, and newfound comfort and luxury led to decadence and immorality from within. Isaiah describes abuses from political corruption to ignoring the underprivileged to exploitation of dwindling land resources by rich estate owners: "Ah, those who add house to house, and join field to field, till there is room for none but you to dwell in the land!" (Isa. 5:8). Against this background, Isaiah has the remarkable vision that initiates his mission: "In the year that King Uzziah died, I beheld my Lord seated on a high and lofty throne"(6:1). In a rare example of visual contact, Isaiah sees God. And he sees the seraphim in attendance, proclaiming God's holiness in words that have become a centerpiece of Jewish liturgy. The verse (6:3) has been rendered: "Holy, holy, holy is the Lord of hosts; the whole earth is full of His glory" (old JPS translation) or "Holy, holy, holy! The Lord of Hosts! His presence fills all the earth!" (new JPS version). Those translations and their like bolster mainstream transcendental theology that sees God's glory as something separate from the world, that comes "down" from God to fill the earthly vessel, inspiring awe in the creatures below.

But the simple Hebrew points in another direction. The key phrase, *melo' kol ha'aretz*, is better read not as an adjective—"the whole earth is full of God's glory"—but as a noun, "the fullness of the whole earth"—that is God's glory! This suggests a very different, more immanental theology. God's glory does not descend from on high to suffuse the otherwise purely physical created world. The Earth and the fullness thereof are the stuff of the Divine Presence; the material is spiritual. God's glory and presence don't fill the world—they are the world! And what is that fullness if not the awe-inspiring diversity of creation and all it contains?

Compare Isaiah with Job, who also received an unexpected revelation. In answer to the question of why a wholly righteous man such as Job suffers so, God answers Job "out of the whirlwind" (chs. 38–41), with a cosmic tour designed to impress upon him the universe's vastness and mysteries. Here, too, it is the unfathomable diversity of God's weird and wonderful, powerful and exotic, creatures that stuns, awes, and exults.

From this revelation, Job realizes the infinitesimal place of human beings within the divine whole and is rendered speechless: "See, I am of small worth.... I clap my hand to my mouth.... I had heard of you with my ears, but now I see you with my eyes. Therefore I recant and relent, being but dust and ashes" (40:4, 42:3–6). Other translations have "I will be quiet, comforted that I am dust" instead of "recant and relent" (Hebrew: *em'as venichamti*), but both express a form of acceptance.

Isaiah, in response "to seeing with his eyes," also becomes aware of his imperfection and inability to communicate: "I am a man of unclean lips" (Isa. 6:5). But for Isaiah, speech is action. As a prophet, he can change the world with his words. For Isaiah, the challenge is not how to live with personal suffering but how to fight the corruption and decadence that come from comfort and prosperity. Isaiah responds to a call to go forth: "my Lord saying, 'Whom shall I send? Who will go for us?' And I said, 'Here am I; send me'" (6:8).

In our day, the lessons of Job and Isaiah complement each other. For many, modernity has muted the experience of the vast natural world that taught Job and the ancients humility. We may have more "knowledge," but we have attained it at the expense of wisdom. And how many of us behave as if "the fullness of the whole Earth" were truly God's own presence and glory? That fullness is being tragically diminished in our lifetimes. If the taking of a single human life, created in the image of God, is understood in Jewish tradition as a diminution of the Divine, then surely the global decimation of biodiversity, the loss of many hundreds of whole species every year, is an issue of vast religious import. Isaiah's political challenges may have been different than these particularly modern threats, but God's answer to his question of "How long?" is eerily apt: "Till towns lie waste without inhabitants, and houses without people; and the ground lies waste and desolate" (6:11).

Isaiah's response was "Here I am," passionately dedicated to repairing the world. What will ours be? It is a challenge worthy of Noah, but here we cannot apply Noah's solution: he saved the world, but he had the explicit backing of God, and clear instructions as to how to act. For us, things are less clear. There is no ark that we can build in order to save species that are disappearing due to destructive human activities. The whole world must be our ark, and the fate of all its passengers is ultimately one fate.

Mazon Ve'chazon—Food and Vision, or the Duties of the Diet

A few main things shape our environments and define our impact on the Earth. One is shelter—how and where we build our buildings, and how we maintain them. Another is transportation—simply how, and how much, we get around. Probably the most basic to human survival, though, fundamental to human cultures around the world and a key nexus of *adam* and *adamah*, is food—what we eat, how and where it's produced, and how it gets to us.

Likewise, few acts are as imbued with as much religious symbolism and stricture as eating. There are few elements that are as connected in people's minds and lives with Judaism and Jewish culture as food. Although for some this is reduced to bagels and lox, the association is not misplaced: all holy days and celebrations have an obligatory festive meal at their center, most festivals have specific foods associated with them, and most important, the dietary requirements of Judaism, the laws of *kashrut,* are a central focus of traditional Jewish observance.

Kashrut is the Jewish category of fit (kosher) food, and though its central components of permitted species, methods of slaughter, and separation of milk and meat are ritualistic in nature, traditional interpretations have also always related to their ethical dimensions, to questions of compassion and respect for life.

Insisting on ethical concerns in eating is far from obvious. In contemporary culture, one's diet is rarely an object of moral analysis. But here is another parallelism between Judaism and environmentalism: both demand that we pay scrupulous attention to what we eat. And in this respect, food is emblematic of the larger category of consumption in general. Our consumer culture keeps us supplied with cheap and plentiful manufactured goods, including a cornucopia of processed foods, but it is difficult to discover on our own how these objects of our consumption contribute to the maintenance of the world, or to its ruin.

Kashrut, however, strictly or historically defined, is of little help in this department. Classically, the moral or ethical dimensions of *kashrut* have been a subcategory of *tza'ar ba'alei chayim,* dealing with the suffering of individual animals, and usually focusing on the method of their slaughter. The first change that needs to be taken into account is that sharp questions of animal welfare arise today as much about the lives of farm animals as in the conditions of their death. Tevye's milk cow was not doped on bovine hormones, and the chickens of the shtetl were free-range. Today, farms are factories where the units of production (i.e., livestock—alive, yes, but *stock*, property, goods) have been rationalized to the utmost, where questions of animal welfare that don't bear directly on output are beside the point.

Preventing cruelty and suffering is a basic human and Jewish value that hardly bears repeating, and it is hoped that the more egregious infringements, such as the force-feeding of geese to produce choice foie gras and the conditions in which calves are raised to achieve tender milk veal, would be roundly denounced. Some rabbis (admittedly a small minority) have indeed declared factory-farmed meat unkosher on these grounds.[19] But as important as that is, it too is focused on the welfare of individual animals. Industrial agriculture, which until now has succeeded impressively in feeding a world of billions, thus staving off neo-Malthusian fears of widespread starvation, has raised a host of questions that have broader, systemic implications, namely, whether the way we raise all our food, including grains, vegetables, fruit, meat, milk, and eggs is *sustainable*.

This "green revolution" was made possible by advances in chemistry that led to the development of artificial nitrogen fixation in chemical fertilizers, and reducing crop damage through pesticides and herbicides. Add to this the use of hormones and antibiotics to enhance animal growth, and all kinds of intensifying technologies to maximize egg, milk, and meat output, and we have the awe-inspiring growth of global food production in the latter half of the twentieth century that has (so far) produced enough to feed everyone, at least in theory. That there are still hungry people in the world is more a function of political problems of distribution, including strife and economic issues, than the sheer quantity of food overall.

Sustainability asks whether these achievements can be sustained over time. Add to the techniques of industrial agriculture the predilection that Western society has for meat, and the specific demands of a heavily meat-based diet, and we get a range of trends that are particularly worrisome. I am referring here both to questions of the health of the world and our responsibility for it and to individual bodily health, or our own obligation to avoid harmful products and situations.

Preserving one's health is not only a good idea—it's "the law." Deuteronomy 4:9 states *v'nishmartem me'od l'nafshotechem*, "take utmost care and watch yourselves scrupulously," which is understood to be a halachic injunction to take care of one's health. One is forbidden to expose oneself to risk or health-impairing agents unnecessarily. The well-known health problems that have been linked to heavily meat-based diets, such as heart disease, diabetes, unhealthy cholesterol levels, and certain forms of cancer, have led many people to reconsider the quantity of meat they consume.

But in terms of environmental sustainability, the negative impacts associated with chemical-based agriculture and intensive livestock raising for heavily meat-based diets are both destructive and wasteful.[20] Although industrial agriculture has so far led to high yields per unit of land, and so is considered quite efficient, the necessity for continual use (and often growing amounts) of chemical additives, in the forms of artificial fertilizers and weed and insect killers, leads to widespread pollution,[21] public health threats (both in ground water and through residues reaching consumers), top-soil erosion, and in general, systematically decreased fertility of the land.

Cattle for beef and dairy raise this problem to an entirely different level. Because of its shocking wastefulness—a meat- and dairy-centered diet requires seventeen times as much land, fourteen times as much water, and more than ten times as much energy as a completely plant-based diet. Consider that it takes up to sixteen pounds of grain to produce one pound of feedlot beef for human consumption. Seventy percent of the grain produced in the United

States and more than one-third of the grain produced worldwide is fed to animals destined for slaughter. The grain fed to animals for meat, milk, and eggs could feed five times as many people if consumed directly by them. Reducing just 10 percent of American beef consumption would free up a quantity of grain equivalent to that needed to feed all the world's people who annually die of hunger.

Furthermore, not only does the tremendous quantity of grains grown to feed animals require enormous amounts of chemical fertilizer and pesticides, but the runoff of cattle wastes from feedlots is also a major source of pollution for ground water and streams. American livestock produce 1.4 billion tons of manure yearly, contributing five times more organic waste to water pollution than do people, and twice as much as that of industry.

Even from this very partial list, one may conclude that we should eat less meat (or none). The question of vegetarianism in Judaism has been a focus of controversy at different times. Whereas many Jewish sources are highly ambivalent about eating meat, general Jewish culture, in particular the cuisines of all Jewish *edot*, ethnic groups, is highly meat-based.

It should be noted that the above data add a new dimension to traditional discussions of the advisability of a vegetarian diet. Previously, the main issue had been the moral right to kill other living creatures for food, and the related question of pain inflicted upon slaughtered animals. Although there is no explicit commandment to eat meat, there is divine permission to do so, and later on eating meat is seen as integral to festival celebrations. As noted earlier, Adam and Eve were vegetarian (see Gen. 1:29–30), but after the Flood, in Genesis 9:3, God says: "Every creature that lives shall be yours to eat; as with the green grasses, I give you all these" (Talmud, *Sanhedrin* 59b).

One of the arguments against vegetarianism is based on the apparent reality reflected in the biblical sources of the antediluvian world. For instance, one reading of the Cain and Abel story is that

Cain was the vegetarian farmer who saw that Abel's slaughtering of lamb was not only acceptable but preferable to his own sacrifice of produce. He took that to be a blanket license to kill other creatures, leading to his murder of Abel.

It has also been interpreted that one of the factors contributing to the lawlessness that led to the Flood was the people's lack of a legitimate outlet for aggression. The permission to eat meat upon repopulating the Earth was meant to answer that need and channel violence into more acceptable forms that would prevent the moral debacle that had occurred previously. Thus, eating meat is seen as a way of expressing important distinctions (animals we kill and eat; people we don't), as well as directing destructive urges.

Early chief rabbi of Israel, Rav Avraham Yitzchak Hacohen Kook[22] and others see this and subsequent permission to eat meat not as divine approbation but as mere concession to the human lust for flesh. In the wilderness, the mainstay of the Israelite diet was manna, and when the people pined, and whined, for meat, God reacted not by gently providing the desired nourishment (as with the manna), but by sending them a huge flock of quail so that they would eat "until it comes out of [their] nostrils and becomes loathsome" (Num. 11:20). Then the people who craved the animal flesh were struck down by a plague with the meat "still between their teeth," and they were buried there at *Kivrot Ha'te'avah*, the "Graves of Lust," or "craving" (ibid., vv. 33–34).

Indeed, in wilderness times, animal slaughter and consumption were linked exclusively to the sacrificial cult (see Lev. 17), tying meat eating to ritual practice. Secular slaughter, or unconsecrated meat *(shechitat chullin)* was prohibited. Settlement in the Land, however, led to an expanded mandate to eat meat in everyday situations:

When the Lord enlarges your territory, as He has promised you, and you say, "I shall eat some meat," for you have the urge to eat meat *(ki te'aveh nafshecha),* you may eat meat whenever you wish. (Deut. 12:20).

This doubly emphasizes the consumption of meat as *basar te'avah,* meat being the object of lust or craving. The Talmud accepts this, and goes further, saying that, ideally, people who desire meat shouldn't go the easy route and buy meat all wrapped up from the market; instead, they should get their hands dirty and participate in the actual act of slaughter:

> The Torah teaches here a rule of conduct, that a person should not eat meat unless he has a special appetite for it. I might think that this means that a person should buy meat in the market and eat it, the text therefore states, "then you may kill any of the cattle or sheep that the Lord gives you." (*Chullin* 84a)

This rather gory image might seem like the opposite of vegetarianism, but in fact it contrasts even more with the way we eat meat today: it makes the procurement of flesh distasteful, or at least so labor-intensive and inconvenient that it would serve to reduce meat consumption drastically. Environmental philosopher (and game warden) Aldo Leopold called this "getting one's meat from God." Although it is impractical in our urban society, a person would gain so much more respect for the animal, the act of slaughter, and the meat that is eaten. It is a world apart from the hamburger at the fast food joint.

The act of eating meat has many layers of significance that bear on the place of the human in the created order. For Leopold, who was an avid hunter, eating meat is an expression of embeddedness in the natural world and its cycles—expressing our trophic niche, as it were. The antelope eats the grass, the lion eats the antelope and eventually becomes grass himself: it's the circle of life. We, then, are no different from the lions. Vegetarianism, according to this view, tries to extend an artificial human morality to the animal kingdom, and thus is "anti-ecological" in that sense (again, I'm talking about hunting, not grocery shopping).

In contrast, Jewish views seem to imply the opposite. Talmud *Pesachim* 49b, for example, states that scrupulous observance of the minutiae of *kashrut* is a condition for eating meat. Eating other animals expresses our difference from and superiority over them (not our kinship with them and their predatory ways). We earn the right to eat meat by avoiding bestial behavior. The laws of *kashrut* help us retain our humanity and therefore safeguard this privilege. Vegetarianism, according to this view, is forced upon us when we lose our moral superiority and therefore no longer have the right to take life and eat meat.

Many discussions of the pros and cons of vegetarianism stop here, at the moral question of killing other creatures. For some, it is the ultimate ideal of *kashrut*: "It is the vegetarian ideal ... that is most consonant with the goal and purpose of Torah to maximize our awareness, appreciation, and sensitivity to the Divine Presence in the world."[23] Messianic times are an ideal, and that is clearly a vision of a vegetarian world, echoing Edenic purity: "The cow and the bear shall graze, their young shall lie down together; and the lion like the ox shall eat straw" (Isa. 11:7).

For others,[24] though, moral vegetarianism is seen as a perversion of Jewish values that equates humans and animals, and prevents us from fully expressing the divine image in our humanity. Although there may be some messianic ideal of non-predation, we are unwise to try to implement that in an unredeemed world. When outspoken vegetarian proponent Isaac Bashevis Singer said that for animals, life is "an eternal Treblinka," he aroused more opposition than support from a comparison many felt to be blasphemous, precisely on these grounds.

Here I leave the moral philosophizing and return to health and sustainability as the important threats associated with extensive meat-based diets. For some, complete vegetarianism is an attractive option, but for the rest, a reasonably doable act is simply to cut down, to expand one's culinary repertoire and options. The current health threats from our meat-based diets stem from overindulgence. Traditionally, too much meat was rarely an issue; the fear was of not having enough for nutritional needs. Most rabbis who recommended the consumption of meat believed that meat was essential for a complete diet.

However, today more than ever before, it is comparatively easy to be a healthy vegetarian. As in the case of many personal practices, it is difficult for individuals to make sweeping changes in their lives when public policy, institutions, or even just the Zeitgeist is unsupportive of alternatives. But that is changing. Richard Schwartz, one of the foremost spokespeople for Jewish vegetarians, suggests that widespread consciousness-raising would go a long way in leading people to confront the issues, for the production and consumption of meat sharply diverge from Jewish mandates to preserve human health, treat animals with compassion, protect the environment, conserve resources, and the like.

We actually "eat" more than food; that is, we consume energy, materials and a host of consumer goods. The discourse on *kashrut,* though, traditionally does not make pronouncements about issues not related to the specific categories of permitted and forbidden foods. This means that by strictly observing *kashrut,* one can actively contribute to negative trends, such as intensive pesticide use to guarantee insect-free greens,[25] and increased use of disposable utensils to avoid *kashrut* doubts. One may be fulfilling the letter of the law of *kashrut,* but is the spirit being honored?

Kashrut is explicitly tied to holiness: when the Torah enumerates permitted and prohibited animals, it concludes: "For I the

Lord am your God; you shall sanctify yourselves, and be holy, for I am holy" (Lev. 11:44). For this reason—that is, the gap between the potential of *kashrut* to help shape our lives in positive and responsible ways and the reality of it not fulfilling that function—the notion of "eco-*kashrut*" was coined, to give voice to the intuition that for food to be truly kosher and a vehicle for holiness, it can't be a product of destructive practices. How can pesticides be deemed "kosher"? How can the most egregious junk food not be a blight on holiness? Food that's bad for the body *and* for the Earth can't be good for the soul.

The apparent originator of this idea is the Jewish renewal mentor, Rabbi Zalman Schachter-Shalomi, who took the traditional idea of injecting consciousness into the automatic act of eating, and then extended it to include the nature of the food and the sustainability of its production. Renewal teacher, rabbi, and social activist Rabbi Arthur Waskow takes this one step further:

> In the society we live in, while food is obviously important, it is not the biggest piece of our economic relationship with the earth. It's not all we eat anymore. We eat coal. We eat oil. We eat electric power, we eat the radiation that keeps some of that electric power going, and we eat the chemicals that we turn into plastic. What does it mean to eat them in a sacred way? What does it mean to say that we're eco-kosher? ... Is it eco-kosher to use electricity generated by nuclear power plants that create waste products that will remain poisonous for fifty thousand years? Is it eco-kosher to ignore the insulation or lack of it in our homes, synagogues, community centers, and nursing homes, so that we burn far more fuel than necessary and drunkenly pour carbon dioxide into the atmosphere, thereby accelerating the heating of our globe? ... I want to suggest that what makes a life-practice eco-kosher may not be a single standard, a

black-white barricade like "Pork is *treyf*"—but rather a constantly moving standard in which the test is: Are we doing what is more respectful, less damaging to the earth than what we did last year?[26]

In our day and age, when our food, like so much of our life, is automated, prefab, or otherwise not a product of love and care for each other and the Earth, a renewed relationship to food, its growth, and its preparation can reinvest a sense of sanctity and concern in this central area of our lives.

Sustainability and Sustenance: How to Keep on Keepin' On

The idea of sustainability, while complicated in application, is simple in theory—to create a society that can sustain itself and its members, materially and spiritually, over time. In traditional societies, such as biblical Israel or indigenous peoples, sustainability was an organizing principle or a working assumption, not a controversial political program or complex set of policies. To use biblical terminology, we desire "to fare well," but not just ourselves, also our children and our children's children; it is a desire to be collectively blessed with "length of days."

It is interesting to note that these two attributes are couched as promises within three very different *mitzvot*, which, together, could be taken as defining the idea of sustainability. The *mitzvot* are: honoring one's father and mother (in Deut. 5:16, a restatement of Exod. 20:12), using honest weights and measures (Deut. 25:15), and sending away a mother bird before taking her eggs or fledglings (Deut. 22:6–7). This "reward" of living well and long has been traditionally understood in one of two ways—as instant, tangible rewards, in the here and now, and as ultimate otherworldly satisfaction in the hereafter—and there have been far-reaching theological disputes over how best to interpret the problematic promise.

We have already read of the apostate Elisha ben Abuya, and how he may have lost his faith in divine justice after witnessing a boy dying tragically after both honoring his father and sending away the mother bird. His grandson, Rabbi Ya'akov Korshai, counters this argument by putting his faith in the justice of the eternal reward. The common denominator of these two seemingly contradictory interpretations is that they are applicable exclusively to the individual, whether the well-being referred to is temporal or eternal. A similar assumption underlies traditional commentators' differing views of the purpose of driving off the mother bird. Maimonides (*Guide for the Perplexed,* section III:48), for instance, says it is for the sake of the (individual) animal, by sparing the mother bird the pain of seeing her offspring taken. Others, like Nachmanides, claim that the commandment is focused rather on the (individual) human being to inculcate humane, compassionate behavior.

Yet why limit the discussion to the individual? The precept has a deep logic, and it becomes more provocatively palatable to contemporary ears when seen as relating to the health and well-being of the collective. Farmer-philosopher Wendell Berry has observed: "This [precept] obviously is a perfect paradigm of ecological and agricultural discipline, in which the idea of inheritance is necessarily paramount. The inflexible rule is that the source must be preserved. You may take the young, but you must save the breeding stock."[27] In short, by all means eat of the fruit, but take care not to destroy the fruitfulness.

This is not only a contemporary exegesis. The fifteenth-century commentator Don Isaac Abravanel (Spain/Italy) states it most clearly in his commentary on this commandment:

> The Torah's intention here is to prevent the possibility of untimely destruction and rather to encourage Creation to

exist as fully as possible.... "In order that you may fare well and have length of days" means that it shall be good for humankind when Creation is perpetuated so that we will be able to partake of it again in the future ... since if we are destined to live for many years on this earth, we are reliant upon Creation perpetuating itself so that we will always have sufficient resources.

This expresses one aspect of sustainability. "Sustainable development" usually refers to an economic system of production and consumption that can sustain itself, and its environmental context over the long term, meaning we live up to our responsibilities to future generations. We need to sustain not only the physical environment and its products but also, perhaps primarily, ourselves, materially and spiritually. Sustainability then becomes intimately linked with the preservation and rejuvenation of sources of physical and spiritual sustenance on every level.

Strikingly, the precise formulation of the biblical verses alludes to both sides: the "quantity"—a society that can sustain itself physically over time ("length of days") without reaching, or breaching, the natural limits of the capacity of the Earth—and the "quality"— a society that can nourish and sustain its members spiritually (that they "fare well"). Our society is far from this simple yet far-reaching ideal. For too long we have enjoyed the fruit and paid no heed to preserving the fruitfulness. One imperative, then, for long and good lives as a society is treating the natural world with reverence and self-restraint.

This point is exemplified in the other two commandments. Honoring our father and mother, our progenitors, honors the idea of giving life and not just taking for ourselves. It rejects an inherently unsustainable throwaway culture in which even the elderly are disposable. Parents and our regard for them help situate us in a great intergenerational chain of being, and they provide a strong statement against the sort of progress that would have us believe the past has no value or meaning.

There is something terrifying about the inner logic of the seemingly benign view that progress is the gradual and continuous improvement of society. If we believe things are essentially always getting better, then (a) there is little of value to be learned from the past, for it is backward and primitive, and (b) we don't have to worry about the future, because it's going to be even better than this glorious age. Past and future and our connections to them and their residents (our progenitors and progeny) are devalued. Sustainability, as a vision and a goal, becomes irrelevant. Why worry about the future when the future surely can take care of itself? Indeed, in such a heavily knowledge-based culture, with the frontiers of that knowledge advancing so quickly that parents find it increasingly difficult even to help their children with their homework, honoring parents is a vote for the importance of wisdom that stems from tradition and experience, rather than from cleverness and data.

Honest weights and measures, symbolic of fairness, justice, and equality, also represent a constitutive characteristic of a society that hopes to create well-being for all its members and endure over the long term. Sustainability captures the two distinctive modes of justice that are becoming increasingly important in the growing mutual engagement of environment and society: the usual, "horizontal," intragenerational justice and the "vertical," intergenerational variety, which demands fairness and equity beyond the quarterly report and the four-year term of office, reaching out to future generations.

All three of these commandments are in fact nothing less than prescriptions for sustaining human society and its place in the natural world. Once again, sustainability also means sustenance: we don't just need an economy that can sustain *itself,* as important and imperiled as that is; we also need a moral and spiritual life that can sustain and nourish *us*. This is the force of the promise in these precepts: not the individual long life of a single person, and not a pie-in-the-sky promise for bliss in the afterlife, but a life and a world of quality and meaning sustained for us and our children after us, and from there to all the world.

And heaven, a dreamed-of better place, *alma de'atei,* the-world-that-is-coming, to use the very evocative Aramaic phrasing, can be, *should be,* that all-too-real world that our children and grandchildren will be inhabiting all too soon, not that other one that our deceased forebears might be in now. As environmental activist David Brower observed, "Environmentalists may make meddlesome neighbors, but they make great ancestors."

Cycles in Time, Sacraments in Life

The previous chapters of this book deal with texts, issues, and values revolving around the mundane and "profane" *(chol)* actions of meeting our physical needs in daily life. These are, of course, crucially important, and they have a potentially huge impact on how we think about our lives in relation to the world, and in turn, how we sustain the world (or not). They express the many dimensions of our *avoda,* the work we do in the world, and *shemira,* the safeguarding needed to keep that labor within sustainable limits.

Life, however, is not summed up by our biological needs and economic relations. Beyond our *avoda* is the question of *menucha,* our rest: how, when, and why we cease from our labors. This is inextricably bound up with how we experience and mark time, how we define and celebrate life and yearly events, and what spiritual dimensions we add to our physical existence. These "spiritual dimensions" are expressed in a number of different areas, which are the focus of this chapter:

- the Jewish calendar and the holidays spread throughout the seasons;
- the weekly Shabbat, and its once seven-yearly societal version, *shmitah,* the sabbatical, or year of "release"; and

- moments of spiritual appreciation and supplication expressed in *berachot* (blessings said over things we enjoy or benefit from) and *tefilla* (prayer, in particular the three daily services).

Other important touchstones in our lives fall under the rubric of the life cycle, including such events as birth (both being born and giving birth), circumcision, coming of age, marriage, death, and burial, each with profound implications for our attitudes toward ourselves, our bodies and souls, and our relationship with the Earth. For instance, it is common in our society to envision life in a linear fashion, with a beginning and an end—birth and death—not unlike a meteor streaking once through the sky.

And yet we speak of the *life cycle* and in many ways conceive of our lives as embedded in some cyclical reality, which presents a very different relationship to the world and its ongoing existence. Whether the cyclicity implied is in the life of a single individual, coming from and returning to dust, as the Bible proclaims, or the reiteration of eternal life in the chain of the generations, the vision is more botanical than astronomical. It is a vision of life generating and regenerating itself, as part of a cosmic process, akin to nature and its renewal in the circle of the seasons and the years, which finds expression in the calendar and our marking of time.

Lu'ach ve'Ru'ach—Of Calendars and Culture, Nature and History

The Jewish calendar has been famously defined by S. R. Hirsch as "the catechism of the Jew." It indeed makes up the warp and weft of Jewish spiritual life, and the calendar's different levels and cycles create a rhythm that gives shape to the experience of days, weeks, months, seasons, and years.[1] The set calendrical components of the *zemanim u'mo'adim,* the appointed times and preordained commemorations, are a "time-out" from the *avoda* of the workaday world, but a "time-in" for reflection and celebration. The crucial complement to these predetermined events is the framework of *berachot,* which are spontaneous or impromptu momentary opportunities for putting on hold the world of utility and functionality, the approach of *appraising,* to cultivate the practice of *praising,* and the virtues of *hakarat hatov,* appreciation and gratefulness for graciousness in the world of Creation.

Time, on some level, is an unbroken stream, and how any given society chooses to break it up and give it structure and meaning is one of the fundamental expressions of its culture. Most of the world is now used to the Gregorian or solar calendar, of 12 months and 365 (and ¼) days, based on the revolution of the Earth around the sun. The Hebrew calendar, with its leap months and other adjustments, seems complex and arcane by comparison. But if it is more complex it is not because it is more primitive—if anything, it is the opposite.

The Hebrew calendar is more complicated than the Western one because it *does* more. Though the solar year, like a lunar calendar, is made up of 12 months (the word *month* comes from "moon"), it has severed all connections with the lunar cycle. Knowing the Gregorian date tells you nothing about the phase of the moon. "Jewish-time" is special in that it is expressed in a lunar-solar calendar, a system of time reckoning that does justice to cycles of the sun *and* the moon.[2] Thus, the Hebrew months all start on the new moon, with the full moon at mid-month, and the 354-day year of 12 lunar months (there being 29.5 days in a lunar month) is filled out with a leap month (second Adar) at periodic times to stay aligned with the solar year. This means that months stay in their respective seasons, and plantings and harvests fall at set times. Indeed, the calendar integrates both large and small solar and lunar cycles: the large solar cycle is the year with its seasons, the small one being the day, from sunrise to sunset and back again; the large lunar cycle is the month, divided into four phases roughly corresponding to seven-day weeks, a small cycle.[3]

Moreover, not only do the holidays mark the harvests and the seasons—Pesach (Passover) in spring, Shavuot (The Feast of Weeks or Pentecost) in early summer, Sukkot (the Festival of Booths) in fall, and (the later instituted) Hanukkah in winter—but the major ones also mark the intersection of central lunar and solar events. For example, Pesach falls on the full moon following the spring equinox, Sukkot on the full moon following the fall equinox, and Hanukkah straddles the new moon closest to the winter solstice. The calculations that make this coordination possible were set down close to two thousand years ago (in a large debt to Babylonian science), making it a work of great astronomical acumen.

But there's more to it than just clever math. The dual nature of the Hebrew calendar expresses itself in other ways as well. It is a commonplace that most Jewish holidays have a natural/agricultural side alongside their historical commemoration. Whereas this was built in with Sukkot and Pesach, it is interesting to see how this came to expression in the festivals where this was not their explicit original character, such as Shavuot and Hanukkah. But we see this interplay of history and nature in other holidays as well. Shabbat, for instance, is marked as both *zecher lema'aseh breishit,* a commemoration of Creation, as well as *zecher leyitziyat mitzrayim,* a commemoration of the Exodus from Egypt.

Likewise, two calendars should have two beginning points, which is exactly what we find. What we call Rosh Hashanah, the start of the year at the beginning of the month of Tishri in the fall, is noted in the Bible as a convocation at the beginning of the seventh month (which may be related to rest and the cycles of seven seen in Shabbat and *shevi'it,* the sabbatical year). Only later did it acquire the character of a new year, one tied to several themes, but crucially including Creation: *hayom harat olam,* "today the world was conceived," as the High Holiday liturgy intones. The biblical new year would have been in Nisan, as it says: "This month shall mark for you the beginning of months; it shall be the first of the months of the year for you" (Exod. 12:2), connected, of course, to the Exodus—not the birth of the created world, but to that of the Jewish people, in history. Indeed, Nisan is listed in the Mishnah, in the tractate of *Rosh Hashanah*, as a new year with the historical significance of marking the reigns of kings.

The relationship of history and nature, so evident in the structure of the calendar, is a central question in Jewish theology and practice in general, especially in the context of renegotiating a relationship between Jewish teaching and the natural world. The deep connections we see to natural cycles in the Hebrew calendar challenge us to re-evaluate the Jewish relationship to the natural world—just as they invite us to re-examine our traditionally oppositional attitudes to other cultures that also have similar deep connections, such as nature-worshiping tribal religions known as paganism.

In their preference for history and reason over nature and a more embodied spirituality, rationalist Enlightenment Judaism tried to dye our pagan roots blue and white, as it were, and emphasized difference and distance from those ancient forms. A more environmentally sensitive perspective on Jewish tradition may be more open to celebrating our cosmic connections and similarities with "the families of the Earth" *(mishpachot ha'adamah)*. The holiday cycle, with its grounding in agriculture and the seasons, is as attuned to the Earth as any pagan tradition, and rituals such as the use of sacred produce of the earth in highly symbolic and suggestive ways (think waving the *lulav* and *etrog* on Sukkot, the holiday when we begin to pray for rain) are clearly of a piece with other fertility rites.

A wonderful expression of all this is the story of Rabbi Zalman Schachter-Shalomi's participation in an interfaith conference one year during the late summer. He went up on the roof of the center to *davven* very early one morning, to say the *shacharit* (dawn) prayer at the first rays of sunlight. He was wrapped in his multi-colored *tallit* (prayer shawl), arm and head swathed in *tefillin* (phy-lacteries), and since it was the month of Ellul, before the High Holidays, he had a *shofar* (ram's horn) to blow. The other confer-ence-goer who ascended the roof at dawn was a Native American, with his own *"davvening"* accoutrements—feathers, beads, and prayer rug. The feeling of commonality was striking, especially as compared with other monotheists and their traditions.

Although there are certainly many issues of great import where Judaism aligns with Christianity and Islam on one side of a divide, with tribal cults on the other, there is no denying the instruc-tive similarities here between traditional Jewish spirituality and so-called pagan rituals, and how they are each suffused with connections to elements and themes from the natural world.

Yamim Tovim—Good Days: The High Holidays and Pilgrimage Festivals

The fact that almost all Jewish holidays have this dual composition, combining historical and natural themes and symbolism, is accessi-bly and ably covered at length elsewhere.[4] Nonetheless, there are a number of central facts and insights regarding these connections with nature that are less obvious and therefore important to pre-sent here.

The holidays of the month of Tishri exemplify just how nuanced these connections with natural cycles can be. The new moon of Tishri is Rosh Hashanah, and the full moon marks the beginning of Sukkot. Between those two, falling after the first quar-ter on the waxing gibbous moon, is Yom Kippur. Later, after the end of Sukkot, on the third-quarter, or waning, crescent moon, is the sep-arate holiday of Shemini Atzeret, a "solemn convocation," marking the end of the harvest celebrations and the pilgrimage. Thus, the entire lunar cycle is embodied right at the onset of the year.

Every one of these appointed times has other environmental connections as well. As mentioned, one interpretation or theme of Rosh Hashanah is the anniversary of nature, the birthday of the world. And Sukkot is, of course, the fall harvest. What of Yom Kippur? Hardly a festival of the great outdoors. Yet there are two perhaps unexpected aspects of the Day of Atonement that are germane here. First, rather than a mythic motif from classical sources, the most striking environmental fact of the observance of the holiday is its contemporary expression in Israel. Because of the near-universal observance of the limitations of the day among the Jewish public in Israel, it is not only a "buy-nothing" day, but it is also nearly completely car-less as well—the latter a function of an informal public norm, not legislation. Urban streets come to life, being reclaimed by people from their usual vehicular masters. Walking and bicycle riding dominate the landscape (for many children the day becomes *yom ofanayim,*"bicycle day"), and the change is widely appreciated. The change in urban air quality alone is startling:

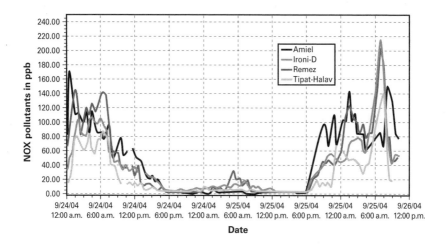

This graph registers the monitoring of nitrous oxide pollutants along several main thoroughfares in the Tel Aviv area: Yom Kippur began on the evening of the 24th of September that year (each column represents a period of 6 hours).[5]

Although cleaner air is a nice perk of the halachic restrictions of the day, the real themes of the day—contrition, atonement, and penitence—are also relevant. It is significant that despite the emphasis on personal soul-searching and *teshuva,* repentance, the main features of the Yom Kippur liturgy, such as the oft-repeated *vidu'i,* confession, and the *Avoda* service, are all phrased in the plural and relate to collective sin and wrongdoing. If we take seriously our responsibilities to the Earth, alongside the traditional categories of *bein adam lamakom,* between us and God, and *bein adam le'chavero,* between humans, surely we should give thought to *teshuva* in the realm of *bein adam le'olam* as well, which represents some of the biggest collective (and private) sins we have. Here we should include transgressions against future generations, from whom it is especially difficult to ask forgiveness. Indeed, some particularly virulent forms of pollutants, such as persistent organic particles (POPs), which last for years in the environment, seem to contradict Ezekiel's dictum that the sins of the parents will not be visited on the children (Ezek. 18:20).

Shemini Atzeret,[6] while a *chag,* holiday, in its own right, is clearly the denouement and completion of the festivities of Sukkot, and with the initial prayer for rain, signifies the beginning of the transition to winter. Sukkot, a peak experience in the middle of the month, represents the completion of a cycle begun the previous Pesach, the holiday of the spring grain *(chag ha'aviv)* and the beginning of the barley harvest, and continued through Shavuot, the wheat harvest and offering of first fruits *(chag ha'katzir, chag ha'bikkurim).* Sukkot is the fall ingathering *(chag ha'asif)* and the only festival explicitly labeled as a time of joy *(zeman simchatenu:* see Lev. 32 and Deut. 16).

Although Sukkot is connected historically to the period of wandering in the wilderness (see Lev. 23:44), it is well nigh incomprehensible apart from the nature motifs of fertility and water. These are expressed in three central components of the holiday. First and most blatant is the building of the *sukkah* (booth or tabernacle) itself. A temporary structure in which we are meant to eat and sleep, it needs to be sturdy enough to shade the burning sun of late summer, but its thatched roof must be open to the moon and stars. As a non-Jewish and outdoorsy friend of mine once said: "Any tradition that makes you sleep outside for a week a year as a religious duty has a lot going for it." The *sukkah* itself has a double symbolism, representing both the temporary dwelling of wandering and the hut of the fruit pickers who work from morning till night and sleep in the fields.

Second are the four species *(minim)*: the *lulav* (palm branch), two *aravot* (willows), three *hadasim* (myrtles), and an *etrog* (citron). Although there are many layers of edifying midrashic exegesis to these symbols, they are first and foremost natural elements that are bound together and ritually waved in the six directions (north, south, east, west, up, down), imploring God for divine sustenance. Call it what you will, but it is a fertility ritual, and while some may balk at this "pagan" rite, there's no reason not to flaunt this amazingly sensual activity that provides such an aesthetic and profound expression of connection to natural cycles, and of the dependence of our own well-being on those cycles and the health of our natural home.

Each of the four species has special ties to the central theme of water: the willows are called *arvei nachal*, willows of the brook, the date palm is emblematic of the desert oasis, and the myrtle is intimately connected with plentiful water (see Isa. 41:17–20 and 55:13). The *etrog,* like all citrus, requires great quantities of water, whether rain or irrigation (see Talmud, *Kiddushin* 3a), and is connected by the midrash to water through the phonetic similarity of the biblical term *pri etz hadar* (literally "the fruit of the goodly tree") and the Greek *hydor* (or hydro-, water; see Talmud, *Sukkah* 35a).[7] This is reinforced by a third element of the *chag,* the water libation and the celebration of Simchat Beit Hasho'eva. Central to the Temple cult, this ecstatic event involved water rituals designed to symbolize, or possibly even to precipitate, divine favor in the form of rain in the coming year. The revelry was a veritable circus, with torches, juggling, and the like, that, according to the Mishnah, was a highlight of the whole year (see e.g., Mishnah *Sukkah,* chs. 4 and 5).

The fall pilgrimage festival of Sukkot is, in essence, the culmination of the holiday cycle begun at the first of the *regalim* (pilgrimage or "foot" holidays), Pesach, in the spring. Pesach, with its intense spring cleaning activity, marks renewal and rebirth, elegantly integrated with the historic birth of the people emerging from the crucible of slavery. Part of the new beginning is the removal of the old grain and fermented and risen foods, making room for the new grain about to be harvested, as the period of the *omer* begins, which connects the two main grain harvests of ancient Israel: the barley harvest begun at Pesach, and the wheat harvest of Shavuot, seven weeks later (see Lev. 23).

Pesach, like Sukkot, is a paradigm example of the Jewish synthesis of history and nature, in theory and in practice. For instance, matzah, the mandatory unleavened bread, is the poor bread of affliction and slavery, or the hastiness of the flight to freedom, yet it's also the new grain, as yet unfermented in the nascent springtime.

Shavuot (Pentecost, literally, "weeks"), the third pilgrimage holiday, didn't originally fit the pattern of merged natural and historical motifs. Biblically, there is no historical event associated with this holiday—it was exclusively agricultural, the festival of the first fruits and the summer wheat. Only later did the Rabbis fill in the blank by connecting it to the giving of the Torah at Sinai, thus situating it between the Exodus of Pesach and the wandering of

Sukkot. This created structural symmetry, but more important, it was a response to the fact that the historical aspects of the holidays would be much more serviceable for Diaspora culture.

Shavuot breaks the mold for another reason. In Leviticus 23, one of the Torah's major accounts of the festival calendar, after the description of the holiday's Temple rituals (verses 15–21), the text inserts a repetition of the commandments of *peah* and *leket,* to leave the corners of the fields and the unharvested gleanings of the crops for the poor. Given the ritual focus of that chapter, this ethical addition is surprising, and it requires an explanation. Because this particular form of support for the poor happens to be relevant during the harvest season of Shavuot, commentators generally gloss this as a mental association, or a reminder that there are social obligations beyond the ritual ones. The reason, however, may be much deeper.

Pesach, with its unleavened bread and arduous dietary restrictions, is clearly in some profound way about food. Sukkot, second only to Pesach in quantity and type of strenuous preparations, focuses on shelter. Both mandate a form of enforced poverty—eating matzah, the bread of affliction, and living in a shack, the most modest of dwellings. These holidays are great social equalizers; fulfilling their two central obligations make the wealthy more like the poor, and no one, rich or poor, is excluded by the celebrations.

The biblical Shavuot is different, the main celebrants being the landowners, those who had grain and fruits to bring to the Temple. As such, this festival is "about" land, a basic element of civilization along with food and shelter. Ideally, everyone is supposed to be a landowner, but the Torah realizes that this would never be the case. The holiday, then, has the dangerous potential of splitting the people between the landed and the landless, and rather than being a "leveler" like Pesach and Sukkot, bringing rich and poor together in a shared experience, it could reinforce and deepen the socioeconomic gap.

The unexpected verse about leaving parts of the harvest for the poor (reinforced in the story of Ruth read on Shavuot) is a poignant reminder of mutual obligation, an admonition that the land should be a source of justice and not division, that the holiday requires an ethic of care, and not just a celebration of wealth. This is a statement about holidays in general: gratitude for our bounteous harvests is best expressed through compassion for those who have not been so blessed—not through closed, self-satisfied convocations of the favored.

But the message regarding the land is even more forceful. Widening gaps between rich and poor are often due to differential access to the land and its benefits. We are no longer talking about a few bushels of grain, however. Real estate is big business: the land has become a commodity, and is traded and speculated rather than husbanded or stewarded. Developers build up dwindling beachfront property, agricultural land is rezoned for upscale residential and commercial complexes, and massive development projects of dubious public value are thrown up. All are a source of profits for some, with many people—and the environment—losing out.

The biblical land ethic, codified in holidays, rituals, and ethics, merged the natural with the social by expressing an inseparable link between the land, its bounty, and its continued well-being, and the need for the care and support of all people.

The Nature of Hanukkah

After the holidays of Tishri and the other pilgrimage festivals, the next significant occasion is Hanukkah. If this winter week of candelabra and spinning tops seems more significant than Shemini Atzeret or Shavuot, it is primarily because of its proximity to Christmas, which has given it somewhat undue prominence in our awareness. Though eight days long, it is considered a minor holiday, post-biblical in origin, and discussed only minimally in the

Talmud. Indeed, the Talmud seems to need basic information when it asks naively "What is Hanukkah?" (*Shabbat* 21). It answers with a story of religious emphasis, about the desecration and rededication of the Temple, and the miracle of the one cruze of pure oil that lasted for eight days. Many supplant or supplement that answer with the political-military story of the victory of Judah Macabee and the Hasmoneans over Antiochus and the powerful Seleucid Greeks, in their fight for independence and freedom from oppression.

Environmentally speaking, though, faced with limited resources and needing to light the menorah of the Temple for its rededication, the Maccabees faced the first great oil crisis, and they found their solution in a unique renewable energy source! Unfortunately, we don't have access to those same technologies to meet our current challenges, and it is forbidden, not to mention unwise, to depend on miracles to solve real-world problems.

But seriously, it's no coincidence that Hanukkah falls toward the end of the *mesik,* the olive harvest in Israel, when oil becomes plentiful. The *nerot* we light on Hanukkah originally referred to oil lamps, not the (petroleum-based) wax candles many of us use today. So here, too, there is an agricultural side to this otherwise historical holiday: the Mishnah (*Bikkurim* 1:6) even mentions Hanukkah as being the last time to bring first-fruit offerings, probably because the olive crop is the last of the seven species to ripen. In other words, olives and olive oil become plentiful just as winter is setting in—when the days shorten and we need it most.

The theme of light and its return is doubly represented on Hanukkah: not only the light of the sun, at the winter solstice, but of the moon as well. The eight-day celebration straddles the new moon of Tevet, and the moon disappears and then reappears during the course of the festival. Like the harvest festivals that are present in many diverse cultures, light (symbolically) is a universal dimension of the holiday that connects us to other peoples and faiths. From Diwali to Santa Lucia Day, many traditions have candle-lighting festivals in winter.

That may sound very "New Agey," but it's actually an ancient realization. The Talmud, in the tractate dealing with idolatrous practices, even hints that the actual origin of the eight days of Hanukkah is as a solstice festival:

> Mishnah: These are the festivities of the idolaters: Calendria and Saturnalia....
>
> Gemara: R. Hanan b. Raba said: "Calendria is kept on the eight days following the [winter] solstice, Saturnalia on the eight days before the solstice...." The Rabbis taught: "When the first Adam saw the day getting progressively shorter, he said: 'Woe is me, for because I have sinned, the entire world is being cast into darkness and returning to chaos! This must be the death that was decreed by Heaven!' He then sat for eight days in prayer and fasting. But as he observed the winter solstice and noted the day getting increasingly longer, he said: 'This must be the way of the world,' and he celebrated an eight day festival. In following years, they became festive days for these and those—some for the sake of Heaven, and some for pagan rites." (Avoda Zara 8a).

Here is a startling rabbinic admission that our Hanukkah and those other festivals go back to that same universal human experience of joy and relief at the return of the light during the darkest of winter.

There is another dimension to this holiday as well, one that definitely touches on environmental issues: the increasing commercialization of Hanukkah, much like its seasonal cousin, Christmas. The infiltration of "consumerist overdose," including the emphasis on quantity in gift-giving, is doubly ironic on Hanukkah, a holiday that represents the triumph of spiritual values over the materialistic culture of Hellenism. That may be a lot of "guilt with the *gelt*" but we do build and preserve the world with both our presence and our presents. The candles of Hanukkah should represent a *ner tamid*, a perpetual, sustainable, nurturing source of light and warmth, and not an *esh ochelet*, a destructive, devouring fire.

The Four Faces of Tu B'Shvat, A New Year of the Trees

Of all the holidays, the festival most associated with a Jewish connection to nature and the environment is Tu B'Shvat, the "new year" of the trees.

On the face of it, scheduling our nature festival in the dead of winter doesn't seem to make much sense. But Tu B'Shvat, the festival of trees and their fruit, didn't start out as a Jewish Earth Day, or even an Arbor Day. And while the almond trees do clothe Israeli hillsides with white and pink blossoms at this time of year, the day isn't about aesthetic nature appreciation. A closer look at the varied "incarnations" of this minor holiday through history reveals four facets of our interdependence with trees and the natural world, which we can contemplate and celebrate.

Through Mishnaic times, Tu B'Shvat, the fifteenth of the Hebrew month of Shvat, was comparable to "Tu B'April" for Americans, a date relevant to calculation and payment of taxes. The exact middle of winter was chosen as the end of the arboreal fiscal year: tithes to the Temple on fruit after this date belonged to the next year. So the Mishnah in tractate *Rosh Hashanah* labels it "the new year of the trees."

The Israelites didn't sweat over tax forms, though, worrying about getting a check to some priestly IRS. Economics and spirituality, environment and society, were more integrated in the ancient Jewish world, and the practice of tithing agricultural produce had deep meaning. Part of the fruitful bounty received from God via trees was returned to God via the priests and the Temple, while part was redistributed to care for the poor.

So one aspect of Tu B'Shvat is *economic* (the body)—we derive physical sustenance from the fruits of nature, quantifiable in economic terms.

After the exile, with no trees of our own from which to tithe, the date's significance waned. Like a tree, the holiday became dormant, only blooming again more than a millenium later. The midrashic inclination of the Jewish people couldn't let the idea of a "new year for trees," with all of its metaphoric potential, wither away without transformation and reinterpretation.

The second efflorescence of Tu B'Shvat came in the wake of the renaissance of Kabbalah in sixteenth-century Safed. Kabbalists taught of the cosmic Tree of the *Sefirot,* the divine emanations, conceived as no less than the blueprint for the creation of the world and a map of the mind of God. With characteristic ritual creativity, their disciples created a Tu B'Shvat seder. They adopted the Pesach Seder's four cups of wine, but added a progression from white to red, symbolizing quiescence to full flowering, or masculine to feminine. Fruits to be eaten at this uniquely vegan feast were also chosen for their metaphysical symbolism, from the gross physicality of peels and pits to the more spiritual realm of pure, unprotected fruit. Together, wine and fruits mark the four worlds, or levels of creation, often labeled as the physical, emotional, intellectual, and spiritual.[8]

Thus, a second dimension of the day is the *spiritual* (the soul)—the natural world is the ground of our spiritual lives, source of symbolism and meaning.

With the Zionist return to the Land, Tu B'Shvat was transformed yet again. In a new act of ritual creativity, Jewish schoolteachers of pre-state Palestine made Tu B'Shvat a day of tree-planting, a festival of reforestation efforts. It is tree-planting, in person or by proxy, that remains the most prevalent observance of

Tu B'Shvat. Although trees have unfortunately become a political pawn in national struggles over the Land, plantings and uprootings taking place on both sides, the visceral significance of actually rooting a tree in the soil establishes an undeniable physical connection with the land.

A third level of meaning is thus the *national-political* (the group)—the world over, trees are powerful symbols of collective identity and pride, rooting themselves and us in the landscape.

Universalizing this connection leads directly to the latest metamorphosis: Tu B'Shvat as Jewish Earth Day. Building on Zionist activism, the day has become a framework for Jews the world over to focus their concern on environmental issues of potentially global import. From ecology we learn that far-off trees in the Amazon basin are integral to our health and well-being, that there is a profound interdependence that informs the world, and that this connection can and should be acknowledged and celebrated in our spiritual lives. And so the mystic seder has gained newfound prominence in observances of the day, reinforced with additional particular and universal materials, and affirming the deep spiritual and physical significance of the natural world in our lives.

The fourth aspect, then, is the *ecological* (the world)—we are part of an interconnected, interdependent, universal web of life.

We come, then, to the *synthesis*—of integrating these fragmented relationships and healing ourselves and the world. Taken alone, each component can easily get out of whack: the economic can become merely utilitarian; the spiritual, overly abstract; and the national risks degenerating into chauvinism. The overarching, contemporary environmental perspective provides a unifying synthesis for our time. In their seder, the kabbalists aimed at uniting all the realms and worlds. In our many-layered Tu B'Shvat, we, too, can strive to integrate and deepen the four interlocking realms that define our relationship to life and land: economic, spiritual, national-political, and ecological—body, soul, group, and world.

Moreover, in celebrating Tu B'Shvat, we can integrate the particular—the personal, fruit-giving tree of the Mishnah and the replanted national trees of Israel—with the universal—the life-giving global trees of the ecosphere and the Life-giving cosmic tree of the Kabbalah. And while Tu B'Shvat gives us a profound festive opportunity to celebrate and reflect on these relationships, in the face of deepening environmental crises in Israel and around the world, we need to affirm and integrate these concepts into our lives much more often than once a year.

Shabbat: A Day of Worldly Rest

When I teach about Shabbat I often begin by asking participants for some general associations they have with the day itself. The initial responses are invariably positive: candles, challah, family, rest, walks in the park. But sooner or later, other feelings crop up: rules, restrictions, obligations, "thou shalt not's." Over and against the very benevolent aspects of the weekly observance, there is another side to the day that arouses indignation and resentment. Yet why should a day so filled with light, holiness, rest, and rejuvenation conjure up such mixed feelings? What is the connection between the "positive" side and the other, often limiting and restrictive side?

I had a Jewish friend in college who became more traditionally Shabbat observant during his studies. That year, he lived near the top of a fourteen-story dorm building. Because riding an elevator is included in the Shabbat prohibition of the use of electricity, he had no choice but to take the stairs all the way up on Friday nights. The first time he did this, finally arriving, huffing and puffing, his (non-Jewish) roommates asked incredulously why he hadn't taken the elevator. His response? "I'm not allowed to (pant, pant), it's the Shabbat (pant), our day of rest."

When we begin to scratch beneath the superficial understanding of "the day of rest," we discover other puzzling features as well:

Shabbat appears in the Ten Commandments, yet it is clearly out of place. It is the only ritual requirement in the Decalogue. Tucked in between the first three commandments, which deal with monotheism and idolatry, and the following six, which regulate relations among people, Shabbat is connected to both categories yet fully part of neither. Is the mere idea of rest and time off so sublime as to merit inclusion in the Ten Commandments?

We are commanded to "rest" (or cease from labor), yet nowhere is the meaning of this spelled out in the written Torah. And thus it is precisely in defining the nature of the work from which we are to refrain that the Rabbis provide us with more details than we might care for. It becomes a violation to pick a flower, write a poem or, later on, flick a switch.

"Are we dealing here with extravagant and compulsive exaggerations of an originally 'sensible' ritual," psychoanalyst Erich Fromm wrote, "or is our understanding of the ritual perhaps faulty and in need of revision?" Fromm's answer was the latter, and he provided the following definition of what is forbidden on the seventh day: "'Work' is any interference by man, be it constructive or destructive, with the physical world. Rest is a state of peace between man and nature."[9] Similarly, Orthodox authority Dr. Isadore Grunfeld defines *melacha*, the particular type of labor forbidden on Shabbat, as "an act that shows man's mastery over the world by the constructive exercise of his intelligence and skill."[10]

This *aggadah* of Shabbat, the theory behind the practice, is hinted at in the commandment itself, for we rest in imitation of the original divine rest that was the climax and cessation of Creation:

> Remember the sabbath day and keep it holy. Six days you shall labor and do all your work, but the seventh day is a sabbath of the Lord your God: you shall not do any work.... For in six days the Lord made heaven and earth and sea, and all that is in them, and He rested on the seventh day;

therefore the Lord blessed the sabbath day and hallowed it.
(Exod. 20:8–11).

God's rest allowed the world to exist without divine intervention. In the same way, Shabbat is as much a respite for the world as it is for the people who observe it. It is a *brit 'olam,* which means both "eternal covenant" and "covenant for (or of) the world." How else can we understand a day of joy and rest that prohibits labor-saving devices and involves frequent inconvenience—but by seeing that something other than human needs is paramount?[11] Historian and former chancellor of the Jewish Theological Seminary, Ismar Schorsch, sums up this message: "The regimen of rest is meant to restrict our strength as much as to restore it, to deflate our arrogance as much as to ennoble our spirit."[12]

In the narrative of the Creation story, the Shabbat is an independent creation, in many ways superseding the human, created before it. As the midrash quoted earlier states, the human was created on the eve of the Sabbath, in order that he submit immediately to the mitzvah of Shabbat.

The link between the commandment and the Creation story indicates how Shabbat rest contrasts with creative labor. As opposed to the anthropocentric Creation story at the beginning of Genesis, Shabbat implies an approach that can be labeled biocentric, demanding that humans abstain from both domination *and* stewardship of the world. It is forbidden to mine and chop down trees, but also to water or weed one's garden. Thus the stairs instead of the elevator, and all the other rules and restrictions.

These do not negate the other great sources of joy (the *oneg Shabbat,* the pleasure or delight of the Shabbat), including good food, wine, and physical love. Indeed, the restrictions help create the leisure, the unoccupied time to enjoy them fully. But there is in some sense a balancing act of sorts between personal enjoyment (rest and recreation in the Western sense) and fulfillment of a higher ideal, the creative and spiritually aware cessation of labor, which includes both gainful employment and also intentional intervention in the natural world.

But the focus is not only on the natural world. Shabbat is indeed presented as being woven into the very fabric of Creation, preceding the existence of the people of Israel, and thus acquiring a certain trans-historical quality. But there is another, more historical and political side, as represented in the version of the Decalogue in Deuteronomy (5:12–15). There, the Shabbat is presented in connection with the memory of slavery and of freedom from bondage. Therefore Shabbat is (also) a *zecher leyitziyat mitzrayim,* a remembrance of the Exodus, and one of its purposes is explicitly "so that your male and female slave may rest as you do" (v. 14).

Thus Shabbat is not only a personal, spiritual act of *imitatio dei* in relation to the world, but it is a social act as well. Slaves rest, which means that slavery itself is not absolute, and domestic animals too are given a day of freedom that expresses an inalienable right to existence beyond human hierarchy and need. Shabbat, with all its rules and regulations, is anything but reactionary: it suggests a more egalitarian social order that for one full day a week trumps structural power relations.

So we see that those "stuffy" Shabbat restrictions serve several purposes. They prevent us from becoming workaholics, and help to carve out time for family, study, and reflection. By applying to everybody, they reinforce community and commonality. The day becomes defined by natural events, from the dusk of one sunset to the stars that appear following the next sunset, creating a day whose tempo is not tied to industrial and mechanical demands. Thus, we are able to see ourselves as creatures, rather than creators, which has both ecological and social ramifications. Orthodox rabbi and philosopher David Hartman says of the seventh day:

> The setting of the sun [on Friday night] ushers in a unit of time where the flowers of the field stand over and against man as equal members of the universe. I am forbidden to pluck the flower or to do with it as I please; at sunset the flower becomes a "thou" to me with a right to existence regardless of its possible value for me. I stand silently before nature as before a fellow creature of God and not as a potential object of my control, and I must face the fact that I am a man, and not God. The Sabbath aims at healing the human grandiosity of technological society.[13]

More specifically, then, what are these restrictions? Although they are not spelled out in the Bible, the Mishnah (*Shabbat* 7:2) enumerates thirty-nine distinct categories of *melachot* (though it does not explain or justify them), from plowing, sowing, and baking to writing, building, and carrying objects from one domain to another.

Modern scholars suggest a sociological approach that breaks these categories down into several orders, which form an "itemized description of the indispensable bases of organized human life."[14] These are:

- the order of bread (everything connected to growing and processing grain and cooking food),
- clothing (processing wool into cloth, weaving, and sewing),
- written matter (including obtaining and processing hides into parchment, writing, and erasing),
- shelter and the organization of space.

Those calculated interventions in our world, which make us civilized, powerful masters of our environment, are defined as that which we should not do in our observance of Shabbat, the day on which we revert to creatures focusing on being, not creators intent on making, doing, having.

A more "religious" explanation is proffered in the Gemara (*Shabbat* 49b), where the *melachot* are midrashically derived from the building of the *mishkan,* the Tabernacle. Interestingly, this extraordinarily important legal construction technically stems from a word in a single verse in the Book of Exodus, where elaborate rules and regulations for the construction of the Tabernacle are presented, immediately followed by the injunction: "Nevertheless, you must keep My Sabbaths" (31:13). That "nevertheless" (in Hebrew simply *ach,* a curt two-letter conjunction) means that the important mission of constructing the *mishkan* does not override the Shabbat and its restrictions. Thus, it was concluded that the specific categories of labor that should be prohibited on the Shabbat are exactly the things necessary for constructing the *mishkan.*

This legalistic exposition was turned into almost poetic theology by Abraham Joshua Heschel, who wrote eloquently of the centrality of time and its sanctification in Judaism. Those things that are required in order to construct sacred space (the *mishkan*) are precisely those that are forbidden in order to create Shabbat, sacred time. Sacred time becomes here a photographic negative of sacred space, and the Shabbat "a cathedral in time," to use his evocative phrase. Heschel writes:

> To set apart one day a week for freedom, a day on which we would not use the instruments which have been so easily turned into weapons of destruction ... a day on which we stop worshiping the idols of technical civilization, a day on which we use no money, a day of armistice in the economic struggle with our fellows and with the forces of nature—is there any institution that holds out a greater hope for man's progress than the Sabbath?[15]

The Shabbat, then, is full of hope, but also full of challenge. There's a reason why the Shabbat ideal is a difficult one. As

Schorsch puts it, it "restricts our strength" and "deflates our arrogance." It is not anti-human, but it does promote a different conception of what human fulfillment looks like. Arguably, the difficulties many of us have with these aspects of Shabbat observance are similar to the resistance that exists to general environmental values: reigning ourselves in, conquering our impulses, and redefining the role of the material in our lives and our conception of the components of the good life.

Shabbat is to time what a nature preserve is to space. Both are "places" marked with distinct boundaries. In both, the soul of the human "visitor" is refreshed, while the natural order is preserved in its unviolated form. Outside the boundaries, we do not seek to negate civilization, the realm of human action, and make the whole world a preserve. But ideally the values experienced inside the "fence" will influence how we view the world beyond, and our role in it.

Shmitah—The Radical Social-Environmental Vision of a Yearlong Sabbath

What Shabbat does for the week, the concept of *shmitah* does for the cycle of years. While the ideal of *shmitah* ("year of release," or sabbatical year) is enormously inspiring, and is invariably touted as one of Judaism's premier environmental concepts, whenever the *shmitah* year arrives in Israel, it's a huge problem. The commandment described in Leviticus 25:1–7 mandates letting the land owned by Jews in their own country lie fallow every seventh year:

> When you enter the land that I assign to you, the land shall observe a sabbath of the Lord. Six years you may sow your field and six years you may prune your vineyard and gather in the yield. But in the seventh year the land shall have a sabbath of complete rest, a sabbath of the Lord: you shall

not sow your field or prune your vineyard.... But you may
eat whatever the land during its sabbath will produce.

The fourfold repetition of the term *sabbath* in this short passage makes obvious the resemblance and connection to the
Shabbat, iterating the cycle of seven, now on a yearly rather than a
weekly scale. The parallels are striking:

On the Sabbath, both humans and animals are freed from
the grind of domestication; all technology, right down to the
kindling of fire, is taboo. In the sabbatical year, the land
itself is allowed to revert to a state of wildness. Sabbath,
sabbatical, and jubilee are all eruptions of wildness into the
humdrum of the technical and economic order.[16]

This was not seen as some intriguing idea, but as an objective need
of the land. It is asserted in 2 Chronicles 36:21 that the Babylonian
exile happened precisely because the Israelites did not observe
shmitah, letting the land rest during the previous era. It was the
land itself that exiled Israel, and Israel would be in exile "until the
land paid back its sabbaths."

But *shmitah*, or *shevi'it* ("the seventh" as the relevant
mishnaic tractate is called), is more than just a Shabbat for the
land: in an agricultural society, a year off for the land is also a yearlong sabbatical for most of the populace. Indeed, the biblical *shmitah* is a stirring example of an entire society choosing to live at a
significantly lower material standard for a year in order to devote
itself to more spiritual pursuits than the daily grind. The vision is
more revolutionary still, with its radical egalitarian thrust: all the
produce of the land that grows by itself must be free to all (even
animals have equal access), and all loans are to be forgiven, allowing people in debt an opportunity to start over (Exod. 23:10–11,
Deut. 15:12).

As in the dual theme of Shabbat, of creation and liberation, rest for the world and for the social order, here too we see the inseparable connection between agricultural practice that allows natural regeneration and a purely economic idea, which can allow personal and societal renewal.

So what's the problem? Well, these days, who can afford not to work for one full year? And how can we feed ourselves without agriculture for a whole year? How can we share our dearest resources with *everybody*? When seen thus, as a problem, *shmitah* invites solutions that bypass the original intent, whether the fictitious sale of land to non-Jews or the dependence on food raised by them.

The entire observance of the precept has become a subcategory of *kashrut:* People ask whether food is grown according to the rules, not whether the society doing the producing and consuming is "kosher." It certainly isn't seen as a model for addressing burning social and environmental issues. It has become another source of tension for and among Jews; it is another wall separating us by degree of religious observance. And the social and ecological significance is all but lost.

It should be noted that *shmitah* observance was never easy, and the more radical the vision, the more unlikely its application. Gerald Blidstein notes that some interpretations in Tannaitic times went so far as to require the tearing down of fencing—that is, completely abolishing private property for the year. Rabbi Judah the Prince, redactor of the Mishnah, called for the annulment of the *shmitah* year because its implementation was so arduous (J. T. *Demai,* 3.1, 22a). "The potency of *shevi'it* has been its historical doom," writes Blidstein.[17] The jubilee year *(yovel)* was even harder, requiring a complete "reset" of the ancient Israelite economy, with all land transactions being nullified, and everyone returning (in theory) to their preassigned ancestral holdings. It may never have been implemented at all in the way described (see Lev. 25).

But what if we looked at *shmitah* not as a problem but as a solution, and then considered which problem it is meant to solve? In that light, *shmitah* becomes a political statement of social and environmental import, raising deep questions about the nature of a healthy and sustainable life—for individuals, society, and the land.

For instance, currently only academics have a sabbatical year. Why? Our "affluent" society actually decreases leisure and family time, as more people not only choose to work but also feel compelled to work, in order to afford what society says they should have. Consumerism necessitates "producerism" to keep both supply and demand high. Yet as *shmitah* hints, people are indeed like the land: for both, when overwork leads to exhaustion, we engineer continued "vitality" not with true renewal, but with chemicals.

Just as silence is an integral part of speech, punctuated periods of fallowness are crucial for guaranteeing continued fertility. There's no reason why only an intellectual elite should benefit from a year of learning, reflection, and regeneration. The original sabbatical was for farmers, not physicists. And making each year *shmitah* for one-seventh of the labor force would also be a creative way to combat unemployment.

Variations on the sabbatical idea are actually cropping up with surprising force and relevance with calls for moratoria on certain types of problematic scientific research, European initiatives to remit debts of Third World countries, and growing opposition to unfettered economic and technological growth.

The fact that the very idea of any sort of technological moratorium or attempt to gain control over the frenetic pace of economic development seems hopelessly utopian only emphasizes the problem. Technical innovation outstrips ethical deliberation, and human lives are adapted to fill corporate "needs." Contemporary society is a sorcerer's apprentice, whose tools have taken on a life of their own, leaving us to run behind, trying to catch up. The environment seems to be quintessentially a thing of space, a physical thing that surrounds us. Although the *shmitah* is focused on land, it determines how we relate to time as well. The frenetic pace of our lives—determined by economic and technological considerations, and not organic or ecological ones—is as much a part of the environmental crisis as pollution is.

The sabbatical principle, dictating periods of enforced restraint, rededication, and redistribution, presents a compelling alternative to business as usual. Limiting the share that production and consumption have in our lives will create the space for higher pursuits. The economy must not be an engine that runs itself, disengaged from social and environmental concerns, but a conscious expression of our spiritual and moral values. Money and land are not personal property to be accumulated; they are divine abundance channeled through us to be shared for the benefit of all.

As a problem, *shmitah* has become of interest to limited sectors of the Jewish people. As a solution, it can serve as a bridge to all those seeking answers to pressing social and environmental problems. It is extremely hard for us to critique a world view from the inside, and to imagine that things can be different. The ancient institution of *shmitah* and the religious language in which it is couched are an urgent message from a distant time that can provide a much-needed challenge to the prevailing Zeitgeist. Perhaps the specific solutions that the *shmitah* idea suggests will not be deemed practical, but they can provide much-needed help in formulating the crucial questions.

Blessings and Worship: From Appraising to Praising

Although the system of *mitzvot* in its entirety is meant to shape the life of the "religious" or "traditional" Jew, there are a number of particular practices that outwardly mark a Jew as "observant," such as keeping kosher and observing Shabbat and the holidays (especially the restrictions). One of the most central or indicative rituals in this regard, though, is regular prayer, whether reciting the liturgy of the services at the set daily times or the saying of *berachot*, blessings, at the appropriate occasions. The inclusion of these sacramental observances in this book may be surprising at first, because in the great triad of human-world-God, they seem to relate exclusively to the human-God relationship and thus would have very little to say about the world, and the human-world relationship. Prayer and blessings are the mandated professing of certain doctrinal beliefs that for some are deep expressions of their personal faith, and for others are simply not relevant. It is precisely here that "environmental readings" can add meaning to otherwise obtuse texts.

For instance, the second paragraph of the Shema prayer, taken from Deuteronomy 11:13–21 and recited twice daily, speaks of the heavens closing up, denying rain if the Jewish people do not observe the commandments, a rather difficult claim to justify in a modern scientific world view. But contemporary Jewish environmentalists, no less modern or scientific in their outlook, read this text as a poignant warning: our moral and economic behavior indeed impacts the natural world, and we can maintain or impair the continued well-being and fertility of natural systems through our personal and collective choices.

Beyond creative (re-)interpretation, we can explore how traditional Jewish prayer and blessings can challenge us and stretch our understanding of environmental sensibility and sensitivity. It should be noted at the outset that while the language and examples that will be referred to are indeed "religious," the sensitivity that it is so important to cultivate is not limited by that rubric.

The fixed liturgy, known as the *keva* (the set form), and its rote recitation often seem distant from devotional adulation, but the key concepts here are indeed spiritual-emotional ones: appreciation and gratitude, wonder and awe, amazement and reverence.

Abraham Joshua Heschel wrote that the cultivation of these experiences and attitudes is one of the great true teachings of religion in general, and one of the keys to the regeneration of humanity in the modern world:

> Among the many things that religious tradition holds in store for us is a *legacy of wonder.* The surest way to suppress our ability to understand the meaning of God and the importance of worship is *to take things for granted.* Indifference to the sublime wonder of living is the root of sin.... The beginning of our happiness lies in the understanding that life without wonder is not worth living. What we lack is not a will to believe but a will to wonder [emphasis Heschel's].[18]

How do we develop this "will to wonder"? How do we make sure we not only remember to appreciate but that we also remember *how* to appreciate? These connect to the expressions of *kavana,* the intention or inwardness of praying. If *keva* relates to the text of the prayer, *kavana* focuses on the experience of the pray-er. Jewish prayer is made up of the synthesis of the two. Experience is central to the act of prayer, for liturgy is not a text to be read but rather an activity to be performed. And it is precisely the fixed, almost canonical, nature of the text, and its frequent ritualized repetitive performance, that gives it such psychic power, and also authority.

The idea of prayer as performance is a field of inquiry unto itself,[19] but I will mention a few important aspects here. For instance, two of the three daily prayers are mandated at the rising and setting of the sun. They even take their names from these natural phenomena: *shacharit,* from *shachar* (dawn), and *arvit* (or *ma'ariv*) from *erev* (evening). It is especially meritorious to begin the morning prayer at *netz* (literally, "spark"), the very first glint of light as the sun appears over the horizon.

The congregational section of *shacharit* begins with the *Barchu* call to prayer, and with the *yotzer* blessing, which speaks of creation in general, and the divine grace of the sun and its light in particular:

> Praised are You, YHVH, our God, ruler of the universe, who fashions light and creates darkness, makes peace and creates all things.[20] In Your mercy, You shine on the earth and its inhabitants, and in Your goodness You daily renew the work of Creation. How manifold are Your works, YHVH, You have fashioned them all in wisdom. The earth is filled with Your creations.... To the Ruler, who lives and endures ... who in His goodness daily renews the work of Creation, as it is written: "Who makes the great lights, for His steadfast love endures forever" (Pss. 136:7).... Praised are You, creator of lights.

Most remarkable is the twice-repeated idea that God, in God's goodness, daily renews the work of Creation. In other words, creation was not a one-time event, but is something that is happening all the time, and it is an expression of the divine goodness that exists for creative processes to be renewed.

This dawn paean is bookended with a parallel text from the evening service, also directly following the initial call to prayer:

> Praised are You, YHVH, our God, ruler of the universe, whose word causes the evening to commence (*ma'ariv aravim*, literally, "'dusks' the dusk"), opens gates in wisdom, and in understanding changes the time and sets the succession of the seasons, and arranges the stars in their patterns in the heavens according to His will. Creator of day and night, rolling the light away from before the darkness, and the darkness from before the light, causing the day to

pass and bringing on the night, and distinguishing between day and night ... Praised are You, who causes the evening to commence.

These are just two examples of inspiring nature themes in liturgy that direct our attention to what is going on around us. Heschel, the great preacher of awe and radical amazement, was known on occasion to have entered an evening class, commenting breathlessly, "Gentlemen, a momentous event has just occurred!" "What? What?" all the rabbinical students would be wondering. "The sun has just set," he would respond.

A significant part of the liturgy comes from the great "nature poetry" of the Bible, to wit, the Psalms. Masterpieces such as Psalm 104, Psalm 19, and many others are part and parcel of the Jewish prayer experience. These hymns and other texts have been integrated into the weekday and Shabbat liturgy, such that recognition and thanks for the world around us in all its intricate and miraculous workings is part of the fabric of Jewish life.

Likewise, the deep significance of the moon and sun for the Jewish calendar and holidays is celebrated liturgically in a number of different ways. The new moon is considered a momentous event and announced in the synagogue on the Shabbat before its appearance, together with a prayer for life and health. Rosh Chodesh, the day of the new moon and thus "the head of the month," is a minor holiday, with a special *musaf,* additional service, and other observances. The moon is the focus of the *Kiddush Halevana* prayer, said outdoors, any night the waxing moon is visible, between the third and fifteenth of every month. The sun, too, has its own blessing, *Birkat Hachama,* said a little less frequently, only once every twenty-eight years, on April 8 (because it is based on an exclusively solar cycle). The next blessing of the sun will be in 2009.

There are other aspects of "nature" that we would hardly class as sublime, but they merit their own blessings and liturgy, expanding all that we stop to appreciate. A different part of the morning service, said upon arising and whenever one goes to the bathroom, is essentially a psalm of the plumbing, that is, being grateful that all our internal machinery works:

> Praised are You, YHVH, our God, Ruler of the universe, who fashioned the human body in wisdom, and created in it all kinds of openings and tissues. It is revealed and known that if one of them opens or closes [when it is not supposed to] it would be impossible to exist and stand before You. Praised are You, YHVH, healer of all flesh, who acts wondrously.

The blessings for eating and drinking and other acts from which we derive benefit are a different form of liturgy known as *Birkot Hanehenin*, "the blessings of enjoyment." As opposed to other forms of benedictions, which are to be recited at prescribed times, either during a prayer service or before the performance of a mitzvah, these *berachot* are essentially a set form for spontaneous reactions of wonder and thanksgiving for experiences of various aspects of nature. The best known of these *berachot* are the blessings before and after eating, including the Motzi, the blessing said when eating bread and an entire meal, and the *Birkat Hamazon*, the grace after meals. These not only express appreciation for the earth's/God's bounty, but they are also a formal act of gaining permission to consume that bounty, which is not automatically ours.

The idea, based on Deuteronomy 8:7–10, is that food grown on God's land requires actual transfer of ownership: "It is forbidden to enjoy anything of this world without a *beracha*, and whoever does so commits sacrilege *(ma'al)*" (Talmud, *Berachot* 35a). Contrast this with liberal theories of property rights, which view resources and raw materials as ownerless objects that we appropriate through labor, with relatively few limitations.

Traditionally, one says a blessing before eating anything, from a sip of water to a seven-course meal. These blessings make interesting and important distinctions between breads, grains, and types of fruits and vegetables, showing a sophisticated and intricate relationship with the earth and its produce. The Rabbis distinguished between fruits of the ground (vegetables) and of trees, between species grown in the Land of Israel and other foods, all of which serve to give us an opportunity to deepen our awareness of what we are eating and where it came from.

Perhaps less well known are other *berachot* that are recited on a whole host of occasions. There are separate *berachot* for smelling different aromatic things: spices, trees, herbs, fruit, and oils. Upon seeing lightning, shooting stars, deserts, mountains, or even a sunrise, we praise God, who is still "doing the work [or deeds] of Creation." A different blessing for hearing thunder speaks of God's "power and might which fill the world." Upon seeing a rainbow, we praise God for remembering the covenant and keeping the divine promises to us. There is even an amazing *beracha* for seeing a deformed creature, expressing appreciation for God creating diversity in the world. Similarly, there are *berachot* for good news (for God's beneficence) and for bad (acknowledging "the true judge"), and for seeing heads of states and great scholars (Jewish and non-Jewish).

There is another *beracha* that is to be recited at the sight of beautiful creatures and trees: *Barukh shekakhah lo be'olamo*— "Blessed is the One whose world is thus." This includes beautiful creatures of all sorts: people (non-Jews, even idolators, as well as Jews) and all sorts of beasts. In J. T. *Berachot* 13b and c, it is related of Rabban Gamliel that he recited this blessing upon seeing a beautiful Roman woman, no less one of God's handiworks.

As Midrash *Tanhuma* says, a person who does not feel and express this appreciation is considered dead, "for he sees the sun shining and does not bless 'the Creator of light'; he sees the sun setting and does not bless God 'who brings on the evening'; he eats and drinks and offers no blessings" (*Tanchuma Beracha* 7). All in all, while observance is no guarantee for being observant, it becomes more than a good idea to stop and smell the flowers. Like sleeping outdoors on Sukkot, it's a mitzvah.

Ironically, it may be precisely the calendar and the holidays, whose very structure is deeply rooted in the seasons and the natural world, that has contributed to a certain Jewish alienation from nature throughout history. The seasons, the harvests, and the rain for which we fervently hope are connected to a particular place, the Land of Israel. Thus, to pray for rain when there's snow on the ground, or to celebrate the harvest festival with semitropical fruits from halfway around the world, may connect you to nature in a faroff place, but it simultaneously distances you from the local environment and the natural world that is right outside the window. It is to this central question of the nexus of Judaism and environmentalism, the connection to the Land and the possibilities of a Jewish sense of place, that we now turn.

6

The Land of Israel and a Jewish Sense of Place

Over the last thousand-plus years, Judaism has largely developed in relation to and under the influence of the dominant religious cultures of Christianity and Islam. While there are, of course, many commonalities and points of contact among the three "faiths," we often mistakenly think of Judaism in categories and terms of reference taken from those traditions. For instance, the labeling of Judaism as a "faith," or even a "religious culture," as opposed to, say, a civilization or an ethnic-national group, is a partial view imposed from without, not a comprehensive frame native to Jewish experience.

In exploring the fruitful encounter between environmentalism and Jewish sources and practices, we have seen some of the unique contributions of Jewish teachings, some of which have no relevance to the idea of religion, theology, or religious faith as commonly understood. Specific regulations regarding land use and urban planning, or the proper treatment of hazardous waste, fall into different modern disciplines than what we are used to thinking of as connected to synagogue and church. But these, too, are "Judaism."

The very name "Judaism" (from the Latin *Judaismus*) seems to suggest some sort of ideology, like capitalism and communism, not a cultural or national identity. It is a Western-Christian epithet, not unlike Mohammedanism, so different from the term Muslims use, Islam. The equivalent Hebrew term *Yahadut* is simply the abstract nominal form of *Yehudi*, a Jew, literally, a descendant of the tribe of *Yehudah*, Judah. The identity is, at its root, not only historical but also tribal.[1]

If "Judaism" is a foreign appellation for what Jews are, do, and believe, what would the native "Jewish" term be? One leading candidate is simply "Torah," the all-encompassing synthesis of law, narrative, and history of God, the world, and Israel. Torah, though, or *Torat Yisrael*, while encompassing quite a bit, does not do the whole job. The term *Am Yisrael*, the nation, people, or even peoplehood of Israel, is no less central a component of a full Jewish identity. Although certain movements or groups have tried to minimize the importance of this idea over the years, it is difficult to imagine a Judaism that negates the mutual responsibility of *klal Yisrael* (the "entirety," or public, of Israel), the sense of common history and shared destiny, as well as other defining features such as unique Jewish languages like Hebrew, Yiddish, and Ladino.

Beyond *Torat Yisrael* and *Am Yisrael*, what sets us off from the other major Western religions is *Eretz Yisrael*, the Land of Israel, and our tenacious connection to it. While there are holy sites and cities in Christian and Muslim traditions, those are transnational, globalizing religious cultures, and neither has one distinct homeland. Ideally, the whole world would become the *dar essalaam*, the realm of peace where Islam holds sway, or the Kingdom of Christ. Their global reach is the result of their active desire to bring their truths to all humanity, and remake the world in the process.

Confusion arises, perhaps, because Jews, too, have achieved global distribution. There are historic Jewish communities, *"mi-Hodu ve'ad Kush,"* from India to Ethiopia (as in Achashverosh's mythic kingdom in the story of Esther), including the Maghreb and the Hijaz, as well as Europe, the Americas, and every other corner of the globe where Western societies have expanded and settled. But in our case, it has been more a fate imposed upon us, a Sisyphean search for safe haven, than a condition actively sought out.

The Land was always present, central to traditional Jewish consciousness, evident in religious observances such as holidays and liturgy, and in a whole class of *mitzvot* that are applicable only in the Land (such as tithes on produce and the entire *shmitah* year). Historically, however, this was more of a spiritual, even "virtual" presence, because the Land was no more than an imagined object of desire and could hardly be a focus of daily care or real responsibility.

Relating seriously to the centrality of the Land in Judaism from an environmental perspective generates our central question here: can we understand Judaism as a *place-based* culture? This may sound surprising or even absurd to some: can the Jewish people, the People of the Book, who have made wandering a veritable art form, be a civilization indigenous to a land and its conditions?

In our generation, the Land has been transformed from a virtual reality into a very concrete one. Israel is no longer a dreamed-of abstraction, but a flesh-and-blood country, with factories, parks, sewage, roads, wildlife, and millions of people—Jews and non-Jews—who call it home. Beyond the political and other issues relevant to the connection of Jews wherever they may be to their own countries and to the State of Israel, the question of the environmental relationship of Jews to land, and of Jews to the Land, is a relatively new one. What does it mean to relate to the important environmental concepts of sense of place and responsibility for one's place as Jews, and specifically, as Jews living comfortably, and apparently permanently, in many places all over the world? And what does that mean regarding our relationship to the Land and to the State of Israel?

Bein Adam *"LaMakom"* — On the Importance of Place

The central environmental emphasis on place, on what might be termed a "localist" approach, requires some justification. Many of the high-profile environmental issues we read about are global: climate change, species extinction, the ozone layer, and rain-forests. Likewise, much environmental work in the world is of a global nature: international treaties, worldwide NGOs such as Greenpeace and the WWF, and broad campaigns around big issues. Moreover, these are not only international developments, for many large national organizations, especially in the United States, function in the same large-scale, top-down way.

Yet this is only one type of environmentalism. These same big issues are often hard to connect to on a personal level, because they are distant from our daily lives. Global issues are often felt to be "somewhere on the other side of the world" problems, and global solutions tend to be technocratic, "one-size-fits-all" obligations in a world of almost unimaginable cultural and ecological difference and variety.

Just as the human race is made up of peoples, languages, and cultures, the world too is not one seamless, undifferentiated whole. It is made up of different locales, terrains, climates, and ecosystems. To ignore or try to erase the differences among peoples is fascist, and it risks the tragic loss of the rich diversity of our species that is at the heart of what it means to be human. Places, too, have identities. Different environments have different qualities and characteristics, and therefore possess different possibilities and needs. Although there are problems of global proportions, there are no solutions that are equally valid at all times for all cultures and places.

Opposite the top-down, policy-driven, national and international initiatives stands the local approach,[2] which claims that environmentalism should be about taking care of places, "reinhabiting" one's locale, including local empowerment, strengthening grassroots participatory democracy, and addressing the central questions of personal values and lifestyles. Here, leading issues are about people and communities, such as urban environments, including transportation, planning, and health, and formulating local policies that are geared to the particularities of place. The connection to place, and the responsibility for it, becomes key on the activist, organizing level and in the personal, emotional, and even spiritual realm.

For most of us, meaningful and effective environmental sensitivity doesn't spring from a vague feeling of identification with the entire planet. People connect with places, with landscapes and surroundings they grow to love and care for. While we like to think of "spaceship Earth" as our home, it is really more a collection of homes, each of which needs to be cared for in varying ways.

In general, modern technological "advances" are no replacement for the cultures of indigenous peoples and the ways of life they have developed and led for hundreds and thousands of years in particular locales.[3] This is precisely the value of indigenous cultures, and the tragedy of their decimation with the onslaught of modernity. Scientific universal "solutions" to land use or other issues of production and consumption are an ill fit at best, and positively disastrous at worst, compared with native wisdom and methods, which all too often are decried as woefully primitive.

Deeply rooted local environmentalism begins with the knowledge and caring that can only come from that natural sense of place, including the technical knowledge and familiarity with the ecology of one's "bio-region," as well as a spiritual connection and sense of belonging, which informs a cultural language and perspective that shapes and is shaped by that place.

Such relationships are possible in serene spots around the globe, where people can peacefully tend homes and lands inherited from ancestors, and local populations can rally around common causes with unchallenged, broad-based consensus. But in other conflict-ridden areas, controversy more than consensus informs everything connected to land and its status as a political, cultural, and economic possession. Likewise, the conflict raises a host of questions for Jews inside and outside of Israel, which makes the notion of a Jewish sense of place more complex. Given the political tensions surrounding Zionism, Israel, and the Palestinians, which focus so much on the issue of land, many Jews are increasingly uncomfortable with Jewish particularism in the face of cosmopolitan (post-)modernity, and in particular the seemingly "primitive" idea of choosing to retain and promote ties to a certain piece of territory in one corner of the world.

Like Maimonides, who claimed that the much-mourned destruction of the Temple enabled Jewish worship to evolve into a higher spiritual plane of verbal prayer as opposed to the animal slaughter necessitated by the sacrificial cult, some nineteenth- and twentieth-century Jewish thinkers and movements made a spiritual and social virtue of cosmopolitanism, out of the historical necessity of exile and landlessness. In Jewish views as diverse as the socialist-internationalist Bund, the religious philosopher Franz Rosenzweig, and the secular literary critic George Steiner, the spiritual sophistication of the Jewish people was seen to be embodied precisely in our ability to dispense with a homeland of soil and borders, and to live in the world at large, or in the text,[4] according to religious or social values.

Some of these earlier approaches are distinct products of the ideologies of the nineteenth century, whose promise of a brave new world and brotherhood of humanity proved later to be tragically illusory. But many who sympathize now with a deterritorialization of the Jewish people are working from a very different paradigm. In the shrinking globalized world of instantaneous telecommunications, and the breakdown of the simplex model of the nation-state, with the growing reality of decentralized or multicultural political confederations, dispensing with "blood and soil" ideologies seems to be the height of enlightenment, if only because they require so much blood in the equation.

The values of rootedness and territoriality are somewhat out of fashion in social thought, because they are seen as reactionary and irredentist, and are part of a range of problems and very few solutions. For environmentalists, however, belonging, in spatial as well as social terms, is the source of responsibility and caring, and therefore can be the basis for progressive activism as well. As social geographer David Harvey writes:

> Territorial place-based identity, particularly when conflated with race, gender, religious, and class differentiation, is one of the most pervasive bases for both progressive political mobilization and reactionary exclusionary politics.[5]

The progressive possibilities provide the starting point for the rest of this chapter, which seeks to explore the idea of Jewish sense of place and "indigeneity" and its implications for Jewish life and environmental values.

On Wandering and Return: The Jew as Native

Some years ago, I participated in a conference at Harvard University on "Judaism and the Natural Environment." Once there, I learned that the conference was one in a series on different religious traditions and the environment. Besides the usual faith traditions that one might expect (Christianity, Islam, Buddhism, etc.), there was a separate conference for indigenous peoples. So, in addition to trying to figure out who got invitations to that one and why (i.e., who are indigenous peoples and what do they have in common?), I had my own gut reaction, which was, "Hey, I want to be—I should be—with those guys!"

My reactions at that conference stemmed from the same feeling that led me to pack up and move to Israel from the United States twenty-plus years ago. My involvement with Zionism, love of Hebrew and Israeli folk culture, and eventually my *aliyah* to a small pioneering kibbutz in the Arava wilderness, was a personal attempt at "reindigenization." That is, having grown up in a typical American suburb, and not feeling "native" there, or connected to anywhere in particular, I wanted to try to root myself in a place that "made sense" for me as a Jew, that was not simply the luck of the migratory draw.

For two thousand years, we Jews have insistently, almost pathologically, prevented ourselves from developing a deep connection to any other spot on the globe—though we have sojourned in most of them. My own personal biography is quite "traditional" in this regard: over the course of my family's past five generations, no one raised children in the same place where he or she had been raised, and most not even in the same country. Each generation had its own reasons for its peregrinations, but the chances are slim that this "tradition" will end with mine.

To put it another way, those nineteenth- and twentieth-century world views, which encouraged universalism and cosmopolitanism (religious or not), connected to an ethos of wandering that is deeply ingrained in Judaism. One could begin with a section of the biblical Book of Numbers and continue it to this very day:

These are the journeys of the children of Israel who went out of the land of Egypt ... From Rameses to Succoth, and from Succoth to Etham and from Mithkah to Hashmonah ... from Lisbon to Livorno ... and from Marrakesh to Marseilles and Montreal ... from Grodno to Brooklyn ... from Brooklyn to Miami Beach ... and from San'a to Jaffa to Los Angeles.

The tradition itself seems to have internalized a wanderer's consciousness: of the five books of the Torah, three and a half take place during that desert displacement. As far as the yearly readings go, no sooner do we arrive at the edge of the Land of Israel at the close of Deuteronomy than the cycle ends, sending us back to the beginning, to Eden with its own exile and resultant eternal wandering. Liturgically speaking, we never enter the Promised Land. An *aliyah,* being called to the reading of the Torah, is an "ascent" only to the text, and is something one *receives,* not something one *does,* as in a physical move to the homeland. Indeed, the text itself, to use Heinrich Heine's apt phrase, became our "portable homeland."

Although Jewish mobility, including the centrality of the text as the ground for Jewish identity, has been an amazing survival strategy that has served us well over the millennia, it is also at the heart of an endemic alienation from the natural world that grew with the lengthening exile. What is striking today is that our rootlessness, although it has its own roots in ancient times, is something very modern. What has historically been the lot of the Jew, for theological reasons, is true of contemporary denizens of the global village everywhere, for sociological ones. The professional ideal for many is the urban nomad, in pursuit of career equivalents of good grazing land. The average American moves ten times during his or her life. The Jewish situation is now fashionable, and therefore that much more attractive, for Jews themselves.

And the state of the environment shows this. Whatever the implications of wandering (mobility) for the Jew (citizen), it can't be good for the physical world. Without a sense of place and a generations-long, rooted connection to a piece of land, real caring and environmental awareness are partial at best. Rootlessness is clearly part of the problem.

Jewish tradition, though, insists on maintaining some sort of consciousness of wanderer: one can assimilate not only in language, dress, and customs, but also in terms of one's sense of place in an environment. Setting down deep collective roots in other lands and landscapes is fraught with peril. This point is developed eloquently by the poet Chayim Nachman Bialik in the form of a "commentary" on the teaching from *Pirkei Avot* about the mortal sin involved in breaking off one's studies to appreciate nature. Bialik wrote the following in his seminal essay *"Halacha and Aggada,"*[6] attributing the idea to Zionist philosopher Ahad Ha'am:

> It is not without significance that the people of Israel, or at least the great majority of them, submitted to the iron yoke of Halachah, and not only that, but actually chose to carry with them into exile a heavy load of laws and ordinances.... And here is what the Halachist himself says: "If a man studies as he walks, and breaks off his study to say 'How lovely is this tree! How lovely is this field!'—Scripture regards him as guilty of deadly sin." Our aestheticists have spent all their ammunition on this unfortunate mishnah: but even here the sympathetic ear will detect, between the lines, the apprehension, the trembling anxiety for the future, of a wandering people which has nothing to call its own but a Book, and for which any attachment of its soul to one of the lands of sojourn means mortal danger.

As long as the Jews were in lands other than their own, connected not to a real homeland but primarily to that "portable homeland," then, yes, rejecting the eternal spiritual inheritance for the sake of a tenuous connection with "one of the lands of their sojourn" is potentially spiritual suicide. According to Bialik, this mishnah is not talking about all of nature—only Diaspora nature. Only that sort of diversion presents a spiritual threat, the implication being that once the Jews return to their land, a new balance can be struck between Torah and *teva* (nature), Creation and Revelation, that can validate both sides of the equation. The

Land—a metonym of all of Creation, but also the special portion of the Jewish people—would take its place alongside the Book as a ground for identity and meaning.

This reconnection resolves other "environmental" dilemmas of Diaspora life. For it is precisely those elements of Jewish religion and culture, which in the Land of Israel express and perpetuate the physical rootedness in land and landscape, that in the Diaspora became highly spiritualized and symbolic. Though calendar, liturgy, and language all bespeak a deep connection to Creation, for Jews outside the Land, this is an abstract connection to a faraway piece of Creation. The extreme example is, of course, south of the equator, where much of Jewish observance borders on absurdity—celebrating the rejuvenating arrival of spring at Pesach while hunkering down at the beginning of autumn or celebrating the winter festival of lights and their renewal under the blazing summer sun.

The North American reality, however, may be different from all other Diasporas, because it includes both the general political situation of integration in a pluralist society and a feeling of truly being at home in the country. To top it off, the new creation of Jewish environmentalism is largely a product of North American Judaism. Indeed, it has been proponents of American "eco-Judaism" that I have chided (only half-jokingly) with the observation that if New England Jews, say, were to put their metaphorical money where there environmental mouths are, they should be celebrating the autumn harvest by marching around the synagogues with native pumpkins and cornstalks, rather than the distinctly subtropical Mediterranean citron and palm fronds, flown in from halfway around the world!

This usually arouses a chuckle, but the question behind it is serious: Jews in history have never significantly adapted calendar or liturgy to reflect local natural reality, or reinterpreted the commandments specific to caring for the Land of Israel *(hamitzvot ha'tluyot ba'aretz)* to apply elsewhere. Should we do so now, in light of rising environmental consciousness and a desire to ground this awareness Jewishly?

The most eloquent response to this challenge came from my friend and colleague Rabbi Bradley Shavit Artson, now dean of the rabbinical school at the University of Judaism:

> All Jews must have a sense of Jewish "bio-regionalism" for Israel and for where they live. I know that my love for California feels a lot like my feelings for the Land of Israel— I feel at home here, that it is my land, in a deeper way than I do anywhere else. The plants, the animals, the seasons— these are mine in more than just the happenstance of birth.
>
> It's striking that the kabbalists discovered the idea of Galut [exile] when they were banished from Spain, and they wrote songs of longing from Israel for their lost homelands. Jews provide an ecological model in their ability to make sanctity portable and to take it anywhere, in their ability to plant roots of loyalty and love over the long term anywhere they have lived. The truth is that I don't feel myself in a cosmic state of Galut, and if I lived in Israel (an attractive idea) I'd feel exiled from California, just as here I miss Jerusalem. Maybe that sense of partial exile is itself a religious environmental value: the world isn't whole, no matter where we live, and we need to work to reestablish Eden anywhere we are.[7]

The image of portable sanctity is compelling. Although it has become well-nigh impossible to imagine the Jewish world without the State of Israel, it is equally difficult to picture that same world without the Diaspora. And this is true for the two sides of the environmental coin as well. The ideal model isn't "rooted identity" *or* "portable sanctity"—it is both, in varying combinations, relations, and dosages in different places and periods. With their respective advantages and disadvantages, they each have something to gain from and something to give to the other. The current structure of the Jewish world should, at best, foster a dynamic dialogic equilibrium between them, because either by itself would be skewed and inadequate.

Perhaps the whole dynamic of wandering and return needs to be reevaluated. They are not linear arrangements of temporary or final unchanging historical states, but rather an ongoing dialectic, a *ratzo veshov,* a "back and forth," a continual ebb and flow that is as much existential and personal as it is historical.

The entire structure of the biblical narrative seems to bear this out—beginning with Adam and Eve, the expulsion from the Garden, and their son Cain, the wanderer, and continuing with the builders of the Tower of Babel and their dispersal, through Abram, who, immediately after receiving the command of *lech lecha* and fulfilling it, leaves the Promised Land for Egypt, a harbinger of what is soon to come. Then Jacob (not without much personal wandering of his own) follows his sons down to slavery in Egypt, only to be redeemed by Moses with the Exodus, leading to the climactic ending of the Torah on the brink of the first national "going home," the (re-)entry into the Promised Land. The Book of Joshua begins with that entry, only to focus later on the impending threat of destruction, followed by the consolation of the possibility of return. The entire Bible ends with the words of the Persian king Cyrus to the remnant of Judah: "Any of you of all his people, the lord his God be with him and let him go up." The last word of scripture is *va'ya'al,* "go up," emigrate to the Land of Israel—make *aliyah* (again, ending before the fulfillment of that promise!). The universalist, pre-Abrahamic motif of exile, wandering, and return subsequently becomes refracted through the prism of Israel's national consciousness, and acquires uniquely Jewish trappings and expressions, which continue down through post-biblical, rabbinic, medieval, and modern times.

Thus the emphasis on the Jewish connection to land and place that I have developed here is not meant to negate other dimensions of the Jewish environmental discussion. The bulk of this book is devoted to general Jewish environmental views and values, and explicates texts and practices that are relevant to all Jews everywhere. Those inspirational teachings and practices are all part of what I would term Judaism's *universal spiritual language* regarding environmental ethics and sensitivity, applicable with no regard—but therefore also no real connection—to locale. They are portable and accessible everywhere, which is their great strength and potential.

But that is not the entire picture, for in addition to this amazing universal spiritual language are components of the tradition that are elements of a *local indigenous culture.* Judaism has the potential, even more than the universal traditions of Islam and Christianity in this regard, to provide a model for deep spiritual ecological living in a set place.

It is a commonplace that Zionism means the modern return of the Jewish people to the Land of Israel. Until now, that statement has generally been thought of in socio-political or historical terms. As I have claimed here, though, the return of a people to a land and the reconnection to that place is an *environmental* claim: Zionism is a Jewish "back-to-the-land" movement. For the first time in two thousand years, the Jewish people—whether we like it or not— have assumed responsibility for a piece of Creation. To put it another way, for most of the history of Halacha, the *peshat* (contextual meaning) of *bal tashchit,* about protecting fruit trees in times of war, was a memory or a metaphor or simply theoretical. Now Jews are fighting real wars, and there are real fruit trees that can be cut down or not. There are also the environmental issues of sewage, hazardous waste, and land-use planning, and though there are some successes, the country and citizens of Israel often fail in fulfilling values such as those discussed here. How well we have discharged the responsibility to our little piece of Creation, and the complexities of the actual Zionist relationship to the environment, will be the topic of the next section.

The Cultural Contradictions of Israeli Environmentalism

From the foregoing paean to Jewish indigeneity and place-based environmental fervor, one would assume that Zionism would have been the "greenest" thing to hit the Middle East. There were, indeed, "environmental" strains to classical Zionist thought and practice, but there were other more modernizing and development-oriented ones as well. One look around the country reveals this complexity. As Israeli activist and environmental chronicler Alon Tal wrote in 2000:

> Naomi Shemer's 1967 song "Jerusalem of Gold" spoke of "mountain air as pure as wine." Today, a thick haze hovers over the Holy City. Scientists predict that Jerusalem's air will soon be as polluted as that of Mexico City.
>
> Zionist farmers have made the desert bloom, and Israel has become an exporter of world-class produce. Yet pesticides now contaminate ground water, taking a serious toll on the health of both wildlife and Israeli farmers.
>
> The State of Israel has enabled the ingathering of millions of Jewish exiles. Yet urban sprawl threatens to pave over much of the promised "land of milk and honey." And when the bridge over the Yarkon River collapsed during the 1997 Maccabiah Games, one athlete drowned—and three died of toxic poisoning.[8]

One could go on: Although Israel is a world leader in solar-energy research and even products, relatively little is implemented, leaving the Israeli economy as oil dependent as ever. Forestation efforts throughout the last century were an example for the world over, yet the aggressive planting practices and predominantly pine forests have had untoward ecological consequences. The pre- and early-State Egged bus service was legendary, and though certain progress has been made in the development of intercity rail service (and one hopes urban light rail as well), Israeli transport policy is unsustainable, allowing a growing dependence on private cars, translating both into air pollution and suburbanization, with all their attendant problems.

Any criticism expressed here is not directed at the tough decisions taken before the founding of the State or in its early years, where the demands of mere survival—laying the foundations of the State, absorbing massive immigration, creating development, establishing security, and other needs—would have challenged the most environmentally sensitive policymakers. But today is a different story.

Although many of Israel's challenges are identical to the threats faced by other countries that have undergone industrialization and urbanization, few nations have sustained such intense economic and population growth in the space of barely a half-century as Israel has. For instance, in the second half of the twentieth century (1950–1999), the world's population grew by a factor of 2.4, from 2.5 billion to 6 billion, while the world GNP (economic production) grew six-fold. In contrast, Israel's population grew four and a half times, from 1.4 to 6.2 million, and Israeli economic activity grew by a whopping factor of twenty-three.

Some of Israel's challenges on this score are a reflection of her unique cultural and political history. Both loving the Land as it is and desiring to change it drastically are Zionist ideals. The popular "Song of the Homeland" *("Shir Lamoledet")* by national poet Natan Alterman, written in the 1930s, famously includes the lines:

We shall build you, beloved country ... and beautify you ...

We shall clothe you in a robe of concrete and cement, and spread out carpets of gardens before you ...

We love you, O Homeland, in battle, in song, and in labor."

Although that catchy refrain of cloaking the land "in a robe of concrete and cement" has become the bugaboo of Israeli environmentalists, it is important to note that the very next words speak of gardens and greenery. The building and the planting were not contradictory, but part of one grand vision of development.

That is one reason why the relationships among environmentalism, cultural values, and social policy in Israel is so complex. The landscape itself is politicized in all sorts of ways. As social critic Yaron Ezrahi writes in his trenchant study of Israeli society, *Rubber Bullets:*

> In this perhaps most contested of all lands—where the three religions have focused their prophesies of destruction and redemption; where the mountains dripping with wine are a blessing and dry land a divine curse; where the heavens declare the glory of God; where temples have been built on the ruins of other temples—in this land, the escape into nature is invariably a political act which denies the existence of one category of human beings while affirming the existence of another, which places one people in nature and another in history. In Israel ... where the earth is but a buffer between past and present, where nature is younger than history, no landscape is a retreat from society, and any scenery is but politics in disguise.[9]

Politics, perhaps, but of what sort? Often it seems that nature and open-space protection embody a *critique* of Zionism and its dominant ethos of modernization and development. When green activists from the SPNI (Society for the Protection of Nature in Israel) and others protest government plans to establish new settlements on the Gilboa, or Jewish ranchers homesteading in the Negev, or the Trans-Israel superhighway, they are often criticized by their opponents as putting nature above the national interest, and are branded as "anti-Zionist."

In contrast to this polemic stance, environmental activities are also seen as Zionist in their own right. Of the SPNI, Alon Tal writes: "(A)lthough political leaders have found some of their demands annoying, they could not help but admire the young idealists as representing the best of the Zionist dream."[10] As mentioned earlier, a love of the Land that would translate into preservation, building both on the growing academic discipline of ecology and on the romantic strains of Zionist thought, such as A. D. Gordon's Tolstoyan call for a spiritual return to nature, also has its cultural legitimacy.

Anthropologist Orit Ben-David emphasizes the idea that conquest and preservation are, in fact, two sides of the same Zionist coin:

> An interesting symbolic shift has taken place in the course of Israeli history, from a struggle against nature to a struggle for protecting nature. At the beginning of the [twentieth] century, while the Israeli pioneers sought to attain recognition for the Zionist enterprise, they waged a struggle against nature.... their fight against nature strengthened their right to ownership, because they expropriated the land from nature, and brought it into the "social" realm.... After the creation of the State of Israel ... the idea of protecting nature emerged. This idea is actually the same thing in a new form. The first conquest was to change nature, the second to preserve it.[11]

It is important to note that these ideological tugs of war are occurring against the background of Israel as a veritable ecological wonderland. And I don't just mean in an aesthetic sense, though Israel of course contains many places of breathtaking beauty. The wonder comes from the sheer quantity of biodiversity in such a small place. Israel measures roughly 20,000 square kilometers (about the size of New Jersey), and yet includes 2,600 plant species (130 endemic ones) and almost 700 vertebrates, including 454 bird species. That's with the arid Negev Desert comprising more than half of the landmass. Compare this to California, lush and rich by all accounts, where only 2,325 plant species exist in its 630,500 square kilometers. All of this prompted Herbert Samuel, the first commissioner of the British Mandate, to praise "the diversity of a continent within the area of a province."[12]

To what can such world-class natural wealth be attributed? To the same reasons Canaan/Israel/Palestine has been so fought over throughout history. At the meeting point of Europe, Asia, and Africa, Israel is a crossroads and a unique biological juncture: it is the southern boundary of northern regions, the northern extremity of southern climes, and the western end of eastern habitats. Add to this the tens of millions of migratory birds that pass over each year, on their way from Europe to Africa and back, and Israel has indeed a richness of flora and fauna of international proportions.

What we would see today as incomparable ecological wealth, however, was seen in the latter years of the nineteenth century by European Jewish immigrants, striving to make lives for themselves in a social and natural environment that was often less than hospitable, as another feature of the *desolation* of the land. Wild beasts (such as bears and alligators—since hunted to extinction) had taken over because humans had not conquered and developed. This idea that the land was "desolate" (in Hebrew, *shomem* or *sh'mamah*), taken as dogma in Zionist historiography, turns out to be not so straightforward. "Desolation" is more of a psychological category than an ecological one.

Geographer Izhak Schnell has written of the several reasons why the land was perceived as desolate by the Jews coming there.[13] First, there are the biblical prophesies of divine retribution and devastation (such as in Lev. 26), which gave Jews a mental image and *expectation* to find the land desolate after being "abandoned" (by them) for two thousand years of exile. Second, immigrants from Europe also came with expectations based on European *images* of nature, which were not fulfilled in a countryside of Mediterranean scrub and maquis.[14] Finally, the self-declared mission of building Jewish bodies and spirits *needed* an environment that also required development and improvement. Through redemptive pioneering efforts, the Land could be returned to its former glory, flowing with milk and honey, just as those same efforts would transform (re-create) the Jews as a native sovereign people. As the popular song has it: *Anu banu artza livnot u'lehibanot bah,* "We came to the Land to build it, and to be rebuilt by it."

However, relegating the evaluation of late nineteenth- and early-twentieth-century Palestine as desolate to subjective expectations, assumptions, images, and needs, powerful though they are, is too facile. Significant deforestation had occurred since Crusader times and under the Ottomans, especially as a result of the war effort during World War I. Economic and real estate conditions in the late Ottoman Empire led to marginal (i.e., un- or under-developed) land, and whether desolate or not, it was certainly economically unproductive in the Western terms the immigrants employed.[15] Furthermore, on the eve of what was to become intensified modernization, population density was low,[16] and agriculture and other technologies were different from those in Europe, easily lending themselves to characterizations of desolation by those predisposed to do so.

Obviously, this is a sensitive point in the often polemical historiographies of Zionist and Palestinian researchers. It is entirely beside the point to try to ascertain whether Palestine as a whole, or any given part, was or was not "desolate." The same scene could be described either as squalid, primitive, subsistence peasants scratching out a living from the barren earth or as self-sufficient indigenous farmers using time-honored traditional methods in their pristine and pastoral landscape. These views are important because in the contemporary debates about environmental preservation and restoration, the question always arises about what it is exactly that we are preserving or restoring: What is the ideal? What is a natural, beautiful, healthy landscape?

This brings us back to the question of the tension between environmental perspectives (or narratives) and Zionism. Zionist ideals of development and building the Land, both past an present, are enlisted in all sorts of anti-environmental ways; as we have seen, it is tempting to describe the encounter of "green" with "blue and white" as one of confrontation. But, of course, the simplistic equations "environmentalism = preservation" and "Zionism = development" are highly distorted and misleading on both sides.

In its commitment to "redemption of the land" *(ge'ulat ha'adamah)*, the internal understanding of Zionism manifests a strong *progressive* narrative, a robust belief in improvement and in having served the land well, even as it contributed to the well-being of the Jewish people. Like other narratives, this is an unspoken "commonsense" motif that most people hold without giving it much thought or exposing it to critical analysis. The creation of a Jewish society, according to this view, has been unambiguously good for the land: Jews have taken the land out of its neglected infertility and restored it to its biblical milk-and-honey state. The perception of the land as previously desolate, or at least wildly under-exploited, is a central component of that tenet.

Environmental narratives, on the other hand, are generally not progressive about how things have gotten better, but *declensionist*. Environmental awareness arises in a context of threat or suffering, of degradation, of a deeply felt sense that things are not as they should be, were, or could be. Simply put: things used to be better, and now they're worse. This is potentially very challenging to the basic redemptive narrative of Zionism. An environmental critique that highlights degradation cannot leave Zionism unscathed.

There are, of course, strong and weak versions of an environmental narrative, the weak accepting the basic progressive narrative, and calling for small corrections in order to realize fully the potential of the national ethos. As long as traditional Israeli environmental campaigns were about limiting the excesses of the Zionist zeal for development, and stuck to open-space protection, or cleaning up pollution, the "anti-Zionist" side was limited in its impact. But a more radical contemporary critique is potentially more comprehensive and societal, including a deep mistrust of the technological ethos of progress, the establishment of strong connections between social and environmental justice, and a critique of things like industrial farming, which had been a jewel in the Zionist crown.

Although challenges from cynical politicians and rapacious industrialists are significant for Israeli environmentalists, the deeper, long-term, cultural changes that need to be made are much harder to address. To a great degree, environmental impact is a function of population and consumption levels. Regarding the former, Israel has the "best of both worlds," combining a developing country's high birth rate with massive immigration usually seen more in the developed world, for a sky-high growth rate of upward of 2.5 percent per year. Most Jews see this as a blessing, and population policy—including pro-natalist child allowances and free immigration (for Jews and their relations)—is one of the most sacred of Israeli sacred cows. But given the country's diminutive size, Israel is well on its way to being one of the most densely populated countries in the world (especially if one discounts the sparsely populated Negev).

Rarely have environmentalists tackled this taboo,[17] and one can say that if there are other reasons for allowing or encouraging unchecked population growth, then the looming negative impact needs to be confronted on the level of wasteful consumption and poor planning. But here, too, we have been deeply affected by our American-influenced mind-set—Israelis are loathe to rethink what are seen as the "achievements" on this front in recent years. Combined factors of memories of deprivation from the Holocaust and, on a very different note, the period of austerity following the establishment of the State, make profligate consumption appear to many to be a basic right. Large houses and SUVs are the new status symbols, disposables of all types are ubiquitous, and Israel is being "malled" like the United States and Europe. Advocating for different measures of wealth and happiness, no matter how they are framed, are seen as calls to return to the "bad old days." Politically, environmental concerns are often shunted aside and are not high on anyone's agenda. The left invariably sees social problems as separate from and more pressing than environmental ones, and the right's political love of (the) land rarely translates into more ecological caring. Both sides of center have blind faith in rapid economic growth to solve all problems.

Although these are formidable (though not insurmountable) challenges on the national level, there have been notable successes by large organizations, including the Israel Union for Environmental Defense, the Society for the Protection of Nature in Israel, the Heschel Center, and the increasing prominence of the umbrella organization of Life and Environment, often in close cooperation with the governmental Ministry of the Environment. Together they have formed a coalition for sustainability that has made some inroads, along with help from improved international standards and demands. Real progress has also been made on the local level, including the successes of local green parties and broad-based coalitions for improving the quality of life and dealing with local issues.

Throughout this section on environmentalism in Israel, there has been barely a word about specifically *Jewish* teachings and values. It might be expected that Israel, in its role as the Jewish state, would implement some of the values discussed in this book. Though there are some positive examples (low levels of hunting, for instance, as an expression of a Jewish value), in general the split between religious and secular groups makes it difficult to promote even very progressive social values taken from Jewish tradition, for fear of religious coercion.

On the other side of the divide, Jews more connected to Halacha and classical sources, both the ultra-Orthodox and the Zionist national religious public, are perceived (and also often see themselves) as being distant from environmental concerns for several reasons. First, the public face of green activism is often left-wing or progressive, which is not the dominant tone of these sectors. Second, to the extent that environmental values are seen to oppose development and settlement construction, which is viewed as the ultimate expression of holy work (the mitzvah of *yishuv ha'aretz*), there will not be widespread support for these causes.

But regardless of their reactions to the above issues, Israelis can't ignore wider-reaching environmental concerns, such as rising rates of respiratory illness and cancer, unsafe drinking water, and contaminated beaches. In a conference organized by Life and Environment, then–Chief Rabbi Bakshi Doron said that responsibility for a sane environment lies on the shoulders of the leaders of the community and that rabbis are responsible for awakening the public's awareness of environmental issues. He emphasized that issues of environmental protection fall within *dinei nefashot* (capital crimes) and therefore are of great significance. While mentioning environmental crises such as the pollution of the Kishon River and air pollution in Haifa, Rabbi Doron, referring to the powerful Torah value of public responsibility for a death due to unknown causes, argued that leaders could not say, "Our hands did not shed this blood and our eyes did not see" (Deut. 21:7).

These are powerful words, and hopefully they can reach a wider public. Environmental causes are often seen as sectoral issues, relevant only to certain populations and interest groups. The environment in Israel has the potential to break out of this stereotype, and be of significance to all Israelis and to Jews the world over. It is thus an important point of contact between Diaspora and Israeli Jews, and also for all Israeli citizens, specifically Jews and Arabs, potentially contributing to a redefinition of the complex and difficult relations between these groups, as well as the very idea of citizenship.

Back to Bridge-Building: The Environment as Deep Common Concern

Environmental activism has come a long way since its contemporary inception in the '60s and '70s. But it still battles all sorts of stereotypes and prejudices. For instance, a common objection is that environmentalism is somehow misanthropic, because it pits human needs against those of nature, and sides with the latter. But using the guiding vision of sustainability, we see that humans and nature are essentially on the same side. We can only flourish together.

There have been other objections along the way, namely that there are more important items on our collective agendas. Here, too, the wide purview of environmental concern has become striking, affirming also that we need jobs and economic well-being, because poverty—especially amid increasing wealth for some—is one of the greatest social-environmental threats there is. But our concern for (economic) well-being can't be limited to this generation alone. As the Native American saying has it, "We mustn't rob our grandchildren to feed our children." The basic, central Jewish desire for justice has to include a concern for future generations, and the opportunities and threats we bequeath to them.

One of the big competitors on the level of national priorities, in Israel and now in the United States as well, is security. Security is a life-and-death issue; it's about protecting ourselves and our children from forces that threaten us. Not fulfilling our obligations in this realm can translate into real disaster. But exactly the same can be said about environmental issues. When the Pentagon publishes reports on global warming because it is considered one of the top security threats facing the United States and the world today, as it did in 2005, we are witnessing a reordering of priorities. Likewise, water and access to it in Israel and the region have always had grave geopolitical ramifications, and yet for some reason there has always been a separation between quantity and quality. The "environmental" issue of water pollution, which contaminates aquifers and ground water, and so significantly reduces available resources, rapidly translates into both a security issue in terms of conflict with Palestinians over dwindling sources and a political concern to find solutions to this perennial problem.

On any given issue there may be a variety of possible positions, but the environment is coming into its own as an overarching consensual issue that has the power to unite disparate groups. In the present context of Jews, Israel, and the environment, one axis of great potential is the Diaspora-Israel connection. The other is a bridge between Israeli Jews and Israeli Arabs.

The present generation of Diaspora Jews, who have grown up in the twenty years since the first intifada, has a different connection to Israel than its forebears did. Their grandparents saw the miracle of Israel coming into being, and their parents celebrated the victory of the Six Day War and agonized over the Yom Kippur War. For this generation, however, the existence and significance of the State of Israel is taken for granted. Coupled with increasing international condemnation of the occupation of the territories and other controversies, this makes Israel a tough sell on American college campuses. Trips through Birthright Israel and other travel experiences may make inroads into revitalizing personal relationships with the country for young Diaspora Jews, but many are in need of new and different ways of connecting to Israel.

The environment might be one of the best new/old connections: it is a strongly held general value, which is deeply relevant to Jewish identity and expression, and it plugs into existing values such as connecting to the land, supporting causes with money and time, and seeing real progress in Israeli society. Connecting to the environmental challenges in Israel also means connecting to people of different ages, political viewpoints, and ethnic backgrounds. Environmental involvement suggests the right blend of the universal and the particular. It ties into the personal passions of many who are fighting for the environment both globally and in their home communities, and it allows young Jews to look at Israel and realize that the Land is theirs as well, that they can make a difference there. As Jewish scholar and activist Gil Troy writes: "Love it or hate it, environmental Zionism has an important role to play in revitalizing Zionism. It can remind us that Zionism needs to be modernized and updated, relevant and diverse, electrifying and subversive."[18] Organizations such as JGEN (the Jewish Global Environmental Network) and the Green Zionist Alliance are working to develop these ties, which can make a real contribution in both directions.

The other role that the environment can play is in relations between Jews and Arabs inside Israel. This may be counterintuitive for some, because the environment is as much a bone of contention between these groups as it is a focus of consensus. For various reasons, such as open-space protection and limitations on commercial development that have adversely affected Arab cities and towns, Israeli Arabs have not only been distinctly underrepresented in Israeli environmental groups, but they have also been actively alienated from the environmental movement as a whole.

Changes in the nature of environmental concern, though, have begun to attract more Arabs. Sustainability promotes environmental justice—fighting differential access to resources and increased exposure to threats—as well as community development and local empowerment, which serve the needs of the Arab public in a variety of ways. After the violence of October 2000, when many coexistence projects that flourished in the Oslo years collapsed due to the feelings of a deep breach of trust on both sides, a number of joint environmental initiatives started to grow or were begun. The general feeling behind these undertakings was that, unlike other more superficial ventures that emphasized mutual understanding or cultural exchange, these projects recognized the real inequality and host of grievances that need to be redressed. Israel is an unsustainable society if there is fear, discrimination, and enmity. Animosity, on both sides, pollutes people's lives no less than chemical contaminants.

Although still only beginning, the idea of working together for the common home is a rallying point for some Jewish-Arab coexistence projects, and it even has the potential to redefine the nature of joint citizenship. Citizenship is not just about rights and equal treatment, though those issues are crucial. In a democracy, citizenship also has to include the possibility for the individual to contribute to the common good. When that is impossible or inhibited, alienation grows and collective responsibility wanes.

For better or for worse, the public good in Israel has been defined according to the Jewish narrative of Zionist return and redemption. Pioneering settlement (known as *chalutziyut*), defending the Land and the people through army service, building the

Jewish economy—all these are not accessible to Arab citizens in general. Enter environmentalism, a movement that is actively trying to redefine the nature of the collective good and become a central focal point of civic virtue. The good of the Land demands other struggles now, defending it in a different way, from different threats, and working for development that is sustainable, for all the country's citizens. This can be a new form of Zionism (though it needn't be labeled as such) that is consonant with an internal Jewish agenda and not repugnant to the Israeli-Jewish mainstream. At the same time, it provides a way for increasing numbers of Israeli Arabs who want to create a more neutral common ground and make the country their own.[19]

This is an important message that provides a counterpoint of sorts to the rest of this book. All other chapters have been about strengthening our "story," bringing Jewish values and teachings to bear on contemporary environmental issues, and emphasizing the worth of relating to them as Jews. All that still stands, and it is the first part of Hillel's dictum: *"Im ein ani li, mi li?"* "If I am not for myself, who will be for me?" But now we have the other half: *"Im ani rak le'atzmi, mah ani?"* "If I am only for myself, what am I?"

We can't only delve deeper and deeper into our own sources, losing touch with those around us. Such a strategy only begets intolerance and prevents us from being true to our highest ideals. Unfortunately, ecological awareness, though it should emphasize the interdependence of all beings, is not immune to bigotry or fanaticism, and a Zionist-inspired environmentalism, with its roots in the Land and the landscape, even more so. There are many who recognize that risk and, reasoning that difference is the source of conflict, argue for abandoning all particularity, thinking that we can all be "just human" together.

But even if that were possible, it would hardly be desirable. The world would be a much poorer, stultifyingly uniform place. And we would still be a very particular type of human: secular, twenty-first century, globalized, and English speaking, stripped of traditions and the wisdom of the ages in confronting new but ageless challenges. Nobody should feel the need to negate or erase his or her own identity and particularity, and the resulting diversity of thought and opinion can only enrich ourselves and our world. We need to strengthen our own story and deepen the wellsprings of our own distinctiveness, even as we open ourselves up to others and their unique contributions and perspectives.

Where to Go from Here: Suggestions for Further Study

"Global warming isn't about carbon emissions; it's about intergenerational equity," remarked Paul Gorman of the National Religious Partnership for the Environment, continuing, "therefore choose life, that you *and your children* may live" (Deut. 30:19). To the long list of values and commitments that define the ideal Jew, we need to add being environmentally aware and active—for our own and our children's sakes, and for the sake of the *olam* (world) desperately in need of *tikkun*.

But on a deeper plane, the environment is not an issue to be added to our already overburdened catalog of causes; it is a perspective, a world view. This book has attempted to sketch both an environmental interpretation of Judaism and a Jewish approach to environmentalism. There is much more to be said: more about Kabbalah and Jewish mystical teachings that are becoming increasingly mainstream, particular denominational views, feminist perspectives and connections, and specific issues that fit into the whole of a new sustainable Judaism.

There is also more that you can *do* yourself. There has been enormous creative initiative in Jewish environmental groups, but there is still potential to be fulfilled: greening your synagogue, setting up a study group on sources mentioned in this book (and below), changing personal and family lifestyles, connecting to organizations at home and in Israel that engage these issues, and more. See the websites listed below for more about how to connect.

This book was not written in a vacuum; it was influenced by and relies upon a gratifyingly growing list of works in this area. Beyond the specific books and authors listed below, the reader is referred to writings of the following thinkers and activists who, together with friends and colleagues listed in the acknowledgments, have had a huge influence on my environmental thinking: Wendell Berry, J. Baird Callicott, Rachel Carson, William Cronon, Rene Dubos, David Ehrenfeld, Abraham Joshua Heschel, Barry Lopez, Bill McKibbon, Gary Paul Nabhan, Bryan Norton, David Orr, and E. F. Schumacher.

The resources below are relevant to the environment and religion in general, and Judaism in particular.

Books

Abram, David. *The Spell of the Sensuous: Perception and Language in a More-Than-Human World.* New York: Pantheon, 1996.

Bernstein, Ellen, ed. *Ecology and the Jewish Spirit: Where Nature and the Sacred Meet.* Woodstock, Vt.: Jewish Lights Publishing, 1998.

Eisenberg, Evan. *The Ecology of Eden.* New York: Knopf, 1998.

Elon, Ari, Naomi Hyman, and Arthur Waskow, eds. *Trees, Earth, and Torah: A Tu B'Shvat Anthology.* New York: Jewish Publication Society, 1999.

Gottlieb, Roger, ed. *This Sacred Earth: Religion, Nature, Environment.* New York: Routledge, 1996.

Kellert, Stephen, and Timothy Farnham, eds. *The Good in Nature and Humanity: Connecting Science, Religion, and Spirituality with the Natural World.* Washington, D.C.: Island Press, 2002.

Oelschlaeger, Max. *Caring for Creation: An Ecumenical Approach to the Environmental Crisis.* New Haven: Yale University Press, 1994.

Schwartz, Richard. *Judaism and Global Survival.* New York: Lantern Books, 2002.

Tal, Alon. *Pollution in a Promised Land: An Environmental History of Israel.* Berkeley: University of California Press, 2002.

Tirosh-Samuelson, Hava, ed. *Judaism and Ecology: Created World and Revealed Word.* Cambridge: Harvard University Press, 2002. This book is part of a larger series called *Religions of the World and Ecology,* sponsored by the Center for the Study of World Religions at Harvard

Divinity School; the series is edited by Mary Evelyn Tucker and John Grim.

Waskow, Arthur, ed. *Torah of the Earth: Exploring 4,000 Years of Ecology in Jewish Thought*. Woodstock, Vt.: Jewish Lights Publishing, 2000.

Yaffe, Martin, ed. *Judaism and Environmental Ethics: A Reader*. Lanham, Md.: Lexington Books, 2001.

Websites

Adamah Fellowship
http://www.isabellafreedman.org/adamah
Adam Teva ve'Din: The Israeli Union for Environmental Defense
http://www.iued.org.il
American Society for the Protection of Nature in Israel
http://www.aspni.org
Arava Institute for Environmental Studies
http://www.arava.org
Canfei Nesharim
http://www.canfeinesharim.org
The Coalition on the Environment and Jewish Life (COEJL)
http://www.coejl.org
EarthKosher
http://www.earthkosher.com
The Eco-Kosher Network
http://www.ecojew.com/ecokashrut
Elat Hayyim: The Jewish Retreat Center
http://jewishretreatcenter.org/overview/ecology_social_change.html
Friends of the Earth Middle East (FoEME)
http://www.foeme.org
Green Course (Megama Yeruca): Israeli Students for the Environment
http://www.green.org.il/cgi-bin/v.cgi?id=green
Hazon
http://www.hazon.org
The Heschel Center for Environmental Learning and Leadership
http://www.heschelcenter.org/index_eng.html
Israeli Ministry of the Environment
http://www.sviva.gov.il (click on "English" in the upper left-hand corner)
The Jewish Global Environmental Network (JGEN)
http://www.jgenisrael.org
Jewish Vegetarians of North America
http://jewishveg.com
Life and Environment: The Israeli Union of Environmental NGOs
http://www.sviva.net (click on "English" in the upper left-hand corner)
The Noah Project (London)
http://www.noahproject.org.uk
The Shalom Center
http://www.shalomctr.org

Simplicity as a Jewish Path
   http://www.jewishsimplicity.org
Teva Adventure
   http://www.tevaadventure.org
The Teva Learning Center
   http://www.tevacenter.org

Notes

Introduction

1. The terms *relevance* and *authenticity* in reference to Jewish textual education are professor Michael Rosenak's.
2. I am indebted to Golan Ben Horin for this compelling interpretation of what it means to do midrash.

Chapter 1

1. *Science* 155 (1967): 1203–1207. He was not, however, the first to deal with these questions. Preceding him were the Islamic scholar Seyyed Hossein Nasr, *The Encounter of Man and Nature: The Spiritual Crisis in Modern Man* (London: Unwin, 1967; rev. ed., Chicago: Kazi Publishers, 1997, from the Gifford Lectures, delivered in 1965–6), and certain essays before that by the Buddhist D. T. Suzuki. The historian Arnold Toynbee and architect Ian McHarg also wrote in a similar vein during that period.
2. The classic statement and documentation of this view is Jeremy Cohen's *Be Fertile and Increase, Fill the Earth and Master It: The Ancient and Medieval Career of a Biblical Text* (Ithaca: Cornell University Press, 1989).
3. David Ehrenfeld's problematic yet suggestive study *The Arrogance of Humanism* (Oxford: Oxford University Press, 1978) is an example of this approach.
4. The glitch in theocentrism is that God is not around in the everyday—people do the interpreting of what God wants, which can deteriorate into simple anthropocentrism.
5. Abraham Joshua Heschel, God *In Search of Man* (New York: Farrar, Straus and Cudahy, 1955), 46.
6. Jeanne Kay, "Concepts of Nature in the Hebrew Bible," in Martin Yaffe, *Judaism and Environmental Ethics: A Reader* (Lanham, Md.: Lexington Books, 2001), 102.
7. See Robert Gordis, "Judaism and the Spoliation of Nature," *Congress Bi-Weekly* (April 1971); Eric Freudenstein, "Ecology and the Jewish Tradition," *Judaism* 19 (1970): 406–414; Norman Lamm, "Ecology and Jewish Law and Theology," in his *Faith and Doubt* (New York: KTAV, 1971).

8. Prof. Steven Schwartzschild, "The Unnatural Jew" first published in *Environmental Ethics*, vol. 6 (1984), reprinted in Yaffe, *Judaism and Environmental Ethics*.

Chapter 2

1. Literally, human and earth (or soil); the nearest English language cognate pairs are "earthling" and "Earth," or "human" and "humus."
2. The midrash of Rabbi Acha in *Bereishit Rabbah* 60:8, which relates to the length of the conversation of Abraham's servant Eliezer with the parents of Rebecca, as compared to the laconic language of commandments of more central importance, stresses the importance of the Book of Genesis as an outline for the moral and ethical laws found in the rest of the Torah.
3. See Robert Alter, *The Art of Biblical Narrative* (New York: Basic Books, 1981), 146.
4. Or suggest harmonizing readings as certain midrashim do—cf., eg., Talmud, *Hullin* 60a.
5. Syntactically, verse 4 is two separate phrases patched together, with the second constituting the introduction to verse 5 and what follows. The graphic layout of the New JPS translation makes this clear. Chapter 2:4b is also the first mention of the name YHVH, introducing a different historical source, or alternatively, a different aspect of divine creativity. Both indicate the contrast between the first and second stories.
6. I have avoided assuming that reading above, because it is reasonably claimed, based on midrashim that emphasize the androgynous nature of that first solitary *adam*, that, verse 2:23 notwithstanding, with no contrasting female, there was also no male before the separation. See Phyllis Trible, "Depatriarchalizing in Biblical Interpretation," in Elizabeth Koltun, *The Jewish Woman: New Perspectives* (New York: Schocken 1987).
7. Joseph Soloveitchik, "The Lonely Man of Faith," *Tradition*, vol. 7, no. 2 (1965).
8. There is a subtle but significant difference in wording between these two blessings: the blessing to be fertile and multiply is said by God of the fish and birds in verse 22, while it is said to the human in verse 28. This could imply that the former possess the blessed quality of fertility as part of their biological nature, whereas for humans it is no less a blessing but a divine charge, implying an element of human judgment.
9. It is also the word used in contemporary Israel to refer to "the occupation" (of the territories)—*hakibush*— with all the attendant connotations.
10. An early reading that expresses the view that this dominion was not an absolute right is the comment in the midrash *Genesis Rabbah* 8:12, used by Rashi in his commentary, which uses a word play to make the point that only if humans are morally worthy will we assume the mantle of dominion; if not, we "descend" below the level of the animals, and will be ruled by them.

11. Although this is not entirely false—small-scale societies that have survived for centuries generally do evince admirable wisdom and practices of sustainability—it is often overstated and problematically ascribed to metaphysical reasons.
12. Quoted in Jeremy Cohen, in Yaffe, p. 77.
13. Whether this accords with evolutionary or physiological data is not entirely clear, or germane. The point of the story is not the prehistorical data (were we gatherers? hunters? both? was the Garden envisioned as a place of work? of leisure?), but the ultimate vision of paradise, the end of days. As Isaiah (cf. ch. 11) prophesied, the ideal world of eternal peace implies no harm to any of God's creatures by any of them, and the idyllic messianic era implies a "re-creation" of this initial paradise (cf. also Hosea 2:20).
14. It is not surprising, however, that a midrash on *tov me'od* rearranges the letters of *me'od, mem-aleph-dalet* to *aleph-dalet-mem: adam,* that it is specifically the human who is deemed good (cf. *Genesis Rabbah* 8).
15. See Jeremy Cohen, *Be Fruitful,* p. 5ff.
16. See also *Genesis Rabbah* 16:5 for explicit midrashic connections.
17. Although the connections among Darwin, intelligent design, and Genesis is a rich and complex topic beyond the scope of this book, it should be noted that the battle lines are not nearly as clearly drawn as we are often led to believe. Take, for instance, three views:

    - The biblical narrative: *adam* from the dust of the ground but with the breath of God, is therefore a dual nature, the middle top of the Great Chain of Being, vs.
    - Renaissance secular humanist view: "I think therefore I am" and "man the measure," at the absolute top of the chain, possessing a unique *ratio,* a deep chasm separating him from other animals, vs.
    - Darwinian evolutionary theory: human as a self-reflective mammal, embedded in the natural world.

    It is the biblical and the Darwinian views that have the most affinity: in many ways, evolutionary thought reinforces the deep biblical value of the organic unity of Creation, over and against a fragmented, mechanistic world view that has come to dominate Western science and social thought.
18. Lawrence Troster, "Created in the Image of God: Humanity and Divinity in an Age of Environmentalism," in Yaffe, p. 178.
19. See, for instance, R. Joseph Albo, *Sefer Ha'Ikkarim,* III:15.
20. Cf. Exodus 3:5, the burning bush, Moses removes his shoes because he is "standing on holy ground."
21. See his essay "Mastery and Stewardship, Wonder and Connectedness: A Typology of Relations to Nature in Jewish Text and Tradition" in *Judaism and Ecology,* ed. Hava Tirosh-Samuelson (Cambridge: Harvard University Press, 2002). There, he goes beyond the biblical text and

shows how the models express themselves in the contemporary thought of Kook, Gordon, Heschel, and Buber.

22. In contrast to the anthropocentric stories of dominion and stewardship in Genesis, in Job, God says essentially the opposite, that the world is beyond human ken. How can we presume to manage the world when we don't know the first thing about how it came into being and its inner workings? This isn't just a message of the insignificance of humanity, though. There is a great deal of joy in the cosmos, joy that we can partake of, and the whole awe-inspiring picture is comforting to Job. See Bill McKibben, *The Comforting Whirlwind: God, Job, and the Scale of Creation* (Grand Rapids, Mich.: Wm. B. Eerdman's, 1994).

Chapter 3

1. In contrast, if spirituality is seen as embedded in the physical, and the physical is always imbued with something deeper, nature may still be a means, but an indispensable one.

2. The general term *afterlife* conflates a number of different concepts: a metaphysical life after death (heaven) or a historical messianic period (in this world), equivalent or not to "the end of days" *(acharit hayamim)*, with or without *techiyat hameitim*, bodily resurrection.

3. The idea of bodily resurrection implies an affirmation of the physical body. If the body were an empty vessel and the soul the totality of the person, there would be no need to reunite the two. All of which is to say that the larger philosophical questions of body and soul, and this world and its transformation, are not cut-and-dried.

4. Of course, this can and has been abused, with religious institutions perpetuating this-worldly oppression and deprivation in the name of heavenly promises.

5. This is an abbreviated exploration of this significant text, taken from a more comprehensive discussion in my "One, Walking and Studying ...: Nature vs. Torah," *Judaism Quarterly Journal* 44 (1995): 146–168, reprinted in Yaffe and in Waskow's *Torah of the Earth*.

6. Elsewhere, Rabbi Shimon said: "If a person ploughs in the ploughing season, and sows in the sowing season, and reaps in the reaping season, and threshes in the threshing season, and winnows in the season of wind, what is to become of the Torah?" (Talmud, *Berachot* 35b). This is a radical departure from the biblical model: "If then you obey the commandments that I enjoin upon you ... I will grant the rain for your land in season.... You shall gather in the new grain and wine and oil." (Deut. 11:13–14). Contrary to Rabbi Shimon, Rabbi Yishmael interprets this verse to emphasize that harvesting nature's bounty is a blessing from God, and therefore one must combine Torah study with *derech eretz* (literally, "the way of the land"), or worldly professions.

7. The significance of these *mitzvot* and their rewards will be discussed at the end of the next chapter in the general context of sustainability.

8. Others claim that the mishnah is not speaking of nature at all, but rather anything that would interrupt Torah study, cf., e.g., the commentary *Magen Avot* (Shimon ben Tzemach Duran, Spain, 1361–1444). But most commentaries emphasize distractions specifically from the natural world.

9. This text bore great interest for Zionist authors as well, and poet Chaim Nachman Bialik's use of this mishnah will be discussed in chapter 6.

10. Zohar part II, Parashat Teruma, p. 127a.

11. The question of the relationship of mysticism to the natural world is complex and requires a separate, book-length treatment. As opposed to the sympathetic portrayal here, other approaches suggest that nature is but a veil to be penetrated, spiritualized, transcended, or negated. See Eliott Wolfson, "Mirror of Nature Reflected in the Symbolism of Medieval Kabbalah," in Tirosh-Samuelson, *Judaism and Ecology,* pp. 303–332.

12. These brief references elide the important historical and philosophical characteristics of the wisdom tradition, and the tension with the covenantal tradition of Deuteronomy and Prophetic writings. But they are part of the Bible and therefore accessible as alternative models. See Stephen Geller, "Nature's Answer: The Meaning of the Book of Job in Its Intellectual Context," in Tirosh-Samuelson, *Judaism and Ecology,* pp. 109–132).

13. Literally, "has made us wiser *than* those creatures." The Hebrew particle can be read as either "than" or "from."

14. See James Lovelock, *The Ages of Gaia: A Biography of Our Living Earth* (New York: W. W. Norton & Co., 1988), or Lawrence Joseph, *Gaia: The Growth of an Idea* (New York: St. Martin's Press, 1990).

15. *The Guide for the Perplexed,* I:72, p. 184.

16. Ibid., II:5, p. 259.

17. For more on deep ecology, see Bill Devall and George Sessions, *Deep Ecology: Living as If Nature Mattered* (Salt Lake City: Peregrine, 1985). According to Rabbi Dan Fink, the Danish philosopher Arne Naess, founder and ideologue of deep ecology, was deeply influenced by Spinoza, who was influenced by Maimonides, and so the similarity may not be coincidental.

18. "On the Judaism of Nature," in *The New Jews,* eds. James Sleeper and Alan Mintz (New York: Random House, 1971). See also Monford Harris, "Ecology: A Covenantal Approach," in *CCAR Journal* 23 (1976): 101–108.

19. All the major denominations—Reform, Conservative, Modern Orthodox—have their roots in the Germany of Kant and *wissenschaft* and are anti-mystical. The rise of Jewish renewal and the *chavurah,* charismatic teachers such as R. Shlomo Carlebach and R. Zalman Schachter-Shalomi, the growth of the academic study of Jewish mysticism, and Jewish feminism have all contributed to changing attitudes toward previously ignored themes in classical

Judaism that are of great relevance in our attitudes toward the natural world.

20. Nasr, quoted in my "*'Alma De'atei'*: The-World-That-Is-Coming—Reflections on Power, Knowledge, Wisdom, and Progress," in *The Good in Nature and Humanity—Connecting Science, Religion, and the Natural World,* ed. Stephen Kellert (Washington, D.C.: Island Press, 2002).

21. See his *A Sand County Almanac* (Oxford: Oxford University Press, 1949, 1968). When he was a game warden, Leopold saw wolves as enemies to be exterminated, because they killed the deer he was trying to protect for the hunters. Only later did he realize that his job should be to preserve the system as a whole, which is different from its constituent parts.

22. A similar schema of wilderness, city, and Arcadian synthesis is developed historically and phenomenologically to great advantage in Evan Eisenberg's insightful *The Ecology of Eden* (New York: Knopf, 1998).

23. The fact that a common name for God is "Place" has implications for our work here, and requires a study in its own right. Classically, this was understood as a negation of pantheism: "God is the Place of the World, but the World is not the Place of God" (*Genesis Rabbah* 68:9), i.e., all of creation does not—*cannot*— contain Divinity.

24. See also the law code, *Shulchan Aruch,* Choshen Mishpat 291, 292, 308, 324.

25. From *Human Values and the Environment,* conference proceedings from Institute for Environmental Studies, University of Wisconsin–Madison, available on the website of the Coalition on the Environment in Jewish Life: www.coejl.org.

26. Hava Tirosh-Samuelson, "Nature in the Sources of Judaism," *Daedalus,* 130: 4 (Fall 2001).

27. As stated in Hosea 2:20: "In that day I will make a covenant for them with the beasts of the field, the birds of the air, and the creeping things of the ground."

28. Joseph Soloveitchik, "The Lonely Man of Faith," *Tradition,* vol. 7, no. 2 (1965).

29. Writing this from Israel, I can't ignore the fact that the issue of destroying trees in times of war, which might seem esoteric in the Diaspora, is painfully relevant here. Jews uproot Arab olive trees (to prevent them being used as cover for attackers, or as spiteful vandalism, and sometimes for economic reasons, to resell to other Jews), and there have been hundreds of incidents of arson against the "Jewish" pine trees in JNF forests (many of which are planted over the ruins of destroyed Arab villages or admittedly used to prevent the expansion of Israeli Arab towns and villages). The Land of Israel has been one of the great silent victims of the century-long conflict in which we are embroiled.

30. Similarly, Talmud *Bava Kamma* 91b states that there is a distinction made between fruit and other trees to teach that given the option, cutting down a non-fruit-bearing tree is preferable.

31. In fact, the distinction between these types of trees is illusory: all trees, by botanical definition, bear fruit, though some may not be humanly edible.
32. Eilon Schwartz calls these the minimalists and the maximalists. See his treatment of the biblical and rabbinic development of *bal tashchit* and a comparison with contemporary environmental ethical discourse in "*Bal Tashchit:* A Jewish Environmental Precept," *Environmental Ethics* 19 (1997): 355–374, and reprinted in Yaffe and Waskow.
33. This is an extension of the protection of the weak: widow, orphan, stranger, poor, and now animal, the ultimate defenseless and voiceless member of society. This is also a form of *chesed shel emet,* true acts of lovingkindness, such as providing for the dead. These are acts of righteousness done to others who have no way of repaying.
34. See also Ze'ev Levy, "Ethical Issues of Animal Welfare in Jewish Thought," in Yaffe.
35. The midrash says that Joseph merited the title *tzaddik* because he "provided sustenance to God's creatures" when he saved Egypt's livestock (along with the people) by storing grain in anticipation of the famine predicted in Pharaoh's dream.
36. Similarly, the *Shehecheyanu* (celebratory) blessing is recited for all new clothes except leather goods, because an animal had to die for our benefit (Rama in his gloss to *Orach Chayim* 223:3).
37. The Roman name. In the midrash, he is referred to as Turnusrufus.

Chapter 4

1. Population Reference Bureau (2005), based on United Nations, *World Population Projections to 2100* (1998).
2. Mathis Wackernagel and William E. Rees, *Our Ecological Footprint: Reducing Human Impact on the Earth* (Gabriola Island, BC: New Society Publishers, 1996). See also www.footprintnetwork.org.
3. See Talmud *Yevamot* 62 and Maimonides, *Hilchot Ishut, "Laws of Marital Relations,"* 15 and 16, which state that even if one has fulfilled the minimum, a person "is commanded by the Rabbis not to desist from procreation while he yet has strength."
4. Alan Durning, *How Much Is Enough? The Consumer Society and the Fate of the Earth* (New York: Worldwatch Institute/Norton, 1992).
5. Ibid.
6. Based on Joe Dominguez and Vicki Robin, *Your Money or Your Life* (New York: Penguin Books, 1992).
7. Garrett Hardin, "The Tragedy of the Commons," *Science* vol. 162 (1968): 1243–1248.
8. See Robert Bullard, ed., *Confronting Environmental Racism: Voices from the Grassroots* (Boston: South End Press, 1993), and R. L. Turner and D. P. Wu, *Environmental Justice and Environmental Racism: An Annotated Bibliography and General Overview* (Berkeley: Institute for International Studies, University of California, Berkeley, 2003).
9. See *Tosefta Bava Kama* 6:15 and Maimonides, *Mishneh Torah*, "Laws of Theft and Loss," 6:13.

10. Hava Tirosh-Samuelson, "Nature in the Sources of Judaism," *Daedalus,* 130: 4 (Fall 2001).

11. See Lewis Mumford, *The Culture of Cities* (New York: Harcourt Brace, 1938, 1970), esp. "The Regional Framework of Civilization" and also Mark Lucarelli, *Lewis Mumford and the Ecological Region* (New York: Guildford Press, 1995).

12. In 2000, household income in American cities averaged less than three-quarters that of their corresponding suburbs. For data on this and other related issues, see Michael Lewyn, "Suburban Sprawl, Jewish Law, and Jewish Values," *Southeastern Environmental Law Journal* 13: 1, (Fall 2004): 1–32.

13. In a world of global warming, ozone holes, and the like, are there any places left that can be considered untouched by human action? See, e.g., William Cronon, "The Trouble with Wilderness, or Getting Back to the Wrong Nature," in ed. Cronon, *Uncommon Ground* (New York: Norton, 1996), and Michael Soule, "The Social Siege of Nature" in eds. M. Soule and G. Lease, *Reinventing Nature?* (Washington, D.C.: Island Press, 1995).

14. In fact, many biblical translations often have "wilderness" for *midbar*—cf. Exod. 17:1 and Num. 14:21, 20:1, "the wilderness of Zin" (also elsewhere, "the wilderness of Sinai"). There is also the negative designation *sh'mamah,* in biblical and modern Hebrew alike, meaning "wasteland."

15. Elie Weisel, *Somewhere a Master: Hasidic Portraits and Legends* (New York: Schocken, 1984, 2005).

16. One of the *chalutzot,* pioneers, of this teaching is the founder of Shomrei Adamah, Ellen Bernstein. See her essay "How Wilderness Forms a Jew," in the volume edited by her *Ecology and the Jewish Spirit* (Woodstock, Vt.: Jewish Lights, 1998).

17. See, for instance, Darrell Posey, ed., *Cultural and Spiritual Values of Biodiversity: A Complementary Contribution to the Global Biodiversity Assessment* (Nairobi, Kenya: UNEP, 2000), and Luisa Maffi, "Linguistic and Biological Diversity: The Inextricable Link," Terralingua Discussion Paper #3 (1998), accessed at www.terralingua.org/DiscPapers/DiscPaper3.html.

18. *Exodus Rabbah* 10:1; versions of this midrash appear in a number of different sources, such as *Shabbat* 77b, *Genesis Rabbah* 10:7, and *Leviticus Rabbah* 22:1.

19. "Today as never before, the cruelty in the livestock trade renders meat eating and true kashrut incompatible," Rabbi David Rosen, in *Rabbis and Vegetarianism,* ed. Roberta Kalechofsky (Marblehead, Mass.: Micah Publications, 1995), pp. 53–60.

20. This whole section owes a great deal to the work of Richard Schwartz. For the sources of the following data, see his *Judaism and Global Survival* (New York: Lantern Books, 2002).

21. The industrial production of fertilizers is also a dirty business. In Israel, one of the main sources of the pollution of the notoriously contaminated Kishon River that flows into Haifa Bay is Haifa Chemicals, whose main product is fertilizer.

22. Rav Kook is seen by many to be the great prophetic voice of Jewish vegetarianism, largely by virtue of an essay of his, "The Vision of Vegetarianism and Peace." Others note that he emphasizes there and elsewhere that the vegetarian ideal is a messianic one, dependent on the spiritual perfection of humanity and, as such, is not immediately applicable. See Kalechofsky's *Rabbis and Vegetarianism*.
23. Rabbi David Rosen, in Kalechofsky, pp. 53–60.
24. See Rabbi J. David Bleich, "Vegetarianism and Judaism," in his *Contemporary Halachic Problems* vol. 3 (New York: KTAV, 1989). Even Bleich admits that "Jewish tradition does not command carnivorous behavior," and that meat "may be eschewed when there is not desire for it."
25. The grand old man of Israeli organic agriculture, Mario Levi, an observant Jew from the religious kibbutz Sde Eliyahu, speaks often of his struggles with the *kashrut* lobby, which supports hyrdoponic, pesticide-laden vegetables, for their guarantee of being completely pest-free. "Kosher but poisoned," he terms it, and calls upon religious consumers and authorities to take into account what those agricultural technologies are doing to the earth.
26. "And the Earth Is Filled with the Breath of Life," *Crosscurrents* 47: 3 (Fall 1997).
27. See his essay, "The Gift of Good Earth," in the book of the same name (San Francisco: North Point Press, 1981).

Chapter 5
1. Also: the 7-year *shmitah* cycle, the 7 x 7–year cycle of the *yovel* (jubilee), the 19-year cycle that aligns the lunar and solar cycles (there are 7 leap years every 19 years), and the 28-year cycle that is the basis for *Birkat Hachamah*, the blessing of the sun, commemorating its creation, which occurs when the spring equinox falls on the beginning of the fourth day (when the sun was created according to Gen. 1), i.e., Tuesday night.
2. The Muslim calendar by comparison is strictly lunar, the opposite of the exclusively solar Gregorian calendar. The Muslim year is comprised of 12 lunar months of 354 days, with no attempt to remain in synch with the (solar) seasons of the year. Thus, the Muslim date "moves" 11 days every year in relation to the Gregorian date.
3. Like the lunar cycle, there are other bodily cycles, such as the menstrual cycle in women. The cycle itself, including the rituals surrounding it, notably immersion in the *mikveh*, ritual bath, has amazing implications regarding personal connections to natural rhythms. For a provocative view of this topic and the body and nature in general from a Jewish ecofeminist perspective, see Irene Diamond and David Seidenberg, "Recovering the Sensuous Through Jewish Ecofeminist Practice" in Waskow, *Torah of the Earth* vol. 2, pp. 245–260.
4. See Arthur Waskow, *Seasons of Our Joy: A Modern Guide to the Jewish Holidays* (Boston: Beacon Press, 1991, 1986), and Michael Strassfeld,

The Jewish Holidays: A Guide and Commentary (New York: Harper and Row, 1985).

5. See the Israeli Ministry of the Environment website: http://www.sviva .gov.il/bin/en.jsp?enPage=BlankPage&enDisplay=view&enDispWhat= Object&enDispWho=Articals^l122&enZone=events

6. For the past thousand years, Shemini Atzeret is combined with Simchat Torah—falling on the same day in Israel, and on two consecutive days in the Diaspora—which is cyclical in its own way as it marks the completion and beginning again of the reading of the Torah in weekly portions.

7. See Arthur Schaffer, "The Agricultural and Ecological Symbolism of the Four Species of Sukkot," in Yaffe.

8. For a beautiful rendition of the text of this seder, and other inspiring materials regarding Tu B'Shvat, see the wonderful Tu B'Shvat anthology, eds. Ari Elon, Naomi Hymen, and Arthur Waskow, *Trees, Earth, and Torah* (New York: JPS, 1999).

9. Erich Fromm, "The Sabbath Ritual," in *The Forgotten Language: An Introduction to the Understanding of Dreams, Fairytales, and Myths* (New York: Holt and Rinehart, 1951).

10. See his *The Sabbath: A Guide to Its Understanding and Observance* (New York: Feldheim, 1980), for a comprehensive overview of the *melachot* and their derivatives.

11. The desire to use prohibited electrical appliances on Shabbat leads to a waste of resources, by leaving them on for the entire 25-hour period or using timers to do the work, emphasizing our continued scientific exploitation of nature, which we are meant to be restraining on this day. This remains an unresolved tension between the lofty *aggadah* and the nitty-gritty of the Halacha.

12. Ismar Schorsch, "Learning to Live with Less," in *Spirit and Nature: Why the Environment Is a Religious Issue,* eds. Steven Rockefeller and John Elder (Boston: Beacon Press, 1992), p. 33.

13. David Hartman, *Individual and Communal Perspectives on Shabbat* (Jerusalem: The Shalom Hartman Institute for Advanced Judaic Studies, 1981), p. 7–8.

14. See Robert Goldenberg, "Law and Spirit in Talmudic Religion," in *Jewish Spirituality from the Bible Through the Middle Ages,* ed. Arthur Green (New York: Crossroad, 1988).

15. *The Sabbath: Its Meaning for Modern Man* (New York: Farrar, Straus, and Giroux, 1951).

16. Evan Eisenberg, *The Ecology of Eden* (New York: Vintage Books, 1998), p. 130.

17. See his "Man and Nature in the Sabbatical Year," *Tradition* 8 (1966): 48–55, reprinted in Yaffe.

18. Heschel, *God In Search of Man,* pp. 43, 46.

19. See, e.g., Lawrence Hoffman, *Beyond the Text: A Holistic Approach to Liturgy* (Bloomington: Indiana University Press, 1989).

20. This sentence is an altered quotation of Isaiah 45:7, where God creates light, darkness, peace, and evil *(bore' et hara').* God in Isaiah and in the

liturgy is clearly presented as the creator of all, allowing no room for demiurges, or the independent existence of evil. For a detailed exposition of liturgy and biblical texts regarding Creation, see Neil Gillman, "Creation in the Bible and the Liturgy," in Tirosh-Samuelson, *Judaism and Ecology,* pp. 133–154.

Chapter 6

1. The term *dat Moshe* (as in the wedding vow, "You are hereby conse-crated to me with this ring according to *dat Moshe ve'yisrael*"), occa-sionally translated as "the Mosaic faith," is literally "Mosaic law," *dat* being a Persian borrowing, appearing in the Book of Esther and referring to royal edicts.
2. This dichotomy is a simplification, and most environmentalists will call for some combination of the two levels. Yet, most individual and group efforts tend to one dimension or the other.
3. I intend no romanticization of indigenous cultures; there's nothing inher-ent in tribal life (including pagan world views) that ensures eco-sensitiv-ity. Many small-scale pagan societies have self-destructed over the millennia due to unsustainable practices (cf., Easter Island and others mentioned in Jared Diamond's recent work *Collapse*). But still, there are many societies, on every inhabited continent, whether hunter-gatherers, semi-nomadic herdsmen, subsistence farmers, or even just healthy rural-based cultures, that have evolved a sustainable relationship with their places without the help of Western technology.
4. See George Steiner, "Our Homeland, The Text," *Salmagundi* 66 (Winter–Spring, 1985): 4–25.
5. Harvey, "From Space to Place and Back Again: Reflections on the Condition of Post-Modernity," in *Mapping the Futures: Local Cultures, Global Change,* eds. J. Bird, B. Curtis, T. Putnam, and G. Robertson (London and New York, Routledge, 1993), p. 4.
6. Translated by Sir Leon Simon, in *An Anthology of Hebrew Essays,* eds. Israel Cohen and B. Y. Michali (Tel Aviv: Massada Publishers, 1966), pp. 368–388.
7. Artson, personal communication, 1995.
8. From Tal, "Israel and Its Environment—The Flip Side of Zionism's Success: Israel's Environmental Woes," COEJL, 2000, available at http://www.coejl.org.
9. Yaron Ezrahi, *Rubber Bullets: Power and Conscience in Modern Israel* (New York: Farrar, Straus, and Giroux, 1997): pp. 48–49.
10. In his environmental history of Israel, *Pollution in a Promised Land* (Berkeley: University of California Press, 2002), p. 119.
11. Ben-David, "*Tiyul* (Hike) as an Act of Consecration of Space" in *Grasping Land: Space and Place in Contemporary Israeli Discourse and Experience,* eds. Eyal Ben-Ari and Yoram Bilu (Albany: SUNY Press, 1997), pp. 141–142.
12. Quoted in Tal, *Pollution,* p. 36.

13. Izhak Schnell, "Nature and Environment in the Socialist-Zionist Pioneers' Perceptions: A Sense of Desolation," *Ecumene* 4: 1 (1997): 69–85.

14. This question of expectation and mental categories is relevant to Euro-American constructions of the Holy Land as well. Many cite as independent and eyewitness proof of the alleged "desolation" of the Land descriptions of primitive conditions found in the travelogues of nineteenth-century visitors to the Near East. These have been convincingly deconstructed as suffering from colonialist and Orientalist prejudices. In particular, Lynne Rogers has written on the problematics of Mark Twain and William Thackeray's revulsion for the Holy Land in relationship to their Christian heritage in "Literary Snapshots," in *The Landscape of Palestine: Equivocal Poetry,* eds. Ibrahim Abu-Lughod, R. Heacock, and K. Nashef (Birzeit, Birzeit Publications, 1999).

15. See also Tal, *Pollution,* chapters 2 and 3 for other relevant data.

16. According to McCarthy: "By modern standards, Palestine was indeed underpopulated," in J. McCarthy, *The Population of Palestine: Population History and Statistics of the Late Ottoman Period and the Mandate* (New York: Columbia University Press, 1990), p. 16. His exhaustive reevaluation of the demographic data resulted in the following numbers: total population in Palestine of 548,854 in 1895–96, and 628,190 in 1905–1906, as compared with 1,942,349 in 1946 (ibid., p. 37).

17. Some have, with predictably little effect. See Daniel Orenstein, "Population Growth and Environmental Impact: Ideology and Academic Discourse in Israel," in *Population and Environment,* 26 (2004): 40–60. Israeli population growth also includes the Arab growth rate—even higher than the general Jewish rate, and this demographic struggle, "the battle of the wombs," is often a justification for the latter. This is a price of the national-ethnic conflict that is beginning to be felt. The idea on both sides that whoever churns out the most babies wins is increasing poverty for some and decreasing quality of life for all.

18. Gil Troy, "A Green Cure for Zionism's Blues," *Forward* (March 8, 2002).

19. For an extensive treatment of Zionism, environmentalism, Jews, and Arabs, see my *Place and the Other—The Place of the Other: Contested Narratives in Environmental Activism Among Jews and Palestinians in Israel* (unpublished PhD dissertation, Hebrew University of Jerusalem, 2005).

Glossary

Sometimes two pronunciations of words are common. This glossary reflects the way that many Jews actually use these words, not just the technically correct version. When two pronunciations are listed, the first is the way the word is sounded in proper Hebrew, and the second is the way it is sometimes heard in common speech, often under the influence of Yiddish, the folk language of the Jews of northern and eastern Europe. "Kh" is used to represent a guttural sound, similar to the German "ch" (as in "sprach").

acharit hayamim (ah-khah-REET hah-yah-MEEM): "The end of days," a trans-historical time period that can mean the time here on earth after human history has come to an end (with or without the advent of the Messiah), or a more metaphysical Edenic time and place.

adamah (ah-dah-MAH): Land, earth, soil. Etymologically related to *adam*—human being.

aggadah (ah-gah-DAH): Legend, lore, philosophy, theory, the non-legal literary materials of rabbinic literature. From a root meaning to say or tell, *aggadah* contrasts with *halacha* (q.v.); together the two make up the body of Torah.

aliyah (ah-lee-YAH or, commonly, ah-LEE-yah): Ascend, go up. *Aliyah* is used to refer to "the ascent" of an individual to recite the blessings at the reading of the Torah during a prayer service, as well as immigration of individuals or groups to the Land of Israel (pre-state Palestine and the State of Israel) to live.

alma de'atei (al-MAH deh-ah-TAY or, commonly, AL-mah deh-AH-tay): "The-world-that-is-coming" (Aramaic), the world to come, *olam haba* (q.v.).

Am Yisrael (AHM yis-rah-AYL): The People of Israel, the Jewish nation.

anthropocentric: A type of reasoning that sees people and our needs as paramount. Compare biocentric.

avoda (ah-voh-DAH): Work, labor, service. Can refer to both physical labor as well as ritual service (as in the Temple).

bal tashchit (BAHL tahsh-KHEET): "Do not destroy," a collection of laws, stemming from the prohibition of chopping down fruit trees in wartime (Deut. 20:19–20) that includes regulations regarding needless destruction, waste, excessive consumption, and overuse.

beracha (b'-rah-KHAH); pl. *berachot* (b'-rah-KHOHT): Blessing. Beginning *baruch ata Adonai,* "Blessed (or "beneficent") are you, God ... " these are liturgical pronouncements expressing praise and gratitude on various occasions.

biocentric: A type of reasoning that sees the needs of ecosystems, all living things or all of nature as paramount. Compare anthropocentric.

Birkat Hamazon (beer-KAHT hah-mah-ZONE): "The blessing of the food," grace after meals.

Birkot Hanehenin (beer-KHOTE hah-neh-heh-NEEN):"Blessings of enjoyment," particular benedictions said on various occasions, such as eating certain foods, smelling aromatic plants and oils, seeing natural phenomena, and others.

brit (b'-REET): Covenant. Refers to the relationship between God and Israel (but also God, humanity and the world—see Gen. 9:8–17). The essence of the covenant is the ongoing relationship between God and the Jewish People, a relationship shaped by Jewish law, prayer, religious thought, questioning God, and other forms of spirituality, including acts of *tikkun olam* (q.v.). Also can be the shortened form of *brit milah* (b'-REET mee-LAH), "the covenant of circumcision," removal of the foreskin on the eighth day, to mark a baby boy's entry into the covenant of Abraham and Israel. (Gen. 17:10–14; Lev. 12:3).

chag (KHAHG): Holiday, festival. Also known as *yom tov,* literally "good day," refers to the appointed seasons of the Jewish year, such as Rosh Hashanah (the New Year), Pesach (Passover), and the others.

chalutziyut (khah-loo-tzee-YOOT): Pioneering. Describes both a period of Israeli history including the establishment of border settlements, draining swamps, paving roads, and making the desert bloom, as well as the general desire to sacrifice for the good of the collective.

chayei netzach (khah-YEI NEH-tzakh): Eternal life, specifically things of lasting spiritual value, such as Torah and devotion to God. Compare *chayei sha'ah.*

chayei sha'ah (khah-YEI shah-AH): Temporal life, specifically things of ephemeral or merely physical utility, such as livelihood and other mundane activities. Compare *chayei netzach.*

chazal (khah-ZAHL): An acronym for *chachameinu zichronam livracha,* "our sages, may their memory be for a blessing." Refers to the rabbis of the Mishnaic and Talmudic periods, roughly from the end of the Second Temple Period around the turn of the era, to the close of the Amoraic period, or the recension of the Babylonian Talmud in the sixth and seventh centuries CE.

cheshbon nefesh (khesh-BONE NEH-fesh): Personal stock-taking, introspection leading to repentance, literally "accounting of the soul."

chol (KHOLE): Profane, mundane, everyday. Contrasts with *kodesh* (holy, set apart), and can also refer to weekdays (as opposed to Shabbat) and the weekdays of the long festivals of Sukkot and Pesach.

ecofeminism: A school of thought and social and political movement that connects the ongoing degradation of the environment with oppression of women, and/or the dominance of androcentric (male-centered) values.

environmental justice: A movement that sees the environment as central to issues of social justice, such as in equal access to vital resources and equal protection from exposure to health-impairing risks.

gashmi (gahsh-MEE); *gashmi'ut* (gahsh-mee-OOT): Materiality, corporeality. From a root related to *geshem* (rain). Compare *ru'ach, ruchani.*

gemilut chasadim (g'-mee-LOOT khah-sah-DEEM): Acts of lovingkindness, such as visiting or taking care of the sick, feeding the hungry, and more. Whereas *tzedaka* (known as charity, but from the root meaning "justice") involves monetary giving, *gemilut chasadim* involves deeper personal involvement.

guf (GOOF): Body. Compare *nefesh.*

hakarat hatov (hah-kah-RAHT hah-TOVE): Gratitude, the virtue of gratefulness for personal favors or bounty bestowed or for the general gifts of life.

Halacha (hah-lah-KHAH or, commonly, hah-LAH-khah): Jewish law or legal material. From the Hebrew word meaning "to walk" or "to go," so denoting the way in which a person should walk through life. Compare *aggadah.*

Kabbalah (kah-bah-LAH or, commonly, kah-BAH-lah); **kabbalistic:** A general term for Jewish mysticism, but more specifically, a specific mystical doctrine that was recorded in the Zohar in the thirteenth century, and then was further elaborated, especially in the Land of Israel (in Safed), in the sixteenth century. From a Hebrew word meaning "to receive," and secondarily, "tradition," implying the receiving of tradition.

kashrut (kahsh-ROOT): Kosher. Fit or proper, especially referring to food. Meat that is kosher is from a permitted animal, slaughtered in a supervised and halachically acceptable manner, and has not been mixed with milk. The idea of "eco-*kashrut*" combines the idea of ethical eating and consumption with the traditional concept of acceptable food and food preparation.

kavana (kah-vah-NAH): Inwardness or intention, especially in prayer. *Kavana* can mean the meaning with which one imbues an action, or the side of prayer that is inspirational or spontaneous. Compare *keva.*

keva (KEH-vah): The set form, the written text of the prayer. *Keva* can sometimes refer to the rote or (overly) ritualized aspect of prayer or religious form. Compare *kavana.*

kilayim (kee-LAH-yeem): The mixture of unlike things, including among others sowing different seeds together and breeding animal hybrids (see Lev. 19:19, Deut. 22:9–11). Some commentators see these laws as a general warning about tampering with the underlying laws of nature.

klal yisrael (k'-LAHL yis-rah-AYL): The collectivity of Israel, the whole people of Israel. *Klal yisrael* encompasses Jewish peoplehood, and the mutual responsibility of Jews for each other and for the whole.

le'ovda uleshomra (lih-ove-DAH oo-lih-shome-RAH): "To work and to watch" (or "to till and to tend," "to serve and preserve"). From Genesis 2:15, the command to primeval Adam to cultivate and guard the Garden, usually interpreted as a call to human stewardship of the earth.

mahloket (makh-LOH-ket): Argument, dispute. The traditional form of Talmudic discourse that involves the back-and-forth exploration of all sides of an issue, the views of different sages, and the recording of majority and minority opinions.

melacha (meh-lah-KHAH): Labor or creative endeavor. There are thirty-nine distinct *melachot* (pl., meh-lah-KHOTE) that are forbidden on Shabbat as representing purposeful intervention in the natural world.

menucha (meh-noo-KHAH): Rest. Over and above physical leisure, *menucha* is what you get when you refrain from engaging in *melacha* (q.v.).

midbar (mid-BAHR): Desert or wilderness. The place the Children of Israel wandered for forty years after the Exodus from Egypt, an experience both humbling and ennobling.

midrash (meed-RAHSH or, commonly, MID-rahsh): From the Hebrew word *darash* (to seek, search, or demand [meaning from the biblical text]); also, therefore, a literary genre focused upon the creative explication of the Bible. By extension, Midrash refers to a body of rabbinic literature that offers classical interpretations of the Bible.

migrash (mig-RAHSH): A field or pasture, especially that open space around a city, as enjoined in Numbers 35, which outlines the form of the Levitical cities, and which later is seen to be applicable to all Israelite cities.

Mishnah (meesh-NAH or, commonly, MISH-nah): The first written summary of "the Oral Law," that is, the laws and customs communicated through example and speech from generation to generation, from approximately the fifth century BCE to the end of the second century CE, when it was edited and committed to writing by Rabbi Judah, the president of the Sanhedrin. The Mishnah is divided into six parts, or orders, organized by topic.

mitzvah (meetz-VAH or, commonly, MITZ-vah); pl. *mitzvot* (meetz-VOTE): Commonly used to mean "good deed," but in the more technical sense, denoting any commandment from God, ritual or ethical. Tradition lists 613 *mitzvot* in the Torah.

nefesh (NEH-fesh); pl. *nefashot* (neh-feh-SHOTE): Soul. The spiritual component of the human. Compare *guf*.

olam haba (oh-LAHM hah-BAH): The world to come, the afterlife. Usually refers to the place the eternal soul goes after death.

olam hazeh (oh-LAHM hah-ZEH): This world—the physical, historical world in which we live.

Pirkei Avot (pihr-KAY ah-VOTE): Literally, "Chapters of Our Fathers," but more commonly translated as "Ethics of Our Fathers" or "Ethics of the

Sages." It is a tractate of the Mishnah, where it is called *Avot* and is placed at the end of the order of Nezikin (Damages). It consists of rabbinical maxims, and ethical sayings about how to live one's life.

poskim (pose-KEEM); *p'sak* (p'-SAHK): Legal decisors, legal decision (adjudication, or legislation). Refers to individuals, recognized rabbinical authorities, and the method whereby they decide individual *halachot*.

progress: Improvement or betterment. Refers to a doctrine, widely assumed in the Western world that our society and things in general are always improving or moving forward, and thus that our lives are in some absolute sense "better" than those of our forebears. The implicit connection of the idea of progress with economic growth as a measure of social improvement is highly problematic from both an environmental and religious point of view.

regalim (reh-gah-LEEM): The pilgrimage holidays, Sukkot, Pesach, and Shavuot, during which it was mandated to go up to the Temple in Jerusalem for the special festival offerings (see Lev. 23 and Deut. 16). From the word *regel,* "foot."

Rosh Chodesh (rohsh KHOH-desh): The new moon, the beginning of the month. Now a minor festival (Num. 28:11ff.), at times it might have been seen as comparable in importance to Shabbat (Isa. 1:13; Amos 8:5).

ru'ach (ROO-ahkh); *ruchani* (roo-khah-nee): Spirit, spiritual. From the word for "wind." Compare *gashmi, gashmi'ut.*

Shabbat (shah-BAHT): Sabbath, from a word meaning "to desist [from work]" and thus "to rest." The Shabbat commences on Friday evening, before sunset, and ends on Saturday evening after sunset. Shabbat first appears in the opening chapters of Genesis, tied to God's rest after the Creation of the world, and is mandated in the Decalogue.

shevi'it (shih-vee-EET): "The seventh," referring to the seventh year, or the *shmitah* year (q.v.). Also the name of the tractate of the Mishnah explicating the laws of the *shmitah* year.

shmitah (shmee-TAH): The sabbatical year or year of "release," wherein the land was to rest from human cultivation and remain fallow, and all debts between individuals remitted. See Leviticus 25, Exodus 23, and Deuteronomy 15.

sugya (SOOG-yah): A unit of Talmudic text, a discrete dispute or topic in the Talmud.

sukkah (soo-KAH or, commonly, SOOK-ah): A temporary hut or booth, built for the Festival of Sukkot (soo-KOTE). During Sukkot, one is meant to eat and sleep in the *sukkah,* symbolic of the wandering of the Children of Israel in the wilderness.

sustainability: The overall vision of the environmental movement. A sustainable society is one that integrates social, environmental, and economic concerns of health and justice, and can both *sustain itself* over time, living up to responsibilities to future generations, as well as *sustain and nourish* its members, materially and spiritually, in the present and in the future.

tachrichin (takh-ree-KHEEN): The simple linen shroud that is the clothing of a dead body for burial.

Talmud (tahl-MOOD or, commonly, TAHL-m'd): The name given to each of two great compendia of Jewish law and lore compiled from the first to the sixth centuries CE, and ever since, the literary core of the rabbinic heritage. The Talmud Yerushalmi (y'roo-SHAL-mee), also called Jerusalem Talmud or Palestinian Talmud, is the earlier one, a product of the Land of Israel generally dated about 400 CE. The better-known Talmud Bavli (BAHV-lee), or Babylonian Talmud, took shape in Babylonia (present-day Iraq), and is traditionally dated about 550 CE. When people say "the Talmud" without specifying which one they mean, they are referring to the Babylonian version. The word Talmud comes from the Hebrew root meaning "to learn" and, in a different form, "to teach."

techiyat hameitim (tih-khee-YAHT hah-may-TEEM): The resurrection of the dead. A doctrine connected to the vision of the Messianic era, wherein souls are returned to their bodies and live again on earth.

tefilla (t'fee-LAH or, commonly, t'FEE-lah): Prayer. *Tefilla* can refer to individual spontaneous prayer or supplication, or to one of the mandated prayer services, such as *shacharit* (shah-khah-REET or, commonly, SHAH-khah-reet), the morning service; *mincha* (meen-KHAH or, commonly, MIN-khah), the afternoon service; and *ma'ariv* (mah-ah-REEV or, commonly, MAH-ah-reev), the evening service.

teva (TEH-vah): The medieval and modern Hebrew word for nature, referring to the non-human parts of the world, as well as to the orderly working and underlying structure and rules of the world.

tikkun olam (tee-KOON oh-LAHM): Literally, repairing or mending the world. From the Lurianic doctrine of mending the cosmic rupture that occurred at Creation through the intentional observance of *mitzvot*, *tikkun olam* now commonly refers to Jewish forms of social action.

Torah (TOH-rah): Instruction, teaching, or direction. In its narrowest meaning, Torah refers to the first five books of the Bible, the *Chumash* (khoo-MAHSH or, commonly, KHUH-m'sh), "five-fold" book, thus making it the first part of the Tanakh, the Hebrew Bible. The second part is the Prophets *(Nevi'im)*, and the third is the Writings *(Ketuvim)*. In this sense, the Torah is sometimes used to refer to the parchment scroll on which these books are written for public reading in the synagogue. Later, during rabbinic times (approximately the first to the sixth centuries CE), the Tanakh is referred to as the Written Torah (Torah *she-bikhtav*), in contrast to the Oral Torah (Torah *sheb'al peh*), which consists of ongoing interpretations and expansions of the meaning of the Written Torah as well as the customs that evolved over time among the Jewish people and ultimately got written down, in large measure, in the Mishnah and Talmud (q.v.). The term Torah is used also, by extension, to mean all Jewish sacred literature, including books written in the Middle Ages, the modern period, and even contemporary times. Thus, one is "studying

Torah" when one is studying these texts as well as classical Jewish literature.

tragedy of the commons: An analysis proposed by the biologist Garrett Hardin of the collapse of unmanaged common-pool resources whereby individual rational choice by participants trying to better their situation leads to overall worsening for all (structurally equivalent to "the prisoner's dilemma" in game theory). Many environmental problems, from littering to overfishing to global warming, are examples of the tragedy of the commons.

Tu B'Shvat (TOO b'-SHVAHT): The fifteenth of the midwinter month of Shvat. Mentioned in the Mishnah (*Rosh Hashanah* 1:1) as a new year for trees regarding the tithing of fruit. Later, building on the symbolic significance of trees and of different kinds of fruit, was imbued with mystical meaning. A seder, based on the Pesach Seder, was also composed. More recently, Tu B'Shvat has become a time of tree planting, especially in Israel, and a day to focus general ecological concerns.

tza'ar ba'alei chayim (TZAH-ahr bah-ah-LAY khah-YEEM): The pain of living beings. Refers to the values and laws regarding kindness to animals and their proper treatment.

tzaddik (tsah-DEEK): A righteous or just person.

tzedek (TZEH-dek): Justice. A form of this word, *tzedakah* (tzeh-dah-KAH or, commonly, tzeh-DAH-kah), refers to acts of charity.

tzimtzum (tzeem-TZOOM): Contraction. Refers to the doctrine of the Lurianic Kabbalah of the need for God to contract the divine self in order to "make room" for the Creation.

Zionism: The national liberation movement of the Jewish people. Founded in the nineteenth century (drawing on the historical Jewish consciousness of peoplehood), Zionism was a product of (or a response to) European nationalism, and called for a return of the Jewish people to the Land of Israel and the establishment there of a Jewish state, with a renaissance of the Hebrew language and Jewish culture. There have been various schools of Zionist ideology, including socialist, religious, political, and cultural. Each has a different agenda, and a different relationship to central questions, such as the continuing role of the Jewish Diaspora, the role of religion in the state, and the place of Arab citizens of Israel. Zionism remains a force in Jewish life today, focusing on the centrality of the State of Israel and its support in Jewish identity.

Index

activism, environmental: Jewish engagement and, 109; perception of in Israel, 224; sustainability and, 225; *tikkun* (repair) and, 218, 231–232
Adnei Kesef, 53
affluence, consumption and, 119
afterlife belief, 71–72
Alter, Robert, 35, 36
Alterman, Natan, 216–217
animal rights limitations, 105
animals, man's relationship to: Bible and, 44–45; environmental vs. religious perspectives on, 53–58
animals, treatment of: animal rights limitations and, 105; environmental sensibility and, 107; humility and, 106; obligations and, 104–106; *pikuach nefesh* (mandate to save lives) and, 102, 104; Torah and, 103, 105–106; *tzadikkim* (righteous ones) and, 105
anthropocentrism, White, Lynn, Jr. and, 16–18
Artson, Bradley Shavit, 8, 212
avoda (work), duty and, 47–49
avot nezikin (damages), 128

bal tashchit (do not destroy): consumption and, 120–121; Jewish environmental values and, 93, 100; restraint and, 108
behavior, moral and economic, prayer and, 193
berachot (blessings). *See* blessings; prayer/blessings
Berry, Wendell, 15
Between Man and God, 22
Bialik, Chayin Nachman, 210
Bible: man's relationship to animals and, 44–45; meat eating and, 154–156; urban land use and, 136; urban life and, 135; wandering/mobility (Jewish) and,

213; wilderness and, 140–143; *See also creation references; specific stories;* Torah
biblical cubism concept, 35, 36
biocentrism (eco-centrism), Jewish teachings and, 81–82, 96
biodiversity: E. O. Wilson and, 142; Jewish environmental values and, 113, 117, 144–149; Nachmanides and, 146; State of Israel and, 219; wilderness and, 143–145
blessings: related to nature, 166; *See also* prayer/blessings
Book of Education. See Sefer Hachinuch
Breuer, Mordechai, 36
brit (covenant) concept, 83, 92
building and destruction, *bal tashchit* and, 108
Bunim, Simcha, 58
burial, Jewish, 122

Cain and Abel, shepherd/farmer conflict, 60–61
calendar, Jewish: history/nature and, 167–170; holidays, harvests, seasons and, 168–169; Jewish ecological life and, 167–169; Jewish teachings/natural world and, 169; significance of sun and moon, 196; spiritual life and, 166–168; spiritual needs and, 165, 166
carnivory, Creation and, 44–45
challenges, environmental. *See* issues, current
charity, environmental causes and, 30, 134
cheshbon nefesh (soul searching), and caring, 5
city: environmental issues and, 64; Bible and, 60, 63–65; symbolic significance of, 64; *See also specific "urban" references*

commandment to honor parents: sustainability and, 159–163; treatment of natural world and, 161–163

commons: concept *(migrash)*, 136–137; issues surrounding, 129–131; Maimonides and, 137

compassion, treatment of animals and, 106

consumption: advertising and, 125–127; affluence and, 119; *bal tashchit* (do not destroy) and, 120–121; by consumer class, 123*t;* diet and, 123*t;* dissatisfaction and, 119–120; environmental issues in Israel, 223; fulfillment and, 124–125, 124*t;* guidelines, 120–122; Hanukkah and, 178–179; human body and, 120–121; issues, current, 118–126; limits on, 120; material culture and, 123*t; Pirkei Avot* and, 119; population and, 118; transportation and, 123*t;* waste and, 127

consumption guidelines: *bal tashchit* (do not destroy) and, 120–121; Jewish burial and, 122; Maimonides and, 122; *Mishneh Torah* and, 122; *Pirkei Avot* and, 119; Talmud and, 121–122

contraction *(tzimtzum)*, moral responsibility and, 58

coveting, 125–127. *See also* consumption; sufficiency

Creation: carnivory and, 44–45; focus on work, 59; Genesis 1 vs. Genesis 2, 38–42; Genesis 2, 37–38; history and, 58–66; humanity and, 2; multiple versions of, 35–36; partnership between God and his creations, 66–67; Shabbat and, 51–53, 185; sunlight, *shacharit* and, 195–196; Talmud midrash and, 51–53; technology and, 19

Creation story, later chapters of Genesis: Cain and Abel (shepherd and farmer conflict), 60; first city, 60; Noah and the Flood, 61, 64; Tower of Babel (Generation of Division), 63–65

crises, environmental: extinction, 11; global warming, 12; perception of, 13–14; poverty, 12; resource depletion, 11; urban issues, 12; widening social gap, 12

cubism, biblical, concept, 35, 36

cultural values and social policy, 217

current issues. *See* issues, current

damages: *avot nezikin* concept, 128; classes of, 128; pollution and, 129; "Tragedy of the Commons" and, 129–131; waste and, 128

desolation, State of Israel and, 219–221

destruction and building, *bal tashchit* and, 108

development, State of Israel and, 222

dialogic approach *(asmachta)*, to environmental issues, 6

Diasporic Jewish life: environmental sensibility and, 210–212; Jewish alienation from nature and, 28

Diasporic Jews and Israelis: environmental causes and, 225; need for cooperation between, 225–230

diet: consumption and, 123*t;* environmental issues and, 150–151; Jewish culture and, 150; laws regarding *kashrut* and, 150; overeating and, 124; sustainability and, 151–152; *tza'ar ba'alei chayim* (prevention of cruelty to animals) and, 150–151

diets, chemical-based, sustainability and, 152

diets, meat-based: Halacha and, 152; health preservation of and, 152–154; Jewish teachings and, 154–156; sustainability and, 152, 157; wastefulness and, 152–153

Disraeli, Benjamin, 53, 55, 56

divine anthropology, (God's-eye view of people), 35

divine reward and punishment concept, 83–84

dominion of humans, Genesis 1 and, 42–47

duties of humans, Genesis and, 47–49

Earth, theories and writings, 81–82

ecological life, Jewish calendar and, 167–169

Ehrlich, Paul, 23

Eliezer, R., 87

environment: bases of Jewish disconnection from, 28–29; building and destruction and, 108; complexity of, 107–111; Jewish engagement and, 107–111, 138; Jewish values and, 138; nature vs., 11; restraint and, 111; *tikkun* (repair) concept and, 108–111; values and, 108; Yom Kippur restrictions and, 171

environmental activism, Zionism and, 109, 218, 224, 225, 231–232 environmental crises: Wendell Berry and, 15; State of Israel and, 225

environmentalism: defined, 12; traditional beliefs and, 30–31

environmental legislation, 129–131

environmental perspectives, Zionist ideals, 221

environmental sensibility: sense of place and, 85, 204–206; stewardship concept and, 84

Environmental World Summit (2005), Johannesburg, 12

erosion, ancient world and, 2

ethical issues: obligations concerning nature, 88–89; protection of the weak, 81

Ethics of the Sages. *See Pirkei Avot*

exile: Jewish disconnection from environment and, 28; Jewish sense of place and, 206–207

extinction, 11, 144, 146–147

Ezrahi, Yaron, 217

family size, 115–118

food production, sustainability and, 161

Fox, Michal Smart, 57

freedom: environmental movement and, 134; justice and, 132

Freudenstein, Eric, 25

Fromm, Erich, Shabbat and, 183

fulfillment, consumption and, 124–125, 124*t*

Gaon, R. Saadya, 44

gemilut chasadim (lovingkindness), environmental causes and, 30

Genesis (chapters 1 and 2): concept of nature (Genesis 2), 41–42; dominion (Genesis 1), 42–47; dominion of humans and (Genesis 1), 42–47; human duties (Genesis 2), 47–49; humanity and Creation and, 33–35; stewardship (Genesis 2), 47–52

Genesis, differences between two chapters: content and style, 41; environmentalism and, 43; Genesis 1 and 2: comparative readings, 36–42; good and evil, 40; order of Creation, 38–39; physical environment, 40–42; relations of sexes, 41

global warming, 12

Gordis, Robert, 25

Gorman, Paul, 147, 231

Great Chain of Being, 18–19

Grunfeld, Isadore, 183

Guide for the Perplexed, 45, 81–82, 160; *See also* Maimonides

Halacha: *bal tashchit* (do not destroy) and, 91; preservation of health and, 152; Jewish environmental values and, 3, 132, 146; Jewish law and, 7; land-related issues and, 88–92; rescuing innocents from harmful acts, 91; treatment of nature during war and, 93; trees and, 98; Yom Kippur and, 170

Halacha and Aggada, 210

Hanukkah: consumption and, 178–179; natural themes and, 176–179

Hardin, Garrett, 129

harvests and seasons, Jewish holidays and, 168–169

Harvey, David, 207

Hasidic focus, 29

health preservation: Halacha and, 152; meat-based diets and, 152–154; vegetarianism and, 152–154, 156–157

heaven, belief in, 73–74

Heschel, Abraham Joshua: Creation and, 21–22; "divine anthropology" and, 35; keva and, 194; Shabbat and, 187

hiddushim (innovations), 11

Hirsch, Samson Raphael: Jewish calendar and, 166; urban issues and, 137–138

"Historic Roots of Our Ecologic Crisis." *See* White, Lynn, Jr.

history: Creation story and, 58–66; Jewish calendar and, 167–170; nature and, 74

holidays, Jewish, themes and symbols: Hanukkah, 176–179; moon/sun significance of, 196–197; Pesach, 174, 175; Rosh Hashanah, 170, 171; Shabbat, 182–188; Shavuot,, 174; Shemini Atzeret, 170–171; *shmitah*, 188–192; Sukkot, 170–174; Tu B'Shvat, 179–182; Yom Kippur, 170, 171

human body: *bal tashchit* (do not destroy) and, 120–121; consumption and, 120–121

humanity: Creation and, 2, 33–35; love of/sustaining world and, 92

human-nature relationships, complexity of, 20–22, 68–69

Ibn Ezra, Abraham, 90; relationship between people and trees, 95–96; stewardship concept and, 90
immigration, State of Israel, 222, 224
Israel, Land of: as concept, 203; connection between holidays and calendar, 199; environmental concepts and, 203; Jewish natural world teachings and, 201; Jewish sense of place and, 201–207; as real place, 203; unique connection of all Jews to, 202–203
Israel, State of: beauty/ecological wealth of, 219–220; biodiversity, 219; culture/social policy/environment and, 217; desolation, 219–221; development and, 222; Diaspora and, 212; environmental awareness in context of hardship, 222–223; environmental challenges, 222–224; environmental issues and, 215–219, 222–225; environmental priorities of, 226; Jewish environmental values and, 224; Jews/Arabs and, 227–228; national priorities, 226; population policy, 222–223; relevance to Jewish identify, 227; security, 226; Zionism, modernization and, 227
issues, current: consumption, 118–126; justice and, 132–134; land use, 131–138; population, 114–116; resource allocation, 135; urban life, 131–138
issues, environmental: compartmentalization and sustainability, 134–135; consumption, 223; Israeli priorities and, 226; Judaism and, 1–6, 51; kashrut and, 157–159; population growth and, 222–223; as rallying point for Jews and Arabs, 227–228; shelter, 149; State of Israel and, 215–219, 222–226; Torah and, 2; See also diet references
issues, related: cultural values and social policy, 217; Jewish environmental engagement, 107–111; Jewish sense of place, 85, 199, 201, 203, 206; social policy and cultural values, 217; Zionism, 214–215
issues, underlying, 3, 4

Jewish-Arab (Israeli) relationship: environmentalism and, 229; environmental justice and, 228;

environmental movement improving, 229–230; hindrances to, 228–229
Jewish cultural-historical background: alienation from nature and, 74–78; sense of place and, 85
Jewish environmental values: concepts of, 25; urban sprawl and, 138; wilderness and, 140–143
Jewish sense of place. See sense of place
Jewish teachings supportive of environmental concerns: bal tashchit (do not destroy), 93; biocentrism (ecocentrism) and, 81–82; brit, 83, 92; concept of brit between God and nature after Flood, 92; divine reward and punishment, 83–84; Land of Israel, 201; mishnah, 78; Pirkei Avot, 76; Psalms, 82–83; Talmud, 76
Joshua, R., 87
Judaism, unnatural, 25–31
justice, environmental: environmental movement and, 132–134; Jewish-Arab coexistence and, 228; protection of future generations and, 226

Kabbalah, environmentalism and, 29, 58
kashrut, environmental issues and, 157–159
Kaspi, Ibn, 53, 55
Kay, Jeanne, 25
keva (the set form), 193–194

Lamm, Norman, 25
land: access to resources, 176; commodity vs. community, 20
Land of Israel. See Israel, Land of
land-related issues, Halacha and, 88–92
landscapes, patriarchs and, 88
land use, 131–138
legal and moral issues, 88–92. See also Halacha
legislation, environmental, 129–131
Leopold, Aldo, 54, 84, 155
leovda uleshomra (work and protect) concept, 47–49
Lonely Man of Faith, 41. See also Soloveitchik, Joseph
Lovelock, James, 81

Maimonides: commons and, 137; consumption guidelines, 122; coveting and, 126; Guide for the Perplexed, 45, 81–82, 160; Mishneh Torah, 98
material culture, consumption and, 123t
meat eating. See diets, meat-based

messianic times, reasons to sustain the world, 92
Mishneh Torah, 98, 122
mitzvot (commandment) and natural world, 88–89
moral responsibility, contraction *(tzimtzum)* and, 58
Mumford, Lewis, urban issues and, 137–138

Nachmanides, 44
National Religious Partnership for the Environment, 231
natural world: ethical obligations and, 88–89; interdependence between humans and in Bible, 62; Shabbat and, 184–185; as source of wisdom and morality, 80; treatment of, 161–163
nature: dominion vs. stewardship, 79–80; environment vs., 11; humanity and, 88; protection of the weak and, 81; *tikkun* (repair) concept and, 109–111; Torah and, 74–77; Tu B'Shvat and, 179; uses of, 94
nature, Jewish alienation from: cultural-historical background and, 74–78; Diasporic Jewish life from and, 28; emphasis on study (Torah), 74–78; Land of Israel connection of holidays and calendar, 199; need to overcome, 77, 78; repair *(tikkun)* needed, 78; rift between Torah and nature, 77–78; solutions for, 77–78
needs, spiritual, 165–166
Noah and the Flood: Creation story, later chapters, 64; interdependence between humans /natural world (theme), 62
Noahide laws of general morality, 45, 61–63

olam haba (the afterlife), 71–72
Orit, Ben-David, Zionism, 218
overconsumption, coveting and, 125–127. *See also* consumption; sufficiency
overeating, 124

pagan rituals, traditional Jewish spirituality and, 28, 170
partnership between God and his creations, 66–67
patriarch landscapes, 88
Periodic Report on Yom Kippur, 171*t*

perspectives on humans/creation, 23–24
Pesach, 174, 175
Philo (Greco-Jewish philosopher), 127
pikuach nefesh (mandate to save lives), animals and, 102, 104
Pirkei Avot, 73; consumption and, 119; Torah and nature, Mishnah on, 74–75; wilderness and, 142
policy, State of Israel: cultural/social/environmental, 217; population, 222–223
pollution: ancient world and, 2; in Israel, 171–172, 171*t*, 225; "Tragedy of the Commons" and, 129–131; Yom Kippur and, 171, 171*t*
population: the Bible and, 116–117; consumption and, 118; family size and, 115–118; growth in Israel, 222, 224; growth rate and, 114*t*, 115; policy in Israel, 222–223; problem bases, 114–115; standard of living and, 115–116; sustainability and, 114–116, 117
possessions of others, accountability for, 91
poverty, environment and, 12
prayer/blessings: as ritual, 192–199; behavior, moral and economic, 193; food, 197–199; natural elements and, 87–88
preservation: conquest and, 218; development and, 97; war and, 93–97; Zionist ideals and, 221
procreation commandment, 46
protection: future generations and, 226; *shemira* concept and, 47–48; of the weak, 81
Psalms, 82–83

rain, 85–87
recreation, wilderness and, 139–140
religion: environmental degradation and, 18; environmental movement and, 13
Religious Partnership for the Environment, 147
religious vs. secular Israeli groups, 224–225
repair *(tikkun)*. *See tikkun* (repair) concept
representation, justice and, 132
resources: access to and justice, 132–133; allocation of, 135; depletion of, 11; land access and, 176

responsibility/humility, Talmud midrash and, 51
resurrection *(techiyat hameitim)*, 73
rights of the poor, legislation and, 134
Rosh Hashanah, 170, 171
Rothschild, Fritz, 22
Rubber Bullets, 217

Schwartzschild, Steven, "Unnatural Jew" and, 26–31
security, Israeli national priorities and, 226
Sefer Hachinuch, 67–68, 100–101
self-regulating organism, theories regarding Earth, 81–82
sense of place: complexity of for Jews, 206; environmental sensibility and, 85, 204–206; impact of Jewish exile and, 206–207; Jewish alienation from nature and, 199; Jewish identity and, 207; Jewish mobility and, 207–215; Land of Israel and, 201–207; Zionism and, 208, 214–215
settlements *(chalutziyut)* impact on Jewish-Arab relations, 228
Shabbat: Abraham Joshua Heschel and, 187; Creation and, 51–53, 185; Eric Fromm and, 183; natural world and, 184–185; nature and, 76; social act of, 185–186; spiritual needs and, 165; theme and symbolism and, 182–188; theory behind practice of, 183–184; urban sprawl and, 138
shacharit, sunlight and, 195–196
Shemini Atzeret, 170–171, 172
shepherd/farmer conflict, Cain and Abel, 60–61
shmitah (sabbatical): as an environmental concept, 188–189; holidays, Jewish, natural/historical themes, cycles, symbolism, 188–192; as opportunity to solve social and environmental issues, 191–192; societal renewal and, 189; as spiritual concept, 189; spiritual needs and, 165
social acts, Shabbat and, 185–186
social policy and cultural values, 217
Society for the Protection of Nature in Israel (SPNI), 218
Soloveitchik, Joseph, 36, 41
spiritual life, Jewish calendar and, 166–168
standard of living, population and, 115–116

State of Israel. *See* Israel, State of
stewardship concept: Abraham Ibn Ezra and, 90; as environmental ethical ideal, 50–51; environmental sensibility and, 84; responsibility for saving the Earth and, 89–90
suffering, prevention of, 89
sufficiency: excess and, 123; obesity and, 123; recycling and, 123; Talmud and, 121
sukkah, Sukkot (fall harvest), environmental aspects of, 173–174
Sukkot (fall harvest), 170–174
sustainability: commandment to honor parents and, 159–163; diet and, 151–152, 157; environmental activism and, 225; environmental agenda and, 11; environmental issue compartmentalization and, 134–135; food production and, 161; population and, 114–116, 117; urban sprawl and, 135
sustaining the world, messianic times and, 92

Tal, Alon, 215
Talmud: consumption guidelines and, 121–122; discussion on study vs. action, 8; Jewish law and, 7; meat-eating and, 155–156; sufficiency and, 121; "Tragedy of the Commons" and, 129–131; waste and, 127–128
technology, mastery over creation and, 19
territorial-based identity, David Harvey and, 207
theories related to environmental issues, 81–82
tikkun (repair) concept: defined, 77–78; imperfections of nature and, 109–111; Jewish environmental engagement and, 108–111; Zionism and, 218
tohu, why world was created and, 68
Torah: accountability for possession of others, 91; animals/treatment and, 103; environmental issues and, 2; limitations on destruction during war and, 94–95; meat eating and, 155; nature and, 74–77; *teva* vs., 74; *See also* Bible; Halacha
Tower of Babel, 63–65
traditional beliefs, Jewish disconnection from environment and, 29
"Tragedy of the Commons," 129–131
transportation, consumption and, 123t

trees: treatment of shade vs. fruit, 96, 98–99; peacetime treatment of, 98–100; army treatment of, 94–97; Tu B'Shvat and, 179–182

Troster, Lawrence, 57

Tu B'Shvat: ecological significance of, 180, 181–182; economic significance of, 180; national-political significance, 181; nature/environment, connection to, 179; spiritual significance of, 180–181; trees and, 179–182

tza'ar ba'alei chayim (prevention of cruelty to animals), 101–103, 150–151

tzadikkim (righteous ones), animals and their treatment and, 105

tzedakah (charity), 30

tzimtzum (contraction), moral responsibility and, 58

"Unnatural Jew," 26–31

urban immorality, Biblical history and, 61

urban issues: environmental crises and, 12; Lewis Mumford and, 137–138; Samson Raphael Hirsch and, 137–138

urban life: Bible and, 135; current environmental issues and, 131–138

urban sprawl, 135, 136, 138

values, Jewish environmental: activism *(tikkun)* and, 231–232; *bal tashchit* (do not destroy) and, 93, 100, 101; biodiversity and, 144–149; concept of, 25; Halacha and, 132, 146; justice and, 132–134; nature and protection of the weak, 81; religious vs. secular Israeli groups and, 224–225; State of Israel, 224; *tza'ar ba'alei chayim* (prevention of cruelty to animals) and, 101–103; urban sprawl and, 138

view of humans *(adam):* divine image and, 57–58; God vs. animal, 55–57;

uniting heaven and earth (angels or apes), 54–58

wandering/mobility (Jewish): alienation from nature and, 209–211; Bible and, 213; reconnection to nature upon return from Diaspora, 210–211; sense of place and, 207–215

war: limitations on destruction during, 94–95; preservation of nature and, 93–97; trees and, 94–96

waste: consumption and, 127; damages and, 128; disposal, 127–128; Talmud and, 127–128; "Tragedy of the Commons" and, 129–131

water, Sukkot and, 173–174. *See also* rain

White, Lynn, Jr., 14–18, 20, 25.

Wiesel, Elie, 142

wilderness: Bible and, 140–143; biodiversity and, 143–145; Jewish values and, 140–143; *Pirkei Avot* and, 142; recreation and, 139–140

Wilson, E. O., 142

work, human: concept of, 59–60; duties of humans and, 47–49; the garden and, 59

Yom Kippur, 171; air pollution in Tel Aviv, 171–172, 171*t;* environmental restrictions and, 171; Halacha and, 170

Zionism: Ben-David Orit and, 218; environmental activism *(tikkun)* and, 218; environmentalism and, 215–225; environmental narrative and, 221–222; ideals, 221; Jewish disconnection from environment and, 28–29; modernization and, 227; preservation and conquest and, 218; sense of place and, 208

Zohar Hadash, 49

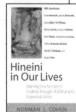

Congregation Resources

The Art of Public Prayer, 2nd Edition: Not for Clergy Only *By Lawrence A. Hoffman*
6 x 9, 272 pp, Quality PB, 978-1-893361-06-5 **$19.99** *(A SkyLight Paths book)*

Becoming a Congregation of Learners: Learning as a Key to Revitalizing
Congregational Life *By Isa Aron, PhD; Foreword by Rabbi Lawrence A. Hoffman*
6 x 9, 304 pp, Quality PB, 978-1-58023-089-6 **$19.95**

Finding a Spiritual Home: How a New Generation of Jews Can Transform the
American Synagogue *By Rabbi Sidney Schwarz*
6 x 9, 352 pp, Quality PB, 978-1-58023-185-5 **$19.95**

Jewish Pastoral Care, 2nd Edition: A Practical Handbook from Traditional &
Contemporary Sources *Edited by Rabbi Dayle A. Friedman*
6 x 9, 528 pp, HC, 978-1-58023-221-0 **$40.00**

Jewish Spiritual Direction: An Innovative Guide from Traditional and Contemporary
Sources *Edited by Rabbi Howard A. Addison and Barbara Eve Breitman*
6 x 9, 368 pp, HC, 978-1-58023-230-2 **$30.00**

The Self-Renewing Congregation: Organizational Strategies for Revitalizing
Congregational Life *By Isa Aron, PhD; Foreword by Dr. Ron Wolfson*
6 x 9, 304 pp, Quality PB, 978-1-58023-166-4 **$19.95**

Spiritual Community: The Power to Restore Hope, Commitment and Joy
By Rabbi David A. Teutsch, PhD 5½ x 8½, 144 pp, HC, 978-1-58023-270-8 **$19.99**

The Spirituality of Welcoming: How to Transform Your Congregation into a
Sacred Community *By Dr. Ron Wolfson* 6 x 9, 224 pp, Quality PB, 978-1-58023-244-9 **$19.99**

Rethinking Synagogues: A New Vocabulary for Congregational Life
By Rabbi Lawrence A. Hoffman 6 x 9, 240 pp, Quality PB, 978-1-58023-248-7 **$19.99**

Children's Books

What You Will See Inside a Synagogue
By Rabbi Lawrence A. Hoffman and Dr. Ron Wolfson; Full-color photos by Bill Aron
A colorful, fun-to-read introduction that explains the ways and whys of Jewish
worship and religious life.
8½ x 10½, 32 pp, Full-color photos, HC, 978-1-59473-012-2 **$17.99** *For ages 6 & up* *(A SkyLight Paths book)*

The Kids' Fun Book of Jewish Time
By Emily Sper 9 x 7½, 24 pp, Full-color illus., HC, 978-1-58023-311-8 **$16.99**

In God's Hands
By Lawrence Kushner and Gary Schmidt 9 x 12, 32 pp, HC, 978-1-58023-224-1 **$16.99**

Because Nothing Looks Like God
By Lawrence and Karen Kushner
Introduces children to the possibilities of spiritual life.
11 x 8½, 32 pp, Full-color illus., HC, 978-1-58023-092-6 **$16.95** *For ages 4 & up*

Also Available: **Because Nothing Looks Like God Teacher's Guide**
8½ x 11, 22 pp, PB, 978-1-58023-140-4 **$6.95** *For ages 5–8*

Board Book Companions to *Because Nothing Looks Like God*
5 x 5, 24 pp, Full-color illus., SkyLight Paths Board Books *For ages 0–4*

What Does God Look Like? 978-1-893361-23-2 **$7.99**

How Does God Make Things Happen? 978-1-893361-24-9 **$7.95**

Where Is God? 978-1-893361-17-1 **$7.99**

The Book of Miracles: A Young Person's Guide to Jewish Spiritual Awareness
By Lawrence Kushner. All-new illustrations by the author
6 x 9, 96 pp, 2-color illus., HC, 978-1-879045-78-1 **$16.95** *For ages 9 and up*

In Our Image: God's First Creatures
By Nancy Sohn Swartz 9 x 12, 32 pp, Full-color illus., HC, 978-1-879045-99-6 **$16.95** *For ages 4 & up*

Also Available as a Board Book: **How Did the Animals Help God?**
5 x 5, 24 pp, Board, Full-color illus., 978-1-59473-044-3 **$7.99** *For ages 0–4* *(A SkyLight Paths book)*

Holidays/Holy Days

Rosh Hashanah Readings: Inspiration, Information and Contemplation
Yom Kippur Readings: Inspiration, Information and Contemplation
Edited by Rabbi Dov Peretz Elkins with Section Introductions from Arthur Green's These Are the Words
An extraordinary collection of readings, prayers and insights that enable the modern worshiper to enter into the spirit of the High Holy Days in a personal and powerful way, permitting the meaning of the Jewish New Year to enter the heart.

RHR: 6 x 9, 400 pp, HC, 978-1-58023-239-5 **$24.99**
YKR: 6 x 9, 368 pp, HC, 978-1-58023-271-5 **$24.99**

Jewish Holidays: A Brief Introduction for Christians
By Rabbi Kerry M. Olitzky and Rabbi Daniel Judson
5½ x 8½, 144 pp, Quality PB, 978-1-58023-302-6 **$16.99**

Leading the Passover Journey: The Seder's Meaning Revealed,
the Haggadah's Story Retold *By Rabbi Nathan Laufer*
Uncovers the hidden meaning of the Seder's rituals and customs.
6 x 9, 224 pp, HC, 978-1-58023-211-1 **$24.99**

Reclaiming Judaism as a Spiritual Practice: Holy Days and Shabbat
By Rabbi Goldie Milgram
7 x 9, 272 pp, Quality PB, 978-1-58023-205-0 **$19.99**

7th Heaven: Celebrating Shabbat with Rebbe Nachman of Breslov
By Moshe Mykoff with the Breslov Research Institute
5⅛ x 8¼, 224 pp, Deluxe PB w/flaps, 978-1-58023-175-6 **$18.95**

The Women's Passover Companion: Women's Reflections on the
Festival of Freedom *Edited by Rabbi Sharon Cohen Anisfeld, Tara Mohr, and Catherine Spector*
Groundbreaking. A provocative conversation about women's relationships to Passover as well as the roots and meanings of women's seders.
6 x 9, 352 pp, Quality PB, 978-1-58023-231-9 **$19.99**

The Women's Seder Sourcebook: Rituals & Readings for Use at the
Passover Seder *Edited by Rabbi Sharon Cohen Anisfeld, Tara Mohr, and Catherine Spector*
Gathers the voices of more than one hundred women in readings, personal and creative reflections, commentaries, blessings, and ritual suggestions that can be incorporated into your Passover celebration.
6 x 9, 384 pp, Quality PB, 978-1-58023-232-6 **$19.99**

Creating Lively Passover Seders: A Sourcebook of Engaging Tales, Texts & Activities
By David Arnow, PhD 7 x 9, 416 pp, Quality PB, 978-1-58023-184-8 **$24.99**

Hanukkah, 2nd Edition: The Family Guide to Spiritual Celebration
By Dr. Ron Wolfson. Edited by Joel Lurie Grishaver.
7 x 9, 240 pp, illus., Quality PB, 978-1-58023-122-0 **$18.95**

The Jewish Family Fun Book: Holiday Projects, Everyday Activities, and Travel Ideas
with Jewish Themes *By Danielle Dardashti and Roni Sarig. Illus. by Avi Katz.*
6 x 9, 288 pp, 70+ b/w illus. & diagrams, Quality PB, 978-1-58023-171-8 **$18.95**

The Jewish Gardening Cookbook: Growing Plants & Cooking for Holidays
& Festivals *By Michael Brown* 6 x 9, 224 pp, 30+ b/w illus., Quality PB, 978-1-58023-116-9 **$16.95**

The Jewish Lights Book of Fun Classroom Activities: Simple and Seasonal
Projects for Teachers and Students *By Danielle Dardashti and Roni Sarig*
6 x 9, 240 pp, Quality PB, 978-1-58023-206-7 **$19.99**

Passover, 2nd Edition: The Family Guide to Spiritual Celebration
By Dr. Ron Wolfson with Joel Lurie Grishaver 7 x 9, 352 pp, Quality PB, 978-1-58023-174-9 **$19.95**

Shabbat, 2nd Edition: The Family Guide to Preparing for and Celebrating the Sabbath
By Dr. Ron Wolfson 7 x 9, 320 pp, illus., Quality PB, 978-1-58023-164-0 **$19.99**

Sharing Blessings: Children's Stories for Exploring the Spirit of the Jewish Holidays
By Rahel Musleah and Rabbi Michael Klayman
8½ x 11, 64 pp, Full-color illus., HC, 978-1-879045-71-2 **$18.95** *For ages 6 & up*

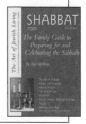

Inspiration

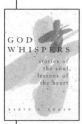

God's To-Do List: 103 Ways to Live Your Purpose for Doing God's Work on Earth
By Dr. Ron Wolfson 6 x 9, 150 pp, Quality PB, 978-1-58023-301-9 **$15.99**

God in All Moments: Mystical & Practical Spiritual Wisdom from Hasidic Masters
Edited and translated by Or N. Rose with Ebn D. Leader
5½ x 8½, 192 pp, Quality PB, 978-1-58023-186-2 **$16.95**

Our Dance with God: Finding Prayer, Perspective and Meaning in the Stories of Our
Lives By Karyn D. Kedar 6 x 9, 176 pp, Quality PB, 978-1-58023-202-9 **$16.99**

Also Available: **The Dance of the Dolphin** (HC edition of *Our Dance with God*)
6 x 9, 176 pp, HC, 978-1-58023-154-1 **$19.95**

The Empty Chair: Finding Hope and Joy—Timeless Wisdom from a Hasidic Master,
Rebbe Nachman of Breslov Adapted by Moshe Mykoff and the Breslov Research Institute
4 x 6, 128 pp, 2-color text, Deluxe PB w/flaps, 978-1-879045-67-5 **$9.95**

The Gentle Weapon: Prayers for Everyday and Not-So-Everyday Moments—
Timeless Wisdom from the Teachings of the Hasidic Master, Rebbe Nachman of Breslov
Adapted by Moshe Mykoff and S. C. Mizrahi, together with the Breslov Research Institute
4 x 6, 144 pp, 2-color text, Deluxe PB w/flaps, 978-1-58023-022-3 **$9.99**

God Whispers: Stories of the Soul, Lessons of the Heart By Karyn D. Kedar
6 x 9, 176 pp, Quality PB, 978-1-58023-088-9 **$15.95**

An Orphan in History: One Man's Triumphant Search for His Jewish Roots
By Paul Cowan; Afterword by Rachel Cowan. 6 x 9, 288 pp, Quality PB, 978-1-58023-135-0 **$16.95**

Restful Reflections: Nighttime Inspiration to Calm the Soul, Based on Jewish Wisdom
By Rabbi Kerry M. Olitzky & Rabbi Lori Forman 4½ x 6½, 448 pp, Quality PB, 978-1-58023-091-9 **$15.95**

Sacred Intentions: Daily Inspiration to Strengthen the Spirit, Based on Jewish Wisdom
By Rabbi Kerry M. Olitzky and Rabbi Lori Forman 4½ x 6½, 448 pp, Quality PB, 978-1-58023-061-2 **$15.95**

Kabbalah/Mysticism/Enneagram

Awakening to Kabbalah: The Guiding Light of Spiritual Fulfillment
By Rav Michael Laitman, PhD 6 x 9, 192 pp, HC, 978-1-58023-264-7 **$21.99**

Seek My Face: A Jewish Mystical Theology By Arthur Green
6 x 9, 304 pp, Quality PB, 978-1-58023-130-5 **$19.95**

Zohar: Annotated & Explained
Translation and annotation by Daniel C. Matt; Foreword by Andrew Harvey
5½ x 8½, 176 pp, Quality PB, 978-1-893361-51-5 **$15.99** *(A SkyLight Paths book)*

Cast in God's Image: Discover Your Personality Type Using the Enneagram and Kabbalah
By Rabbi Howard A. Addison
7 x 9, 176 pp, Quality PB, Layflat binding, 20+ journaling exercises, 978-1-58023-124-4 **$16.95**

Ehyeh: A Kabbalah for Tomorrow
By Arthur Green 6 x 9, 224 pp, Quality PB, 978-1-58023-213-5 **$16.99**

The Enneagram and Kabbalah, 2nd Edition: Reading Your Soul
By Rabbi Howard A. Addison 6 x 9, 192 pp, Quality PB, 978-1-58023-229-6 **$16.99**

Finding Joy: A Practical Spiritual Guide to Happiness By Dannel I. Schwartz with Mark Hass
6 x 9, 192 pp, Quality PB, 978-1-58023-009-4 **$14.95**

The Flame of the Heart: Prayers of a Chasidic Mystic By Reb Noson of Breslov. Translated by
David Sears with the Breslov Research Institute 5 x 7¼, 160 pp, Quality PB, 978-1-58023-246-3 **$15.99**

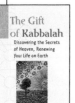

The Gift of Kabbalah: Discovering the Secrets of Heaven, Renewing Your Life on Earth
By Tamar Frankiel, PhD 6 x 9, 256 pp, Quality PB, 978-1-58023-141-1 **$16.95;**
HC, 978-1-58023-108-4 **$21.95**

Kabbalah: A Brief Introduction for Christians
By Tamar Frankiel, PhD 5½ x 8½, 208 pp, Quality PB, 978-1-58023-303-3 **$16.99**

The Lost Princess and Other Kabbalistic Tales of Rebbe Nachman of Breslov
The Seven Beggars and Other Kabbalistic Tales of Rebbe Nachman of Breslov
Translated by Rabbi Aryeh Kaplan; Preface by Rabbi Chaim Kramer
Lost Princess: 6 x 9, 400 pp, Quality PB, 978-1-58023-217-3 **$18.99**
Seven Beggars: 6 x 9, 192 pp, Quality PB, 978-1-58023-250-0 **$16.99**

See also *The Way Into Jewish Mystical Tradition* in Spirituality / The Way Into... Series

Life Cycle
Marriage / Parenting / Family / Aging

Jewish Fathers: A Legacy of Love
Photographs by Lloyd Wolf. Essays by Paula Wolfson. Foreword by Rabbi Harold Kushner.
Honors the role of contemporary Jewish fathers in America. Each father tells in his own words what it means to be a parent and Jewish, and what he learned from his own father. Insightful photos.
10¾ x 9⅞, 144 pp with 100+ duotone photos, HC, 978-1-58023-204-3 **$30.00**

The New Jewish Baby Album: Creating and Celebrating the Beginning of a Spiritual Life—A Jewish Lights Companion
By the Editors at Jewish Lights. Foreword by Anita Diamant. Preface by Rabbi Sandy Eisenberg Sasso.
A spiritual keepsake that will be treasured for generations. More than just a memory book, *shows you how—and why it's important*—to create a Jewish home and a Jewish life. 8 x 10, 64 pp, Deluxe Padded HC, Full-color illus., 978-1-58023-138-1 **$19.95**

The Jewish Pregnancy Book: A Resource for the Soul, Body & Mind during Pregnancy, Birth & the First Three Months
By Sandy Falk, MD, and Rabbi Daniel Judson, with Steven A. Rapp
Includes medical information, prayers and rituals for each stage of pregnancy, from a liberal Jewish perspective. 7 x 10, 208 pp, Quality PB, b/w photos, 978-1-58023-178-7 **$16.95**

Celebrating Your New Jewish Daughter: Creating Jewish Ways to Welcome Baby Girls into the Covenant—New and Traditional Ceremonies *By Debra Nussbaum Cohen; Foreword by Rabbi Sandy Eisenberg Sasso* 6 x 9, 272 pp, Quality PB, 978-1-58023-090-2 **$18.95**

The New Jewish Baby Book, 2nd Edition: Names, Ceremonies & Customs—A Guide for Today's Families *By Anita Diamant* 6 x 9, 336 pp, Quality PB, 978-1-58023-251-7 **$19.99**

Parenting As a Spiritual Journey: Deepening Ordinary and Extraordinary Events into Sacred Occasions *By Rabbi Nancy Fuchs-Kreimer*
6 x 9, 224 pp, Quality PB, 978-1-58023-016-2 **$16.95**

Parenting Jewish Teens: A Guide for the Perplexed
By Joanne Doades 6 x 9, 200 pp, Quality PB, 978-1-58023-305-7 **$16.99**

Judaism for Two: A Spiritual Guide for Strengthening and Celebrating Your Loving Relationship *By Rabbi Nancy Fuchs-Kreimer and Rabbi Nancy H. Wiener; Foreword by Rabbi Elliot N. Dorff* Addresses the ways Jewish teachings can enhance and strengthen committed relationships. 6 x 9, 224 pp, Quality PB, 978-1-58023-254-8 **$16.99**

Embracing the Covenant: Converts to Judaism Talk About Why & How
By Rabbi Allan Berkowitz and Patti Moskovitz 6 x 9, 192 pp, Quality PB, 978-1-879045-50-7 **$16.95**

The Guide to Jewish Interfaith Family Life: An InterfaithFamily.com Handbook
Edited by Ronnie Friedland and Edmund Case 6 x 9, 384 pp, Quality PB, 978-1-58023-153-4 **$18.95**

Introducing My Faith and My Community
The Jewish Outreach Institute Guide for the Christian in a Jewish Interfaith Relationship
By Rabbi Kerry M. Olitzky 6 x 9, 176 pp, Quality PB, 978-1-58023-192-3 **$16.99**

Making a Successful Jewish Interfaith Marriage: The Jewish Outreach Institute Guide to Opportunities, Challenges and Resources *By Rabbi Kerry M. Olitzky with Joan Peterson Littman* 6 x 9, 176 pp, Quality PB, 978-1-58023-170-1 **$16.95**

The Creative Jewish Wedding Book: A Hands-On Guide to New & Old Traditions, Ceremonies & Celebrations *By Gabrielle Kaplan-Mayer* 9 x 9, 288 pp, b/w photos, Quality PB, 978-1-58023-194-7 **$19.99**

Divorce Is a Mitzvah: A Practical Guide to Finding Wholeness and Holiness When Your Marriage Dies *By Rabbi Perry Netter; Afterword by Rabbi Laura Geller.* 6 x 9, 224 pp, Quality PB, 978-1-58023-172-5 **$16.95**

A Heart of Wisdom: Making the Jewish Journey from Midlife through the Elder Years
Edited by Susan Berrin; Foreword by Harold Kushner
6 x 9, 384 pp, Quality PB, 978-1-58023-051-3 **$18.95**

So That Your Values Live On: Ethical Wills and How to Prepare Them
Edited by Jack Riemer and Nathaniel Stampfer
6 x 9, 272 pp, Quality PB, 978-1-879045-34-7 **$18.99**

Meditation

The Handbook of Jewish Meditation Practices
A Guide for Enriching the Sabbath and Other Days of Your Life
By Rabbi David A. Cooper Easy-to-learn meditation techniques.
6 x 9, 208 pp, Quality PB, 978-1-58023-102-2 **$16.95**

Discovering Jewish Meditation: Instruction & Guidance for Learning an Ancient
Spiritual Practice *By Nan Fink Gefen*
6 x 9, 208 pp, Quality PB, 978-1-58023-067-4 **$16.95**

A Heart of Stillness: A Complete Guide to Learning the Art of Meditation
By David A. Cooper 5½ x 8½, 272 pp, Quality PB, 978-1-893361-03-4 **$16.95** *(A SkyLight Paths book)*

Meditation from the Heart of Judaism: Today's Teachers Share Their
Practices, Techniques, and Faith *Edited by Avram Davis*
6 x 9, 256 pp, Quality PB, 978-1-58023-049-0 **$16.95**

Silence, Simplicity & Solitude: A Complete Guide to Spiritual Retreat at Home
By David A. Cooper 5½ x 8½, 336 pp, Quality PB, 978-1-893361-04-1 **$16.95**
(A SkyLight Paths book)

The Way of Flame: A Guide to the Forgotten Mystical Tradition of Jewish
Meditation *By Avram Davis* 4½ x 8, 176 pp, Quality PB, 978-1-58023-060-5 **$15.95**

Ritual/Sacred Practice/Journaling

The Jewish Dream Book: The Key to Opening the Inner Meaning of
Your Dreams *By Vanessa L. Ochs with Elizabeth Ochs; Full-color illus. by Kristina Swarner*
Instructions for how modern people can perform ancient Jewish dream practices
and dream interpretations drawn from the Jewish wisdom tradition.
8 x 8, 128 pp, Full-color illus., Deluxe PB w/flaps, 978-1-58023-132-9 **$16.95**

The Jewish Journaling Book: How to Use Jewish Tradition to Write
Your Life & Explore Your Soul *By Janet Ruth Falon*
Details the history of Jewish journaling throughout biblical and modern times, and
teaches specific journaling techniques to help you create and maintain a vital journal,
from a Jewish perspective. 8 x 8, 304 pp, Deluxe PB w/flaps, 978-1-58023-203-6 **$18.99**

The Book of Jewish Sacred Practices: CLAL's Guide to Everyday & Holiday
Rituals & Blessings *Edited by Rabbi Irwin Kula and Vanessa L. Ochs, PhD*
6 x 9, 368 pp, Quality PB, 978-1-58023-152-7 **$18.95**

Jewish Ritual: A Brief Introduction for Christians
By Rabbi Kerry M. Olitzky and Rabbi Daniel Judson
5½ x 8½, 144 pp, Quality PB, 978-1-58023-210-4 **$14.99**

The Rituals & Practices of a Jewish Life: A Handbook for Personal Spiritual
Renewal *Edited by Rabbi Kerry M. Olitzky and Rabbi Daniel Judson*
6 x 9, 272 pp, illus., Quality PB, 978-1-58023-169-5 **$18.95**

The Sacred Art of Lovingkindness: Preparing to Practice
By Rabbi Rami Shapiro 5½ x 8½, 176 pp, Quality PB, 978-1-59473-151-8 **$16.99**
(A SkyLight Paths book)

Science Fiction/Mystery & Detective Fiction

Mystery Midrash: An Anthology of Jewish Mystery & Detective Fiction
Edited by Lawrence W. Raphael; Preface by Joel Siegel
6 x 9, 304 pp, Quality PB, 978-1-58023-055-1 **$16.95**

Criminal Kabbalah: An Intriguing Anthology of Jewish Mystery & Detective Fiction
Edited by Lawrence W. Raphael; Foreword by Laurie R. King
6 x 9, 256 pp, Quality PB, 978-1-58023-109-1 **$16.95**

Wandering Stars: An Anthology of Jewish Fantasy & Science Fiction
Edited by Jack Dann; Introduction by Isaac Asimov
6 x 9, 272 pp, Quality PB, 978-1-58023-005-6 **$16.95**

More Wandering Stars: An Anthology of Outstanding Stories of Jewish Fantasy and
Science Fiction *Edited by Jack Dann; Introduction by Isaac Asimov*
6 x 9, 192 pp, Quality PB, 978-1-58023-063-6 **$16.95**

Spirituality

The Adventures of Rabbi Harvey: A Graphic Novel of Jewish Wisdom and Wit in the Wild West *By Steve Sheinkin*
Jewish and American folktales combine in this witty and original graphic novel collection. Creatively retold and set on the western frontier of the 1870s.
6 x 9, 144 pp, Full-color illus., Quality PB, 978-1-58023-310-1 **$16.99**

Ethics of the Sages: *Pirke Avot*—Annotated & Explained
Translation and Annotation by Rabbi Rami Shapiro
5½ x 8½, 192 pp, Quality PB, 978-1-59473-207-2 **$16.99** *(A SkyLight Paths book)*

A Book of Life: Embracing Judaism as a Spiritual Practice
By Michael Strassfeld 6 x 9, 528 pp, Quality PB, 978-1-58023-247-0 **$19.99**

Meaning and Mitzvah: Daily Practices for Reclaiming Judaism through Prayer, God, Torah, Hebrew, Mitzvot and Peoplehood *By Rabbi Goldie Milgram*
7 x 9, 336 pp, Quality PB, 978-1-58023-256-2 **$19.99**

The Soul of the Story: Meetings with Remarkable People
By Rabbi David Zeller 6 x 9, 288 pp, HC, 978-1-58023-272-2 **$21.99**

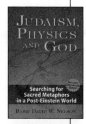

Aleph-Bet Yoga: Embodying the Hebrew Letters for Physical and Spiritual Well-Being
By Steven A. Rapp. Foreword by Tamar Frankiel, PhD and Judy Greenfeld. Preface by Hart Lazer.
7 x 10, 128 pp, b/w photos, Quality PB, Layflat binding, 978-1-58023-162-6 **$16.95**

Entering the Temple of Dreams
Jewish Prayers, Movements, and Meditations for the End of the Day
By Tamar Frankiel, PhD, and Judy Greenfeld
7 x 10, 192 pp, illus., Quality PB, 978-1-58023-079-7 **$16.95**

Does the Soul Survive? A Jewish Journey to Belief in Afterlife, Past Lives & Living with Purpose *By Rabbi Elie Kaplan Spitz; Foreword by Brian L. Weiss, MD*
6 x 9, 288 pp, Quality PB, 978-1-58023-165-7 **$16.99**

First Steps to a New Jewish Spirit: Reb Zalman's Guide to Recapturing the Intimacy & Ecstasy in Your Relationship with God *By Rabbi Zalman M. Schachter-Shalomi with Donald Gropman* 6 x 9, 144 pp, Quality PB, 978-1-58023-182-4 **$16.95**

God in Our Relationships: Spirituality between People from the Teachings of Martin Buber *By Rabbi Dennis S. Ross* 5½ x 8½, 160 pp, Quality PB, 978-1-58023-147-3 **$16.95**

Judaism, Physics and God: Searching for Sacred Metaphors in a Post-Einstein World
By Rabbi David W. Nelson 6 x 9, 368 pp, Quality PB, inc. reader's discussion guide, 978-1-58023-306-4 **$18.99**;
HC, 352 pp, 978-1-58023-252-4 **$24.99**

The Jewish Lights Spirituality Handbook: A Guide to Understanding, Exploring & Living a Spiritual Life *Edited by Stuart M. Matlins*
What exactly is "Jewish" about spirituality? How do I make it a part of my life? Fifty of today's foremost spiritual leaders share their ideas and experience with us.
6 x 9, 456 pp, Quality PB, 978-1-58023-093-3 **$19.99**

Bringing the Psalms to Life: How to Understand and Use the Book of Psalms
By Daniel F. Polish 6 x 9, 208 pp, Quality PB, 978-1-58023-157-2 **$16.95**;
HC, 978-1-58023-077-3 **$21.95**

God & the Big Bang: Discovering Harmony between Science & Spirituality
By Daniel C. Matt 6 x 9, 216 pp, Quality PB, 978-1-879045-89-7 **$16.99**

Minding the Temple of the Soul: Balancing Body, Mind, and Spirit through Traditional Jewish Prayer, Movement, and Meditation *By Tamar Frankiel, PhD, and Judy Greenfeld*
7 x 10, 184 pp, illus., Quality PB, 978-1-879045-64-4 **$16.95**
Audiotape of the Blessings and Meditations: 60 min. **$9.95**
Videotape of the Movements and Meditations: 46 min. **$20.00**

One God Clapping: The Spiritual Path of a Zen Rabbi *By Alan Lew with Sherril Jaffe*
5½ x 8½, 336 pp, Quality PB, 978-1-58023-115-2 **$16.95**

There Is No Messiah ... and You're It: The Stunning Transformation of Judaism's Most Provocative Idea *By Rabbi Robert N. Levine, DD*
6 x 9, 192 pp, Quality PB, 978-1-58023-255-5 **$16.99**

These Are the Words: A Vocabulary of Jewish Spiritual Life
By Arthur Green 6 x 9, 304 pp, Quality PB, 978-1-58023-107-7 **$18.95**

Spirituality/Lawrence Kushner

Filling Words with Light: Hasidic and Mystical Reflections on Jewish Prayer
By Lawrence Kushner and Nehemia Polen
5½ x 8½, 176 pp, HC, 978-1-58023-216-6 **$21.99**

The Book of Letters: A Mystical Hebrew Alphabet
Popular HC Edition, 6 x 9, 80 pp, 2-color text, 978-1-879045-00-2 **$24.95**
Collector's Limited Edition, 9 x 12, 80 pp, gold foil embossed pages, w/limited edition silkscreened print, 978-1-879045-04-0 **$349.00**

The Book of Miracles: A Young Person's Guide to Jewish Spiritual Awareness
6 x 9, 96 pp, 2-color illus., HC, 978-1-879045-78-1 **$16.95** *For ages 9 and up*

The Book of Words: Talking Spiritual Life, Living Spiritual Talk
6 x 9, 160 pp, Quality PB, 978-1-58023-020-9 **$16.95**

Eyes Remade for Wonder: A Lawrence Kushner Reader *Introduction by Thomas Moore*
6 x 9, 240 pp, Quality PB, 978-1-58023-042-1 **$18.95**

God Was in This Place & I, i Did Not Know: Finding Self, Spirituality and Ultimate Meaning 6 x 9, 192 pp, Quality PB, 978-1-879045-33-0 **$16.95**

Honey from the Rock: An Introduction to Jewish Mysticism
6 x 9, 176 pp, Quality PB, 978-1-58023-073-5 **$16.95**

Invisible Lines of Connection: Sacred Stories of the Ordinary
5½ x 8¼, 160 pp, Quality PB, 978-1-879045-98-9 **$15.95**

Jewish Spirituality—A Brief Introduction for Christians
5½ x 8¼, 112 pp, Quality PB, 978-1-58023-150-3 **$12.95**

The River of Light: Jewish Mystical Awareness
6 x 9, 192 pp, Quality PB, 978-1-58023-096-4 **$16.95**

The Way Into Jewish Mystical Tradition
6 x 9, 224 pp, Quality PB, 978-1-58023-200-5 **$18.99**; HC, 978-1-58023-029-2 **$21.95**

Spirituality/Prayer

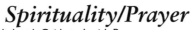

Pray Tell: A Hadassah Guide to Jewish Prayer
By Rabbi Jules Harlow, with contributions from many others
8½ x 11, 400 pp, Quality PB, 978-1-58023-163-3 **$29.95**

Witnesses to the One: The Spiritual History of the *Sh'ma* By Rabbi Joseph B. Meszler; Foreword by Rabbi Elyse Goldstein 6 x 9, 176 pp, HC, 978-1-58023-309-5 **$19.99**

My People's Prayer Book Series

Traditional Prayers, Modern Commentaries *Edited by Rabbi Lawrence A. Hoffman*
Provides diverse and exciting commentary to the traditional liturgy, helping modern men and women find new wisdom in Jewish prayer, and bring liturgy into their lives. Each book includes Hebrew text, modern translation, and commentaries from all perspectives of the Jewish world.

Vol. 1—The *Sh'ma* and Its Blessings
7 x 10, 168 pp, HC, 978-1-879045-79-8 **$24.99**

Vol. 2—The *Amidah*
7 x 10, 240 pp, HC, 978-1-879045-80-4 **$24.95**

Vol. 3—*P'sukei D'zimrah* (Morning Psalms)
7 x 10, 240 pp, HC, 978-1-879045-81-1 **$24.95**

Vol. 4—*Seder K'riat Hatorah* (The Torah Service)
7 x 10, 264 pp, HC, 978-1-879045-82-8 **$23.95**

Vol. 5—*Birkhot Hashachar* (Morning Blessings)
7 x 10, 240 pp, HC, 978-1-879045-83-5 **$24.95**

Vol. 6—*Tachanun* and Concluding Prayers
7 x 10, 240 pp, HC, 978-1-879045-84-2 **$24.95**

Vol. 7—Shabbat at Home
7 x 10, 240 pp, HC, 978-1-879045-85-9 **$24.95**

Vol. 8—*Kabbalat Shabbat* (Welcoming Shabbat in the Synagogue)
7 x 10, 240 pp, HC, 978-1-58023-121-3 **$24.99**

Vol. 9—Welcoming the Night: *Minchah* and *Ma'ariv* (Afternoon and Evening Prayer) 7 x 10, 272 pp, HC, 978-1-58023-262-3 **$24.99**

Vol. 10—Shabbat Morning: *Shacharit* and *Musaf* (Morning and Additional Services) 7 x 10, 240 pp, HC, 978-1-58023-240-1 **$24.99**

Theology/Philosophy/The Way Into... Series

The Way Into... series offers an accessible and highly usable "guided tour" of the Jewish faith, people, history and beliefs—in total, an introduction to Judaism that will enable you to understand and interact with the sacred texts of the Jewish tradition. Each volume is written by a leading contemporary scholar and teacher, and explores one key aspect of Judaism. *The Way Into...* series enables all readers to achieve a real sense of Jewish cultural literacy through guided study.

The Way Into Encountering God in Judaism
By Neil Gillman
For everyone who wants to understand how Jews have encountered God throughout history and today.
6 x 9, 240 pp, Quality PB, 978-1-58023-199-2 **$18.99**; HC, 978-1-58023-025-4 **$21.95**
Also Available: **The Jewish Approach to God:** A Brief Introduction for Christians
By Neil Gillman
5½ x 8½, 192 pp, Quality PB, 978-1-58023-190-9 **$16.95**

The Way Into Jewish Mystical Tradition
By Lawrence Kushner
Allows readers to interact directly with the sacred mystical text of the Jewish tradition. An accessible introduction to the concepts of Jewish mysticism, their religious and spiritual significance and how they relate to life today.
6 x 9, 224 pp, Quality PB, 978-1-58023-200-5 **$18.99**; HC, 978-1-58023-029-2 **$21.95**

The Way Into Jewish Prayer
By Lawrence A. Hoffman
Opens the door to 3,000 years of Jewish prayer, making available all anyone needs to feel at home in the Jewish way of communicating with God.
6 x 9, 224 pp, Quality PB, 978-1-58023-201-2 **$18.99**

The Way Into Judaism and the Environment
By Jeremy Benstein
Explores the ways in which Judaism contributes to contemporary social-environmental issues, the extent to which Judaism is part of the problem and how it can be part of the solution.
6 x 9, 288 pp, HC, 978-1-58023-268-5 **$24.99**

The Way Into *Tikkun Olam* (Repairing the World)
By Elliot N. Dorff
An accessible introduction to the Jewish concept of the individual's responsibility to care for others and repair the world.
6 x 9, 320 pp, HC, 978-1-58023-269-2 **$24.99**

The Way Into Torah
By Norman J. Cohen
Helps guide in the exploration of the origins and development of Torah, explains why it should be studied and how to do it.
6 x 9, 176 pp, Quality PB, 978-1-58023-198-5 **$16.99**; HC, 978-1-58023-028-5 **$21.95**

The Way Into the Varieties of Jewishness
By Sylvia Barack Fishman
Explores the religious and historical understanding of what it has meant to be Jewish from ancient times to the present controversy over "Who is a Jew?"
6 x 9, 250 pp, HC, 978-1-58023-030-8 **$24.99**

Theology/Philosophy

Christians and Jews in Dialogue: Learning in the Presence of the Other
By Mary C. Boys and Sara S. Lee; Foreword by Dr. Dorothy Bass
6 x 9, 240 pp, HC, 978-1-59473-144-0 **$21.99** *(A SkyLight Paths book)*

The Death of Death: Resurrection and Immortality in Jewish Thought
By Neil Gillman 6 x 9, 336 pp, Quality PB, 978-1-58023-081-0 **$18.95**

Ethics of the Sages: *Pirke Avot*—Annotated & Explained
Translation & Annotation by Rabbi Rami Shapiro
5½ x 8½, 208 pp, Quality PB, 978-1-59473-207-2 **$16.99** *(A SkyLight Paths book)*

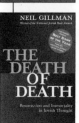

Evolving Halakhah: A Progressive Approach to Traditional Jewish Law
By Rabbi Dr. Moshe Zemer 6 x 9, 480 pp, Quality PB, 978-1-58023-127-5 **$29.95**;
HC, 978-1-58023-002-5 **$40.00**

Hasidic Tales: Annotated & Explained
By Rabbi Rami Shapiro; Foreword by Andrew Harvey
5½ x 8½, 240 pp, Quality PB, 978-1-893361-86-7 **$16.95** *(A SkyLight Paths Book)*

Healing the Jewish-Christian Rift: Growing Beyond our Wounded History
By Ron Miller and Laura Bernstein; Foreword by Dr. Beatrice Bruteau
6 x 9, 288 pp, Quality PB, 978-1-59473-139-6 **$18.99** *(A SkyLight Paths book)*

A Heart of Many Rooms: Celebrating the Many Voices within Judaism
By David Hartman 6 x 9, 352 pp, Quality PB, 978-1-58023-156-5 **$19.95**

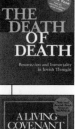

The Hebrew Prophets: Selections Annotated & Explained
Translation & Annotation by Rabbi Rami Shapiro; Foreword by Zalman M. Schachter-Shalomi
5½ x 8½, 224 pp, Quality PB, 978-1-59473-037-5 **$16.99** *(A SkyLight Paths book)*

A Jewish Understanding of the New Testament
By Rabbi Samuel Sandmel; Preface by Rabbi David Sandmel
5½ x 8½, 368 pp, Quality PB, 978-1-59473-048-1 **$19.99** *(A SkyLight Paths book)*

Keeping Faith with the Psalms: Deepen Your Relationship with God Using the Book
of Psalms *By Daniel F. Polish* 6 x 9, 320 pp, Quality PB, 978-1-58023-300-2 **$18.99**;
HC, 978-1-58023-179-4 **$24.95**

A Living Covenant: The Innovative Spirit in Traditional Judaism
By David Hartman 6 x 9, 368 pp, Quality PB, 978-1-58023-011-7 **$20.00**

Love and Terror in the God Encounter
The Theological Legacy of Rabbi Joseph B. Soloveitchik
By David Hartman 6 x 9, 240 pp, Quality PB, 978-1-58023-176-3 **$19.95**;
HC, 978-1-58023-112-1 **$25.00**

The Personhood of God: Biblical Theology, Human Faith and the Divine Image
By Dr. Yochanan Muffs; Foreword by Dr. David Hartman
6 x 9, 240 pp, HC, 978-1-58023-265-4 **$24.99**

Tormented Master: *The Life and Spiritual Quest of Rabbi Nahman of Bratslav*
By Arthur Green 6 x 9, 416 pp, Quality PB, 978-1-879045-11-8 **$19.99**

Traces of God: Seeing God in Torah, History and Everyday Life
By Neil Gillman 6 x 9, 240 pp, HC, 978-1-58023-249-4 **$21.99**

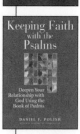

We Jews and Jesus: Exploring Theological Differences for Mutual Understanding
By Rabbi Samuel Sandmel; Preface by Rabbi David Sandmel
6 x 9, 176 pp, Quality PB, 978-1-59473-208-9 **$16.99** *(A SkyLight Paths book)*

Your Word Is Fire: The Hasidic Masters on Contemplative Prayer
Edited and translated by Arthur Green and Barry W. Holtz
6 x 9, 160 pp, Quality PB, 978-1-879045-25-5 **$15.95**

I Am Jewish
Personal Reflections Inspired by the Last Words of Daniel Pearl
Almost 150 Jews—both famous and not—from all walks of life, from all around
the world, write about Identity, Heritage, Covenant / Chosenness and Faith,
Humanity and Ethnicity, and *Tikkun Olam* and Justice.
Edited by Judea and Ruth Pearl
6 x 9, 304 pp, Deluxe PB w/flaps, 978-1-58023-259-3 **$18.99**; HC, 978-1-58023-183-1 **$24.99**
Download a free copy of the *I Am Jewish Teacher's Guide* at our website:
www.jewishlights.com

Current Events/History

The Story of the Jews: A 4,000-Year Adventure—A Graphic History Book
Written & illustrated by Stan Mack
Witty, illustrated narrative of all the major happenings from biblical times to the twenty-first century. 6 x 9, 288 pp, illus., Quality PB, 978-1-58023-155-8 **$16.95**

Hannah Senesh: Her Life and Diary, the First Complete Edition
By Hannah Senesh; Foreword by Marge Piercy; Preface by Eitan Senesh
6 x 9, 352 pp, HC, 978-1-58023-212-8 **$24.99**

The Jewish Prophet: Visionary Words from Moses and Miriam to Henrietta Szold and A. J. Heschel *By Rabbi Dr. Michael J. Shire*
6½ x 8½, 128 pp, 123 full-color illus., HC, 978-1-58023-168-8
Special gift price $14.95

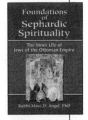

Foundations of Sephardic Spirituality: The Inner Life of Jews of the Ottoman Empire
By Rabbi Marc D. Angel, PhD 6 x 9, 224 pp, HC, 978-1-58023-243-2 **$24.99**

Judaism and Justice: The Jewish Passion to Repair the World
By Rabbi Sidney Schwarz
6 x 9, 250 pp, HC, 978-1-58023-312-5 **$24.99**

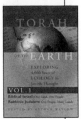

Ecology

Ecology & the Jewish Spirit: Where Nature & the Sacred Meet
Edited by Ellen Bernstein 6 x 9, 288 pp, Quality PB, 978-1-58023-082-7 **$16.95**

Torah of the Earth: Exploring 4,000 Years of Ecology in Jewish Thought
Vol. 1: Biblical Israel: One Land, One People; Rabbinic Judaism: One People, Many Lands
Vol. 2: Zionism: One Land, Two Peoples; Eco-Judaism: One Earth, Many Peoples
Edited by Arthur Waskow
Vol. 1: 6 x 9, 272 pp, Quality PB, 978-1-58023-086-5 **$19.95**
Vol. 2: 6 x 9, 336 pp, Quality PB, 978-1-58023-087-2 **$19.95**

The Way Into Judaism and the Environment
By Jeremy Benstein 6 x 9, 224 pp, HC, 978-1-58023-268-5 **$24.99**

Grief/Healing

Against the Dying of the Light: A Parent's Story of Love, Loss and Hope
By Leonard Fein
5½ x 8½, 176 pp, Quality PB, 978-1-58023-197-8 **$15.99**

Grief in Our Seasons: A Mourner's Kaddish Companion *By Rabbi Kerry M. Olitzky*
4½ x 6½, 448 pp, Quality PB, 978-1-879045-55-2 **$15.95**

Healing of Soul, Healing of Body: Spiritual Leaders Unfold the Strength & Solace
in Psalms *Edited by Rabbi Simkha Y. Weintraub, CSW*
6 x 9, 128 pp, 2-color illus. text, Quality PB, 978-1-879045-31-6 **$14.99**

Jewish Paths toward Healing and Wholeness: A Personal Guide to Dealing with
Suffering *By Rabbi Kerry M. Olitzky; Foreword by Debbie Friedman.*
6 x 9, 192 pp, Quality PB, 978-1-58023-068-1 **$15.95**

Mourning & Mitzvah, 2nd Edition: A Guided Journal for Walking the Mourner's
Path through Grief to Healing *By Anne Brener, LCSW*
7½ x 9, 304 pp, Quality PB, 978-1-58023-113-8 **$19.99**

The Perfect Stranger's Guide to Funerals and Grieving Practices
A Guide to Etiquette in Other People's Religious Ceremonies *Edited by Stuart M. Matlins*
6 x 9, 240 pp, Quality PB, 978-1-893361-20-1 **$16.95** *(A SkyLight Paths book)*

Tears of Sorrow, Seeds of Hope: A Jewish Spiritual Companion for Infertility and
Pregnancy Loss *By Rabbi Nina Beth Cardin*
6 x 9, 192 pp, HC, 978-1-58023-017-9 **$19.95**

A Time to Mourn, A Time to Comfort, 2nd Edition: A Guide to Jewish
Bereavement *By Dr. Ron Wolfson*
7 x 9, 384 pp, Quality PB, 978-1-58023-253-1 **$19.99**

When a Grandparent Dies: A Kid's Own Remembering Workbook for Dealing
with Shiva and the Year Beyond *By Nechama Liss-Levinson, PhD*
8 x 10, 48 pp, 2-color text, HC, 978-1-879045-44-6 **$15.95** *For ages 7–13*

About Jewish Lights

People of all faiths and backgrounds yearn for books that attract, engage, educate, and spiritually inspire.

Our principal goal is to stimulate thought and help all people learn about who the Jewish People are, where they come from, and what the future can be made to hold. While people of our diverse Jewish heritage are the primary audience, our books speak to people in the Christian world as well and will broaden their understanding of Judaism and the roots of their own faith.

We bring to you authors who are at the forefront of spiritual thought and experience. While each has something different to say, they all say it in a voice that you can hear.

Our books are designed to welcome you and then to engage, stimulate, and inspire. We judge our success not only by whether or not our books are beautiful and commercially successful, but by whether or not they make a difference in your life.

For your information and convenience, at the back of this book we have provided a list of other Jewish Lights books you might find interesting and useful. They cover all the categories of your life:

Bar/Bat Mitzvah	Life Cycle
Bible Study / Midrash	Meditation
Children's Books	Parenting
Congregation Resources	Prayer
Current Events / History	Ritual / Sacred Practice
Ecology	Spirituality
Fiction: Mystery, Science Fiction	Theology / Philosophy
Grief / Healing	Travel
Holidays / Holy Days	12-Step
Inspiration	Women's Interest
Kabbalah / Mysticism / Enneagram	

Stuart M. Matlins, Publisher

Or phone, fax, mail or e-mail to: **JEWISH LIGHTS Publishing**
Sunset Farm Offices, Route 4 • P.O. Box 237 • Woodstock, Vermont 05091
Tel: (802) 457-4000 • Fax: (802) 457-4004 • www.jewishlights.com
Credit card orders: **(800) 962-4544** (8:30AM–5:30PM ET Monday–Friday)
Generous discounts on quantity orders. SATISFACTION GUARANTEED. Prices subject to change.